The New Media of Surveillance

The spread of new surveillance technologies is an issue of major concern for democratic societies. More ubiquitous and sophisticated monitoring techniques raise profound questions for the very possibility of individual autonomy and democratic government. Innovations in surveillance systems require equally innovative approaches for analyzing their social and political implications, and the field of critical communication studies is uniquely equipped to provide fresh insights. This book brings together the work of a number of critical communication scholars who take innovative approaches to examining the surveillance dimensions of new media technologies. The essays included in this volume focus on interactive networks, computer generated imagery, biometrics, and intelligent transport systems as sites where communication and surveillance have become virtually inseparable social processes.

This book was originally published as a special issue of *The Communication Review*.

Shoshana Magnet is based at the Institute of Women's Studies at the University of Ottawa, Canada.

Kelly Gates is based at the Department of Communication, University of California, San Diego, USA.

The New Media of Surveillance

Edited by Shoshana Magnet and Kelly Gates

Routledge
Taylor & Francis Group
LONDON AND NEW YORK

First published 2009 by Routledge
2 Park Square, Milton Park, Abingdon, Oxon, OX14 4RN

Simultaneously published in the USA and Canada
by Routledge
270 Madison Avenue, New York, NY 10016

Routledge is an imprint of the Taylor & Francis Group, an informa business

Transferred to Digital Printing 2009

© 2009 Edited by Shoshana Magnet and Kelly Gates

Typeset in Times by Value Chain, India

British Library Cataloguing in Publication Data
A catalogue record for this book is available from the British Library

ISBN10: 0-415-48077-9 (hbk)
ISBN10: 0-415-56812-9 (pbk)

ISBN13: 978-0-415-48077-2 (hbk)
ISBN13: 978-0-415-56812-8 (pbk)

Contents

Acknowledgements

Shoshana Magnet would like to thank Robert Smith, Craig Robertson, Himika Bhattacharya, Jillian Baez, Aisha Durham, Amy Hasinoff, Carolyn Randolph, Darin Barney, Helen Kang and Celiany Rivera Velàzquez for their helpful comments and suggestions.

Communicating Surveillance: Examining the Intersections

SHOSHANA MAGNET AND KELLY GATES

The issue of surveillance is the subject of intensified public and scholarly concern. Journalists, civil libertarians, and scholars in a number of fields all offer critical assessments of the ubiquitous nature of surveillance in modern societies. Theoretical and empirical work on surveillance techniques, practices, and institutions are found in sociology, women's studies, criminology, geography, urban studies, legal and policy studies, and other fields, and collaborative, interdisciplinary research is common. The aim of this volume is to highlight the contributions that the field of communication has made, and can continue to make, to our understanding of surveillance as a set of cultural and institutional practices, and especially as an instrument of social control. In what ways are surveillance practices also communicative practices? How are surveillance functions built into communications media, new and old? What does communication research and theory bring to the study of surveillance, in addition to those insights offered by other disciplines? From consumer research, copyright enforcement, and the surveillance capacity of information communication technologies, to closed-circuit television, interactive media, and the new "rhetorics of surveillance" in television and film (Levin, 2002), communication and media studies have productive interventions to make into the debates about the "surveillance society" (Lyon, 2001).

Of course, the study of surveillance is of necessity an interdisciplinary undertaking, not least because surveillance takes so many different forms. Luckily, the field of communication is one with porous boundaries, and its contributions to the study of surveillance are not confined to communication scholarship, narrowly defined. A recent collection of essays edited by the sociologist Kevin Haggerty and the criminologist Richard Ericson provides ample evidence of this point. The book, titled *The New Politics of Surveillance and Visibility* (2006), contains a number of articles by scholars outside the field of communication that examine intersections between surveillance and the media, including Aaron Doyle's essay on the broadcasting of surveillance footage of crimes, and Serra Tinic's essay on audience research and interactive television. In addition, David Lyon's contribution to the volume examines the role of the mass media, especially television and cinema, in legitimizing ubiquitous surveillance practices and encouraging a culture of voyeurism.

As these examples of surveillance research suggest, the relationship between surveillance and communication – especially the media of communication – is an established and growing object of interdisciplinary concern. The relevance of the field of communication to the study of surveillance stems to considerable extent from its conventional concerns with media and media technologies. In many respects, surveillance technologies *are* media technologies, and in that sense all forms of surveillance beyond direct supervision involve the use of media, from writing and paper to digital video and audio recording devices. There are other productive points of intersection as well. The relationship between the intensification of surveillance and the rise of neoliberalism bears further analysis, and communication scholarship has much to contribute to this debate. The transition to "informationalized capitalism" (Schiller, 2007) depends centrally on the development of new practices of combined state and corporate scrutiny, enlisting new communications technologies born out of the digital convergence of a number of information media – including television, video, and the Internet.

Communication theory provides a rich toolkit for questioning the notion that new information technologies enable improved forms of connectivity, community building and democracy. As John Durham Peters argues, the idea of communication has long been associated with utopian possibilities, and theoretical reflection about communication has consistently maintained that more perfect forms of communication are the answer to many of our social problems. But what exactly is meant by more and better communication, and what are the actual results? Critical investigations into the surveillance capacities of new communication technologies support Peters' contention that assumptions about the inherent problem-solving, community-building capacity of communication "sweep too much under the rug" (Peters, 1999: 6). *The New Media of Surveillance* excavates what is "swept under the rug", highlighting the ways that "more and better" communication has often amounted to amplified forms of institutionalized surveillance and social control. In what follows, we outline some important points of intersection between communication research and the study of surveillance, with the aim of providing a theoretical backdrop for the essays collected in this volume.

Consumer surveillance and new interactive media

One major contribution that communication research makes to the study of surveillance can be found in the wealth of critical scholarship on market research and consumer monitoring. Communication research offers important insights on the relationship between marketing techniques and the drive for intensified forms of consumer surveillance, focusing on the role of information technologies in the market segmentation process. In *The Panoptic Sort* (1993),

Oscar Gandy identified the dispersed and decentralized technological sorting apparatus taking shape along with computerization, using transaction-generated data about individuals in order to classify them according to their presumed economic and political value. His study established the undeniable fact that consumer profiling techniques were functioning in deeply discriminatory ways, structuring the range of choices available to individuals according to the dictates of commodity consumption and corporate profit. Although less critical of corporate profit *per se*, Gandy's colleague Joseph Turow similarly focuses on the forms of discrimination underlying the market research machine. His two major books in this area, *Breaking Up America* (1997) and *Niche Envy* (2007), have taken aim at the fragmentation of US society at the hands of target-marketers and the destructive social consequences of classifying and assigning differential value to consumer groups (and increasingly, to individuals).

As this work suggests, market research and consumer surveillance are special concerns in communication scholarship, not least because they combine the field's longstanding interest in persuasive techniques with a legacy of treating communication as form of information processing.[1] It is the increasingly cybernetic quality of surveillance – the capacity to feed personal data about individuals back into the mechanisms of social control – that distinguishes newer techniques from earlier, less interactive forms of monitoring. Of course, the mass media play a significant role in the feedback loops of surveillance and social control, and the commercial media remain most concerned with monitoring their own markets – or at least part of that market. As Eileen Meehan (1990) shows, the only audience that counted during the network and cable eras of television was the "commodity audience" – that is, the audience most saleable to advertisers. To be sure, things are changing considerably in the field of audience research, thanks to new "interactive" media technologies. Digital video recording (DVR) technology in particular is threatening established models of audience measurement, although not so much because it empowers television viewers to defy highly orchestrated program schedules or to skip over commercials, but because it provides a vehicle for gathering much more precise data on our viewing behaviors – giving programmers a whole new level of information about exactly what we do with the television set, down to when we adjust the volume (Carlson, 2006). But despite these changes, there is not much evidence to suggest that the new forms of audience measurement are any less focused on commercial media's most valuable commodities: people with buying power.

The Internet also introduces new challenges and new opportunities for market research and audience measurement, and new online surveillance techniques raise important questions for communication research. As the Internet became a popular medium in the 1990s, the prevailing argument held that it represented an entirely new playing field, requiring different rules than those that governed established media. Yet, while cyber libertarians insisted that the Internet should be free of the regulatory oversight under which broadcasters had long suffered, private companies established their own regulatory mechanisms by securing control over the Internet "backbone" and domain name system, effectively "ruling the root" as it were (Mueller, 2004). The privatization of the Internet was accompanied by its thorough incorporation into the market system, down to the level of code. The new medium of the web browser, with its "cookies" technology, was specifically designed to automate the collection of personal information (Elmer, 2004), and new Internet tracking companies like DoubleClick and Bluestreak devised ways to turn our online activities into valuable market research data, effectively redefining privacy as a tradable commodity (Campbell and Carlson, 2002).

Without a doubt, the Internet and new ICTs are bringing together persuasive strategies with previously unheard of consumer-tracking techniques. New technologies are enabling the rationalization of social life well beyond the workplace into the spheres of leisure and consumption, as Robins and Webster (1999) have argued. Mark Andrejevic (2007) develops this argument further in his new book, *iSpy: Surveillance and Power in the Interactive Era* (2007). Andrejevic demonstrates how the new culture of media "interactivity" invites us to willingly participate in our own manipulation by freely offering up detailed information about ourselves to marketers – a marketing strategy greatly facilitated by the Internet, mobile phones, and interactive DVR technologies like TiVo. In stark contrast to the utopian promise of "interactive" media technologies for participatory democracy, the reality of this so-called interactivity appears to be nothing more than intensified forms of monitoring aimed at helping marketers develop more effective and efficient forms of consumer persuasion. Serra Tinic (2006) similarly argues that the potential of interactive TV falters in the light of the political-economic reality. Corporate mergers have granted companies unprecedented abilities to use this technology to penetrate the domestic sphere in order to digitally record the actions of audience members as they surf, screen and shop. Interactive TV helps advertisers to further fragment the market – sorting out desirable individuals for participation in this new medium while ignoring the rest.

Police communications and surveillance

If communication research has an established record of examining consumer surveillance and audience measurement techniques, what of its record of research on those forms of surveillance developed for other, non-commercial purposes? In what ways are state and police surveillance practices also communicative practices, involving the use of "interactive" media technologies?

Police use of surveillance technologies is an area of obvious concern to criminologists, and much of the work shares important and under-explored connections to communication research. The history and political economy of telecommunications and computerization has much to offer current debates about warrantless wiretapping, police use of biometrics and other information technologies, and policies like the Communications Assistance for Law Enforcement Act (CALEA), which requires telecommunications carriers to design their equipment, facilities, and services to enable electronic surveillance. In order to understand what is new (and not so new) about new forms of electronic surveillance, it helps to consider the historical record. A rich body of literature addresses the historical development of identification systems, including the incorporation of photography into criminal identification techniques and the corresponding development of archival systems for the organizing criminal files.[2] These archival systems are important predecessors to the database and networking technologies that now underwrite and shape police surveillance practices.

A major contribution to the historical record of these systems comes from James Rule's (1973) landmark study of five bureaucratic surveillance systems in the early seventies. Rule's study provides an invaluable description of the criminal files kept by the British police — and their techniques of information organization and retrieval — just before computerization. Rule also offers a rare glimpse into police use of telecommunications at a particular historical moment. Thanks to new radios in police cars, officers no longer had to find telephone boxes to call in criminal background inquiries when conducting "stop checks." Back at the criminal records office, Rule describes "the steady ringing of telephones and the movement of staff plying back and forth between the phones and the files," although in some cases the teleprinter or telex served as a substitute for the telephone (p. 62). Rule's descriptive account provides an important point of reference for understanding transformations in police surveillance practices, especially the translation of human labor into automated, technical systems.

The labor of surveillance is the heart of policing, and it represents an under-explored area of research.[3] In stark contrast to this dearth of scholarship, the problem of surveillance labor has received an enormous amount of attention from state agencies and other institutions involved in the construction of surveillance architectures, from Bentham to the post-9/11 US (Maxwell, 2005). As highlighted in recent films like *The Lives of Others* (2007) and *Red Road* (2007), surveillance involves considerable work, and special kinds of skills, on the part of its workforce. The labor of surveillance often requires an inhuman level of discipline and detachment, as Richard Maxwell (2005) has shown. Adding an important dimension to this debate, Ericson and Haggerty

(1997) have argued that the modern police are best understood as "knowledge workers" within risk management systems, doing the labor of collecting and processing information well beyond the realm of criminal investigations to support the risk management needs of other institutions, especially the insurance industry. In the process, police officers and other surveillance workers are subject to regimes of scientific management much like other workers, perhaps more so because of the nature of the work they do: "the computer terminal in the patrol car is a time-and-motion study that never ends" (Ericson and Haggerty, p. 432). Research on policing has neglected "how communication rules, formats, and technologies make officers more visible to police supervisors and mangers and to external institutions for which relevant knowledge is routinely produced" (Ericson and Haggery, p. 438). The question of how police officers and other surveillance workers themselves are disciplined through their use of apparatuses of surveillance deserves further attention.

Closed-circuit television

In his analysis of the surveillance practices of the modern nation-state, Anthony Giddens (1987) makes the important distinction between surveillance as the accumulation of coded information (i.e., "dataveillance" to use Roger Clarke's term) and surveillance as direct supervision (of which panopticism is a particular form). If new information technologies have been developed to augment the accumulation of data, closed-circuit television (CCTV) and other audio-visual technologies have been designed to enhance and extend techniques of direct supervision. The 1980s and '90s saw an exponential increase in the use of closed-circuit television by police and private security firms in both the US and Europe for monitoring urban spaces, gated communities, workplaces, and capital-intensive spaces such as banks, malls, and casinos.[4] The intensity of CCTV expansion in the UK in particular caught the attention of sociologists, legal scholars, and civil libertarians, who began to investigate the reasons for this proliferation and its social and political implications. Rather than focusing narrowly on criminological concerns with its effectiveness in reducing crime rates, critical research instead has explored the broader social causes and consequences of the widespread use of video surveillance.[5] Explanations that have avoided the pitfalls of technological determinism have focused on the social factors governing the speed and scale of CCTV deployments, linking the rise of video surveillance to political-economic priorities (especially of neoliberalism) (see Monahan, 2006), governmental strategies (especially risk management) (see McCahill, 2002; Yesil, 2006), and the pathological culture of fear that pervades late modern societies (see Davis, 1992; Bannister, Fyfe, and Kearns, 1998; Graham, 1998).[6]

Building on a long tradition of research, from the work of Raymond Williams (1975) to more recent work by scholars like Anna McCarthy (2001), television studies has important insights to offer the analysis of CCTV as both a technology and a cultural form. Closed-circuit television is an "ambient" form of television, with relevance to issues of media production and reception. Although its status as a "closed circuit" distinguishes CCTV from broadcast television, the images it furnishes occasionally lend themselves to the program formats of television news, documentaries, and voyeuristic reality-based crime shows. But even in its most banal, everyday uses, CCTV is a special kind of media technology in that it mediates direct supervision, enabling the "disembedding" of social relations beyond their immediate context, to use Giddens' terminology. CCTV is central to both crime control and "crime culture TV," as Nic Groombridge (2002) has argued, and the "separation between the rational/bureaucratic elements of CCTV and the affective/aesthetic/entertainment can no longer be sustained" (Groombridge, 2002, p. 37). As a cultural form, CCTV now constitutes a part of the visual repertoire of modern life, embodying a compulsive desire to record time and space, in all its banality, in pursuit of something of interest, while simultaneously overburdening the monitoring institutions with information and threatening to produce what Baudrillard (1980) has called an "implosion of meaning." The questions CCTV raises about the production and manipulation of space and time closely relate to issues examined in communication scholarship at least since Harold Innis's *The Bias of Communication* (1951). Film theorist Thomas Levin (2002) has offered a noteworthy contribution to this discussion in his analysis of the "temporal indexicality" of real-time surveillance video, especially as CCTV becomes part of the language of contemporary cinema.

Media representations of surveillance

The interplay of CCTV with film and other media forms raises an issue of growing concern to both communication and surveillance studies: the convergence between media representations of surveillance and actual surveillance practices. David Lyon's most recent book, *Surveillance Studies* (2007), points to the dialectical relationship between the two, arguing that media representations of surveillance are central to understandings of observation, supervision and inspection. Lyon's analysis of the comic strip *Spiderman*, which he demonstrates is the inspiration for the electronic tagging of criminalized individuals, is one among many of the ways in which media texts inform contemporary surveillance strategies. Companies that sell new surveillance technologies recognise the importance of being familiar with contemporary representations of their products in the popular media. Biometric industry representatives attend films featuring biometric technologies in order to prepare themselves to address consumer anxieties about their products, while at the same time science fiction films serve as the inspiration for the development of new devices (Magnet, 2008). Most recently, billboards that collect personal information about those who look at them, (a product that was formerly restricted to science fiction cinema), were placed in and around Manhattan (Clifford, 2008). In this way, media texts offer critiques of new surveillance technologies while simultaneously naturalizing their expansion. Films like *Gattaca* (Niccol, 1997) and *Minority Report* (Spielberg, 2002) dramatize dystopian societies caught in the grips of police surveillance, while depicting new surveillance technologies as seamlessly functioning systems. In this way, these films paradoxically raise critical questions about surveillance, even as they present authoritative and seemingly non-negotiable visions of the technological future.

Surveillant scopophilia is the hallmark of reality TV, a program genre that offers surveillance itself as mediated spectacle (Andrejevic, 2003). Although the genre has historical precedents, it was the debut of *The Real World* in 1991 that ushered in the reality TV boom – a veritable revolution in television production – as broadcast and cable networks remade their schedules around the cheap-to-produce programming and spun off a slew of specialized subgenres (Oullette and Murray, 2004). Like many program genres, reality TV includes a broad range of textual material, much of which shares affinities with other forms of reality documentation, including news and documentary programming. However, reality TV is decidedly different than these other realist modes of representation. Oullette and Murray distinguish reality TV as "an unabashedly commercial genre united less by aesthetic rules or certainties than by the fusion of popular entertainment with a self-conscious claim to the discourse of the real" (p. 2).

It is this claim to the real that gives reality TV its particular affinity with the surveillance culture, instructing viewers in the work of watching, while simultaneously making them accustomed to the work of being watched (another form of surveillance labor) (Andrejevic, 2002a). The "video verité" style of reality crime dramas like *COPS* encourages viewer identification with police surveillance and voyeuristic pleasure in other people's misery, uncomplicated by any analysis of racism or poverty, as the audience "accompanies" officers as they hunt down petty drug users and sex workers while performing for the camera (Rapping, 2004). If viewers are encouraged to keep a safe psychological distance from the unfortunate folks getting arrested on *COPS*, the same is not true of their relationship to the participants in shows like *The Real World, The Apprentice, Judge Judy*, and *The Bachelor.* Media studies scholars have argued that reality TV encourages viewers to identify closely with the shows' participants – in fact, to envision themselves *as* the participants – articulating new modes of subjectivity more appropriate to an intensively monitored society (Mark Andrejevic, 2002b, 2003; Rachel Dubrofsky, this volume). In her pioneering work on *The Bachelor*, Dubrofsky finds that the surveillance practices of reality TV signal a shift in therapeutic narratives from those that stress self-improvement to those that emphasize self-sameness, where being perpetually watched becomes central to establishing one's consistent identity and sense of self across a range of social spaces. Shows like *The Real World* and *Road Rules* "equate submission to comprehensive surveillance with self-expression and self-knowledge," offering a "kinder, gentler" version of Big Brother and an acceptance of being watched so important to consumer participation in the online economy, as Andrejevic argues (2002b, p. 253).

Surveillance as a ritual of communication

If communication is a "symbolic process whereby reality is produced, maintained, repaired, and transformed," as James Carey theorized, then reality TV is surely doing much more than providing the viewing public with trivial entertainment. Carey's ritual model of communication emphasized its role in the formation and maintenance of community, a theory that has important insights to offer the study of surveillance. Surveillance practices, in all of their technological forms, are part of the cultural rituals of modern societies. Surveillance practices are rituals central to modern statecraft in particular, as the authors published in this volume demonstrate – see, for example, Torin Monahan's examination of intelligent transportation systems and Mark Andrejevic's analysis of ubiquitous computing. State agencies routinely compile information about individuals and groups for the purposes of governance, and surveillance practices are among the central ways in which the state engages with members of the national body. The state's surveillance rituals work to render citizens and aliens "legible" (Scott, 1998) and "verifiable" (Robertson, 2004) to state apparatuses. State surveillance practices are ritual forms of communication aimed at the maintenance of society across space and time.

Yet, like Foucault's conceptualization of power, Carey's ritual model forces us to look beyond state-centered practices of social control to understand the many other ways in which rituals of observation work not only to maintain the established order, but also at times to disrupt or challenge it. In their analysis of US network television news coverage of the "war on drugs," Reeves and Campbell (1994) argue that surveillance practices are an inherent part of the communicative processes that underlie the struggle over "meaning, order, control, and freedom," i.e., part of competing social forces of domination and resistance (p. 33). Network television news embodies these dualistic tendencies. Although generally aligned with those social forces struggling to impose conformity, television news on rare occasions inadvertently becomes "a platform for dissent, an ally of civil disobedience, a whistle-blowing advocate of the disenfranchised, an enemy of tradition" (ibid., p. 34). Here we are reminded of television news coverage from New Orleans after Katrina, as reporters visibly contradicted the bright public pronouncements of the Bush Administration with horrific, real-time footage of the unfolding chaos.[7]

If the ritual model of communication requires us to consider alternative surveillance practices, we should not be fooled into thinking that all of the unintended uses of surveillance technologies amount to emancipatory forms of resistance. A more frightening example of an unintended use of surveillance technology is the cyberstalking spyware used by abusers to stalk their targets.[8] Such computer programs may be covertly installed. Once set up, the software gives the installer second-by-second screen shots of what is happening on the computer that carries the spyware, which in turn can be emailed to the stalker's computer or cell phone. Information transmitted may include email messages or communication sent by an Internet phone. In this way, every moment of the target's day may be tracked – including, for example, email sent to a domestic violence shelter or a call made to a crisis hotline.

Communication, surveillance, and inequality

As the case of cyberstalking suggests, supervisory strategies and their attendant technologies encode systemic forms of inequality, including forms of sexist, racist, and homophobic violence. The ease with which new communications technologies may be used for cyberstalking underscores the close relationship between new technologies and their social context. Another major contribution of communication research to surveillance studies is the attention critical scholars have paid to this relationship, including connections between new ICTs and the reproduction of social inequalities.

For example, Suren Lalvani has theorized the ways in which new technologies codify discriminatory practices of looking. Through his analysis of the production of photographic types - including the bourgeois subject, the criminal object, the primitive other and the ideal worker - Lalvani documents the importance of photography to the growth of surveillance infrastructure. In particular, Lalvani's examination of the role of photography in the production of the laboring body demonstrates that the technology was essential to the development of Taylorism and the scientific management of workers. Photography made it possible to capture movement and simulate realism in ways that allowed for the production of a highly regulated, surveillant apparatus of employee control - "photography" gives the body a visibility that rends it permeable to the operations of a disciplinary regime" (34). Lalvani shows how the photographic medium built on existing inequalities to provide the conditions for the surveillance of working class subjects. The development of photography as a new communications technology was aided by its adoption to surveillance practices in the service of capitalism.

While desirable patrons are targeted by marketing techniques that privilege good consumers, other surveillance techniques render marginalized communities disproportionately vulnerable to policing practices. New surveillance technologies are regularly tested on marginalized communities that are unable to resist their intrusion. A new form of surveillance technology known as a one-way voice intercom system recently made its US debut in Faircliff, a low-income housing complex in Washington, D.C. The hope is that the securitization of this low-income community will encourage wealthy condominium owners to purchase property on the neighboring streets. Staffed by security personnel sitting behind surveillance cameras, who use the one-way intercom to order residents off their own front stoops and the resident's children out of their own yards, the system allows monitors to speak to tenants but does not permit tenants to reply. The anonymous system has already been abused. In one case, a teenage girl who refused to move fast enough when ordered was told to "Get [her] fat ass off the corner" (Jamieson, 2006). This new communications technology is again used to police bodies deemed "out of place," even as those bodies are held static by income disparities and the difficulty of finding affordable housing.

As the Faircliff case suggests, surveillance practices encode existing forms of discrimination, including classism and racism, and even fat phobia. The field of surveillance studies remains concerned with inequality. A special issue of the journal *Surveillance and Society,* edited by Torin Monahan, points to the ways that claims about the democratization of surveillance, in which everyone is understood to be equally subject to surveillance practices, must engage with the ways that surveillance remains tied to existing inequities (2008). The contributors to this book consider how the rituals of surveillance reproduce and deepen existing forms of structural inequality.

Communication, the body, and surveillance

Theorizing the body as a discursive practice and a locus of power/knowledge has been a major theme of communication scholarship, providing important insights for the examination of new surveillance technologies that take the body itself as a source of information. Critical research has investigated the obsessive design and application of visualizing technologies to analyze and define the body's pathologies and productive forces, from photography, film and video to X-rays, sonograms, and medical imaging devices. The body has been at the center of the rationalist tendency towards measurement and quantification, and mapping and measuring the body is central to modern, biopolitical strategies of government.

With advances in network computing and digital technologies, a new set of practices for mapping the body is taking shape. From biometric technologies to the Human Genome Project, the last ten years have seen the emergence of a number of celebrated biomedical and technoscientific initiatives for mapping the body. Most recently, Google announced its latest search engine, Google Body. This new mapping tool is meant to allow the users to search the human body as easily as they search the Internet.

Each new way of visualizing the body has potential surveillance applications, and it is important to consider the ethical implications of making the body a target and source of surveillance. In her contribution, Rachel Hall uses the phrase "the aesthetics of transparency" to describe the state's combined efforts to render the world and the body perfectly visible, flattening three-dimensional interiors into two dimensions with the aim of creating conditions in which there "would no longer be any secrets or interiors, human or geographical, in which our enemies (or the enemy within) might find refuge." As Hall's work suggests, new surveillance technologies produce new understandings of the body, promising to remake bodies into perfectly visible objects. *The New Media of Surveillance* aims to unpack discursive practices that claim to lay the body newly bare.

The contributors

Not only can the field of communication contribute to the study of surveillance, but widespread rituals of surveillance themselves should raise questions about the established research agendas of communication studies. The contributors to this volume build on strong traditions of communication scholarship while also taking important new directions.

In his analysis of the possibilities for surveillance offered by ubiquitous computing, Mark Andrejevic debunks the utopian rhetoric surrounding the promise of computing hyped to be "as free as the air you breathe." Rather than delivering on the promise of the digital sublime, Andrejevic demonstrates that ubiquitous computing promises to force free oxygen into a pipeline structured around the business model of the digital enclosure. Enclosures are spatial configurations that favor surveillance put to work in the service of capital, and Andrejevic reminds us that the digital enclosure "promises little more than the reproduction of the social relations it purports to overcome." Heather Murray's study of biometrics also reveals the ways in which this new communications technology codifies systemic forms of inequality. Grounding the development of biometrics in a specific historical and cultural context that privileges the white, male body as normative, Murray argues that this emerging information technology renders marginalized bodies invisible to the biometric scanner. Understanding that these bodies are made monstrous through their illegibility, Murray asserts that biometrified bodies tell us more about the means of measurement than they do about the truth of bodily identity.

The relationship between communication and transportation – analyzed by communication theorists from Harold Innis to James Carey – is further unpacked by Torin Monahan in his study of intelligent transportation systems. Monahan's analysis of the ways that transportation control centers may be extended by function creep to discipline those suspect bodies, reveals that digitized transportation architecture offers up new possibilities for blurred boundaries between traffic management, law enforcement and security. These bodies-out-of-place are then rendered vulnerable to discipline by transportation infrastructure as a result of their lack of vehicular mobility. Rachel Hall's analysis of the visual culture of surveillance demonstrates that an aesthetics of transparency dominates the US approach to securing the nation. Using the visual culture theory developed by communication scholars, Hall reveals that total visibility is a central preoccupation of the post-9/11 surveillance state. Understanding security in terms of visibility means that new technologies able to flatten interiority into two-dimensional space are required – making human bodies mappable, codeable, and transmissible through time and space.

In her essay examining articulations of the self in reality television, Rachel Dubrofsky notes that this form of programming is giving rise to new forms of subjectivity. Specifically, Dubrofsky argues that the surveillance characteristic of these programs gives rise to a profound change in therapeutic behavior. Whereas older forms of therapeutic culture emphasized the importance of a dynamic self marked by its capacity for transformation, the therapeutic self is marked by stasis. Thus, rather than understanding the healthy self as one that is continually growing and changing, instead, the participants on these television shows aim to keep their identities consistent across time and space, a process that can be verified by the surveillance practices found on these shows.

In "Getting Carded Border Control and the Politics of Canada's Permanent Resident Card," feminist theorist Simone Browne notes that September 11th produced an "identity-industrial complex" in which security industries invest in transforming individuals into data for corporate profit. This is a project which Browne confirms is aligned with the security imperatives of the Global North. Moreover, this venture is one that stratifies some individuals into "subjects" while others are marked only as "bodies" – a racialized, gendered, and nationalized process of social sorting that has grave consequences for those marked for exclusion.

In revisiting James Carey's study of the relationship between communication and transportation, Jeremy Packer (2006) argues for a rethinking of the objects of communication research. "As the means of exerting force, maintaining control, and enacting surveillance are increasingly done through mobile communication technologies," writes Packer, "we have to seriously ask why it is that communication as a field predominantly seems to investigate mass media" to the exclusion of some many other vital communicative forms (p. 94). The contributors to this volume further the aim of expanding the range of inquiry of communication, moving beyond an exclusive concern with the mass media to consider important points of intersection between communication and surveillance, and examining surveillance practices as communicative practices in their own right.

NOTES

1 As Dan Schiller (2007) has noted, in its bid for legitimacy at the outset of the cold war, communication studies incorporated the growing, all-inclusive paradigm of information theory, shifting its emphasis away from mass persuasion and propaganda toward "abstract, formalized discussions of information senders, receivers, and channels" (p. 18).

2 See especially the respective work of John Tagg and Alan Sekula, and the volume *Documenting Individual Identity*, edited by Jane Caplan and John Torpey.

3 In a study of police use of information technologies published in 1992, Peter Manning specifically does not include "a host of means of *enhancing the primary data-gathering capacity* of the police such as surveillance devices, miniaturized tape recording and transmitting machines, drug and alcohol testing kits, video cameras for recording traffic stops, and more systematic tools for crime-scene analysis and data storage and retrieval" (p. 351). His study was narrowly concerned with information processing within police organizations and the impact of IT on police organizational communications. Although he does not explicitly address it as such, the study was more closely related to workplace surveillance research – and Richard Maxwell's (2006) work on the labor of surveillance – than to the literature on police surveillance of the social.

4 Chris Williams (2003) traces use of public CCTV systems in Britain back to the 1960s.

5 For examples of research on the effectiveness of CCTV schemes for crime prevention and reduction, see the contributions in Part Four of Norris, Morran, and Armstrong (Eds.)

(1998). *Surveillance, Closed Circuit Television, and Social Control.* Aldershot: Ashgate. See also Short and Ditton (1995) and Ditton, Short, Phillips, Norris, and Armstrong (1999).

6 For a wide variety of different theoretical and methodological approaches to CCTV, see the special issue of *Surveillance and Society* on the topic (2/3), available online at http:www/surveillance-and-society.org/cctv.htm.

7 Mathiesen (1997) uses the term "synopticism" to refer to the role of the mass media, and especially television, in enabling the many to watch the few, in contrast to "panopticism".

8 See Bob Sullivan (2007 August 14) "High-tech abuse worse than ever." Msnbc.com. Accessible online at http://redtape.msnbc.com/2007/08/leah-lived-for.html. The online responses are incredible and worthy of study.

REFERENCES

Andrejevic, M. (2002a). The work of being watched: Interactive media and the exploitation of self-disclosure. *Critical studies in media communication* 19 (2), 230-248.

—— (2002b). The kinder, gentler gaze of Big Brother: Reality TV in the era of digital capitalism. *New media and society* 4 (2), 251-270.

—— (2003). *Reality TV: The work of being watched.* Landham, MD: Rowman and Littlefield.

—— (2007). *iSpy: Surveillance and power in the interactive era.* Lawrence, KS: University of Kansas Press.

Baudrillard, J. (1980). The implosion of meaning in the media and the implosion of social in the masses," in K. Woodward, (Ed.). *The myths of information: Technology and postindustrial culture.* Madison, WI: Coda Press.

Bannister, J., Fyfe, N. R., & Kearns, A. (1998). Closed circuit television and the city. In C. Norris, J. Moran, and G. Armstrong (Eds.), *Surveillance, closed circuit television and social control* (pp. 21-40). Brookfield, VT: Ashgate.

Caplan, J. (2001). "This or that particular person": Protocols of identification in Nineteenth-Century Europe. In J. Caplan & J. Torpey (Eds.), *Documenting individual identity.* (pp. 49-66). Princeton, NJ: Princeton University Press.

Caplan, J. , & Torpey, J. (2001). Introduction. In J. Caplan & J. Torpey (Eds.). *Documenting individual identity: The development of state practices in the modern world* (pp. 1-12). Princeton, NJ: Princeton University Press.

Campbell, J.E. , & Carlson, M. (2002). Panopticon.com: Online surveillance and the commodification of privacy. *Journal of broadcasting and electronic media* 46 (4), 586-606.

Carey, J. (1989). *Communication as culture: Essays on media and society.* Boston: Unwin Hyman.

Carlson, M. (2006). Tapping into TiVo: Digital video recorders and the transition from schedules to surveillance in television. *New media and society* 8 (1), 97-115.

Cartwright, L. (1995). *Screening the Body: Tracing medicine's visual culture.* Minneapolis: University of Minnesota Press.

Clarke, R. (1994). The digital persona and its application to data surveillance. *Information Society* 10, 77-91.

Clifford, S. (2008). Billboards That Look Back. *New York Times.* May 31. (Last accessed November 30, 2008). http://www.nytimes.com/2008/05/31/business/media/31billboard.html

Davis, M. (1992). *City of Quartz*. New York: Vintage Books.

Doyle, A. (2006). An alternative current in surveillance and control: Broadcasting surveillance footage of crimes. In K. Haggerty & R. Ericson (Eds.), *The new politics of surveillance and visibility* (pp. 199-224). Toronto: University of Toronto Press.

Elmer, G. (2004). *Profiling machines: Mapping the personal information economy*. Cambridge, MA: MIT Press.

Ericson, R. V. , & Haggerty, K. D. (1997). *Policing the risk society*. Toronto: University of Toronto Press.

Foucault, M. (1977). *Discipline and punish: The birth of the prison*. (A. Sheridan, Trans.). New York: Vintage Books.

Gandy, O. H., Jr. (1993). *The panoptic sort: A political economy of personal information*. Boulder, CO: Westview Press.

Giddens, A. (1987). *The nation-state and violence: Volume two of a contemporary critique of historical materialism*. Berkeley, CA: University of California Press.

Giddens, A. (1990). *The consequences of modernity*. Stanford, CA: Stanford University Press.

Graham, S. (1998). Towards a fifth utility? On the extension and normalisation of public CCTV. In C. Norris, J. Moran, & G. Armstrong (Eds.), *Surveillance, closed circuit television and social control* (pp. 89-112). Brookfield, VT: Ashgate.

Groombridge, N. (2002). Crime control or crime culture TV? *Surveillance and society* 1 (1), 30-43.

Haggerty, K. , & Ericson, R. (Eds.) (2006). *The new politics of surveillance and visibility*. Toronto: University of Toronto Press.

Innis, H. A. (1951). *The bias of communication*. Toronto: University of Toronto Press.

Jamieson, D. (2006). Speaker of the house: When these cameras don't like what they see, they let you know about it. *The District Line*. Washington.

Lalvani, S. (1996). *Photography, vision, and the production of modern bodies*. Albany: State University of New York Press.

Laudon, K. C. (1986). *Dossier society: Value choices in the design of national information systems*. New York: Columbia University Press.

Levin, T. Y. (2002). Rhetoric of the temporal index: Surveillant narration and the cinema of 'real time.' In T. Y. Levin, U. Frohne, & P. Weibel (Eds.). *CTRL [SPACE]: Rhetorics of surveillance from Bentham to Big Brother* (pp. 578-593). Cambridge, MA: MIT Press.

Lyon, D. (2001). *Surveillance society: Monitoring everyday life*. Philadelphia, PA: Open University Press.

Lyon, D. (2006). 9/11, Synopticon, and scopophilia: Watching and being watched. In K. Haggerty & R. Ericson (Eds.), *The new politics of surveillance and visibility* (pp. 35-54). Toronto: University of Toronto Press.

Lyon, D. (2007). *Surveillance Studies: An overview*. Cambridge, Polity Press.

Magnet, S. (2008). Encoding the Body: Critically assessing the collection and uses of biometric information. Institute of Communications Research, Urbana-Champaign, University of Illinois at Urbana-Champaign. PhD Dissertation.

Mathiesen, T. (1997). The viewer society: Michel Foucault's 'panopticon' revisited. *Theoretical criminology* 1 (2), 215-234.

Marx, G. (1988). *Undercover: Police surveillance in America*. Berkeley, CA: University of California Press.

Maxwell, R. (2005). Surveillance: Work, myth, and policy. *Social Text* 83, 1-19.

McCahill, M. (1998). Beyond Foucault: Towards a contemporary theory of surveillance. In

C. Norris, J. Moran, and G. Armstrong (Eds.), *Surveillance, closed circuit television, and social control* (pp. 41-68). Aldershot, VT: Ashgate.

McCahill, M. (2002). *The surveillance web: The rise of visual surveillance in an English city.* Portland, OR: Willan.

Meehan, E. (1990). Why we don't count: The commodity audience. In P. Mellencamp (Ed.) *Logics of Television* (pp. 117-137). Biooinington, IN: Indiana University Press.

Monahan, T. (2006). Questioning surveillance and security. In T. Monahan (Ed.), *Surveillance and security: Technological politics and power in everyday life* (pp. 1-26). New York: Routledge.

——. (2008). Editorial: Surveillance and Inequality. *Surveillance and Society.* 5(3): 217-226. (Last accessed November 30, 2008). http://www.surveillance-and-society.org/articles5(3)/editorial.pdf

Mueller, M. (2002). *Ruling the Root.* Cambridge: MIT Press.

Norris, C., Moran, J. , & Armstrong, G. (Eds.). (1998). *Surveillance, closed circuit television and social control.* Brookfield, VT: Ashgate.

Norris, C., Moran, J. & Armstrong, G. (1998a). Algorithmic surveillance: The future of automated visual surveillance. In C. Norris, J. Moran, & G. Armstrong (Eds.), *Surveillance, closed circuit television and social control* (pp. 255-276). Brookfield, VT: Ashgate.

Oullette, L. , & Murray, S. (2004). Introduction. In S. Murray & L. Oullette (Eds.) *Reality TV: Remaking Television Culture* (pp. 1-15). New York: New York University Press.

Packer, J. (2006). Rethinking dependency: New relations of Transportation and Communication. In J. Packer & C. Robertson (Eds.), *Thinking with James Carey: Essays on communications, transportation, history* (pp. 79-100). New York: Peter Lang.

Peters, J. (1999). *Speaking into the Air: A history of the idea of communication.* Chicago: The University of Chicago Press.

Robertson, C. (2004). "Passport please': The U.S. passport and the documentation of individual identity, 1845-1930. Institute of Communications Research, Urbana-Champaign, University of Illinois at Urbana-Champaign. PhD Dissertation.

Robins, K. , & Webster, F. (1999). *Times of the technoculture: From the information society to the virtual life.* New York: Routledge.

Rule, J. R. (1973). *Private Lives and Public Surveillance.* London: Allen Lane.

Schiller, D. (2007). *How to think about information.* Urbana, IL: University of Illinois Press.

Scott, J. C. (1998). *Seeing like a state: How certain scheme to improve the human condition have failed.* New Haven, CT: Yale University Press.

Sekula, A. (1986). The body and the archive. *October 39,* 3-64.

Tinic, S. (2006). (En)Visioning the television audience: Revisiting question of power in the age of interactive television. In K. Haggerty & R. Ericson (Eds.), *The new politics of surveillance and visibility* (pp. 308-326). Toronto: University of Toronto Press.

Turow, J. (1997). *Breaking up America: Advertisers and the new media world.* Chicago, IL: University of Chicago Press.

Turow, J. (2006). *Niche envy: Marketing discrimination in the digital age.* Cambridge, MA: MIT Press.

Williams, R. (1975). *Television: Technology and cultural form.* New York: Schocken Books.

Wise, J. M. (2002). Mapping the culture of control: Seeing through *The Truman Show. Television and new media 3*(1), 29-47.

Yesil, B. (2006). Watching ourselves: Video surveillance, urban space, and self-responsibilization. *Cultural Studies* 20 (4-5), 400-416.

Surveillance in the Digital Enclosure

MARK ANDREJEVIC

RECENTRALIZATION

Pronouncing the untimely death of the desktop computer in an interactive era, *Wired* magazine claimed that, "computing is moving off your machine and into the cloud" (Tanz, 2007). Thanks to Wi-Fi and other forms of always-on connectivity, the article reported, users will no longer need to store their data or even their software applications on personal computers—rather these will be relegated to the ether and conveniently accessed via an increasing range of networked devices: laptops, mobile phones, PDA's, and so on. Our portable storage devices will apparently multiply and then shrink to invisibility, as the information they store expands to fill the space through which we move. In the world of ubiquitous computing, we will dip into these invisible currents of information at will, connected by an electromagnetic umbilicus to an overarching matrix of information and communication. As the futurists at MIT put it, describing their ubiquitous computing initiative, "computation . . . will be freely available everywhere, like batteries and power sockets, or oxygen in the air we breathe" (MIT Project Oxygen, 2004).

As William Gibson, famous for coining the term "cyberspace," has observed, the usefulness of the image of the internet "cloud," "lies in its vagueness, like cyberspace—a word which is also useful for its vagueness" (Holliday & Wieners, 1999). Apparently, one of the term's current uses is to obscure the very concrete shifts in control over information associated with the recentralization of information and communication resources envisioned by the architects of the internet "cloud." Consider, for example, the way in which this airy—or cloudy—rhetoric neatly elides the distinction between the "freedom" of the "oxygen we breathe" and that of electricity. Neither power nor batteries are "free" in the sense of being available to all without any consideration of the ability to pay or of access to economic resources. They both come with a charge, as it were, and so will mobile, ubiquitous, networked computing. The creation of ubiquitous "cloud" computing, which internet ideologist and conservative pundit George Gilder (2006) has described as the manifestation of a "newly recentralized computing architecture," is less a spontaneous eruption of convenience than a business model based on separating users from information and communication resources in order to restructure the terms of access to these resources.

The world envisioned by "cloud" computing is one in which users will rely on privatized communication networks and data storage facilities to access and manage an array of goods and services, from personal documents and music files to online shopping and e-mail. It is presaged by applications like Gmail and Google documents, which provide users with large amounts of storage space on Google's servers to store their personal documents and correspondence. In return for this convenience, Google reserves the right to mine its rapidly expanding databases for commercial purposes. If this business model is still in its infancy, one of its dominant emerging characteristics has become evident—a reliance on the interactive capability of networks to gather information about users. The terms of access to the "cloud" will include the capture and commodification of information about how, when, and where, we make use of its resources, a fact that renders the metaphor doubly misleading. The portrait of user activity made possible by ubiquitous interactivity will not be ephemeral, but increasingly detailed and fine-grained, thanks to an unprecedented ability to capture and store patterns of interaction, movement, transaction, and communication. Patterns of users' Web browsing, for example, could be correlated with those of online shopping, communication, and, eventually, advertising exposure. The information clouds here are far from ephemeral, fleeting forms: their details are captured and fixed in a manner that envisions a mechanical and more prosaic version of Jorge Luis Borges's fictional Funes, "who remembered the shapes of the clouds in south at dawn on the 30th of April of 1882, and . . . could compare them in his recollection with the marbled grain in the design of a leather-bound book which he had seen only once, and with the lines in the spray which an oar raised in the Rio Negro on the eve of the battle of the Quebracho" (Borges, 1999, p. 130).

To counter the misleading image of the internet cloud, this essay proposes the model of *digital enclosure* as a way of theorizing the forms of productivity and monitoring facilitated by ubiquitous interactivity. The model of enclosure traces the relationship between a material, spatial process—the construction of networked, interactive environments—and the private expropriation of information critiqued by Schiller (2007), Boyle (2003) and Lessig (2004). Monitoring, in this context, refers specifically to the collection of information, with or without the knowledge of users, that has actual or speculative economic value. Whereas the promise of universal interactivity is portrayed by the popularizers of the rhetoric of the "digital sublime" (Mosco, 2004) at places like MIT's Media Lab and *Wired* magazine as a form of liberation—freedom from the fiber-optic fetters of the wired world—the model of digital enclosure suggests that ubiquitous interactivity also has the potential to facilitate unprecedented commodification of previously nonproprietary information and an aggressive clamp-down of centralized control over information resources.

Consider two examples of digital enclosures in action: Google's proposed business model for equipping the city of San Francisco with free wireless internet access, and the use of the interactive capability of the internet to enforce increasingly restrictive intellectual property regimes. Google and Earthlink's proposal for "free" Wi-Fi in San Francisco would be financed by the collection of information about the time-space paths of users who log on to their proprietary network. In addition to generating what Mosco (1989) calls "cybernetic commodities" (transactionally generated demographic information about user behavior), this information would allow Google to target users with so-called "contextual advertising"—ads based on their location throughout the course of the day. Google's hope is that users will be more likely to click on ads for nearby commercial outlets: "It could be the difference between seeing an advertisement for Macy's, if a user happens to be in Union Square, or a seafood restaurant if the user is near Fisherman's Wharf" (Kopytoff, 2006, p. C1). Moreover, thanks to its myriad interactive applications, the potential exists for Google to supplement its customization algorithms with information gleaned from users' search engine inquiries, their Gmail accounts, their map requests, and so on. Google has already filed a patent application that, as one account puts it, "involves a system in which targeted ads are served to wireless internet users based on the geographic location of the wireless access point (WAP), as well as the behavior and demographics of the WAP's users, and other criteria" (Telecommunications Industry

News, 2006). Behavior and demographics are, needless to say, umbrella terms wide enough to capture the expanding array of information about users that Google hopes to gather with its proliferating array of services. The creation of an interactive "enclosure"—in this case, one large enough to embrace the entire city of San Francisco—promises to be fantastically productive in terms of its ability to generate, capture, and store personal information. The proposed Wi-Fi network, combined with Google's rapidly expanding data storage and sorting capabilities, makes it possible to gather and process information previously too costly to capture and to transform it into demographic inputs for the marketing process.[1]

If proposed enclosures like Google's Wi-Fi network facilitate information gathering, they also enable unprecedented levels of centralized data control. Consider the example of a friend of mine who stumbled across the limits imposed by interactivity when he tried to play a high-definition DVD he had purchased legally in the United States and then carried halfway around the world with him to Australia. When he attempted to play the high-definition version of the DVD (one of the bonus features) on his laptop computer—which he had also brought with him from the U.S., the region for which the DVD was coded—he was greeted with a pop-up box instructing him to register online. Upon doing so, and entering the code on the DVD case as instructed, he was informed that the movie would not play because he wasn't in the appropriate region: the version he had purchased was to be played exclusively in the US. He did not have to enter his location when he logged on—the network had located him. By going online, he had entered a virtual enclosure that could pinpoint him in space and time in order to regulate his access to data that he had purchased perfectly legally thousands of miles away.

This type of control is made possible by the broadening reach of a digital enclosure that increasingly encompasses erstwhile "stand-alone" devices. If personal computers were once relatively self-contained, the architects of recentralization at places like Google, Yahoo, and Microsoft, envision a networked world in which the governing assumption will be that our machines are in constant contact with a broader network that can be used not just to access information, but to monitor its proper use. One apparent solution to the perceived threat posed by file-sharing to the movie and recording industry is not less interactivity, but *more*. When the devices we use to access content are networked, we may find not only that our consumption patterns can be digitally recorded, but that approved forms of access—such as the type of geographic limitations built into my friend's DVD—can be enforced via computer code (Lessig, 1999) rather than reliance on the goodwill of consumers. When the video iPod goes wireless and interactive by enfolding itself within the embrace of an iTunes-controlled digital enclosure, the likelihood that users will be able to play illegally downloaded or shared movies will plummet. In the era of digital enclosure, information does not "want to be free," it (and the "it" here fetishizes the imperatives of those who control the enclosure) wants to stand and be counted. It also wants to go forth and multiply by disclosing details about itself to those with the technology to monitor, record, store, and manage the resulting metadata. A networked iPod will be able to do more than block unlicensed content, it will also be able to keep track of every detail of users' viewing preferences. Consumers will likely have only the vaguest idea of exactly how much information is being gathered about their listening habits and even less control over what Apple does with the proprietary information about individual behavior it has collected in the "privacy" of its digital enclosure.

This is not an argument about the invasive character of the technology *per se*. It is certainly possible to create networks that do not collect and store detailed information about users. Rather this is an argument about the forms of productive data gathering enabled by private ownership of and control over interactive enclosures, wired or wireless, that render an increasing array of spaces interactive. The model of enclosure highlights the ongoing importance of structures of ownership and control over productive resources in determining the role they play in what Schiller (2007) has described as "the struggle against continuing enclosures of non-proprietary information" (p. 56). The attempt to foreground questions of ownership counters the determinism of those who insist on the *inherently* empowering character of interactive networks and the revolutionary *telos* of the digital era. Such accounts run across the political spectrum from figures like Rupert Murdoch who, upon purchasing MySpace for a half billion dollars observed that, "Technology is shifting power away from the editors, the publishers, the establishment, the media elite. Now it's the people who are taking control . . ." (Reiss, 2006) to mainstream liberals like political consultant Joe Trippi ("the technology is finally here to allow people to reject what they're being given and demand what they want") (Trippi, 2004, p. 235) to left-leaning academics and artists like Celia Pearce ("The digital age introduces a new form of international socialism") (Pearce, 1997, p. 180). The rhetoric of "Third Wave," cyber-euphoric futurism invokes the promise of a silicon revolution that painlessly eliminates the inequities attendant upon the concentration of control over wealth and productive resources by economic and political elites. The key to this hypothetical revolution is not the redistribution of control over material resources, but their supposed irrelevance in an emerging information economy. In the preamble to their "Magna Carta for the Knowledge Age," for example, futurists Esther Dyson, George Gilder, and Alvin Toffler (1996), blithely proclaim that "The central event of the 20th century is the overthrow of matter" (p. 295). The implication of course, is that resource ownership no longer matters. This triumphant idealism persists in the popular media's focus on the gee-whiz gimmickry of ubiquitous computing as well as in the hip radicalism of books like *Netocracy: The New Power Elite and Life after Capitalism* (Bard & Söderqvist, 2002), which proclaims the coming irrelevance of property rights and "ownership of the means of production" (p. 255). Against these persistent remainders of the "digital sublime," the model of digital enclosure seeks to explain why much still depends on who owns and controls the networks, who sets the terms of entry, and who gathers and sorts this information for what ends.

It is crucial, for the purposes of critiquing interactive surveillance practices and regimes of centralized control over information, to consider the physical and dynamic aspects of the notion of enclosure: to describe the construction of, for example, cellular wireless networks as expanding interactive overlays that endow the world around us with interactive capabilities. Such networks might be described as physical enclosures to the extent that they define a particular space and are able to both provide functionality and gather information within the confines of the geographically delimited area they cover. These enclosures are not exclusive—they can overlap with, contain, and be contained by other delimited spaces that facilitate information gathering and transmission. Rather than thinking in terms of unitary exclusive enclosures we can discern layers of enclosures, both virtual and physical, with varying spatial reaches and information scopes—cellular networks overlapping Google's Wi-Fi networks, both of which embrace smart homes or offices equipped with radio-frequency indentification (RFID) systems and are in turn encompassed by GPS satellite systems.

These various enclosures facilitate vastly different types of information gathering and transmission. Whereas the enclosure or "cell" encompassed by a mobile phone network might be able to gather pings from and transmit carrier signals to handsets that pass in and out of range, Google may be able to track movements to a much higher degree of resolution and to correlate these with the content of search engine requests and e-mail correspondence. It is also worth noting that different types of enclosures operate with varying levels of symmetry and transparency: book shoppers who go on Amazon.com are able to view why particular recommendations are being made for them: the information-gathering process is relatively transparent to individual users. This is not always the case when, for example, cell phones are used to gather geographic data about users, or even when Amazon.com conducted an experiment in variable pricing, offering a DVD for a lower price to a user who had not logged on as a repeat customer than to a friend of his who had. In many cases—as when search engines gather information about our Web-surfing behavior—we are largely unaware of what information is being gathered, how, and for what purposes. Every now and then we are provided with a reminder of the monitoring capacity of interactivity—perhaps when we log on to the internet in a foreign country and get a different version of Google news, or find an advertisement related to the content of our e-mail messages on Gmail, and so on.

While futurists celebrate the potentially subversive, empowering, or revolutionary character of the internet, commercial entities are working hard to establish the conditions for what Paul Virilio (2005) has described as the contemporary incarnation of "the great Locking Up of the seventeenth century . . . this time, not on the scale of the asylums or prisons of the Ancient Regime, but on a scale encompassing the whole world" (p. 40). If the creation of enclosures such as those of the prison, the factory, and the asylum referenced by Virilio (following Foucault) facilitated the disciplinary monitoring of inmates and workers, that of the digital enclosure extends the monitoring gaze beyond such institutional walls to encompass spaces of leisure, consumption, domesticity, and perhaps all of these together. If this sounds a touch hyperbolic, consider the ambitious scope of one marketer's prediction about the future of radio-frequency ID tagging—yet another type of interactive enclosure that allows objects to be tracked as they move through space: "Ultimately, we'll be tagging every item in the universe" (Bond, 2003, p. A1). The fantasy of total interactivity, in other words, is also one of complete enclosure.

A DIGITAL ENCLOSURE MOVEMENT

Digital enclosures literalize the physical metaphor of what legal scholar James Boyle (2003) has described as a "second enclosure" movement devoted to the "enclosure of the intangible commons of the mind" (p. 37). In more concrete terms, this process of enclosure refers to a variety of strategies for privatizing, controlling, and commodifying information and intellectual property. As Yochai Benkler (2006) and Dan Schiller (2007) have argued, this process relies not just on expropriation of previously nonproprietary information, but on the construction of an increasingly restrictive legal regime for the enforcement and extension of property rights over a growing range of information. Boyle (2003) offers the example of patent claims for human genes, which has been expanded to include life forms—not just strains of wheat or corn, but also, for example, cats with hypo-allergenic fur. The movement he describes, driven by attempts to profit from the commodification of information, is omnivorous and Borg-like in its drive toward total assimilation: "In the new vision of intellectual property . . . property should be extended everywhere—more is better. Expanding patentable and copyrightable subject matter, lengthening the copyright term, giving legal protection to 'digital barbed wire' [encryption] even if it is used to protect against fair use" (Boyle, 2003, p. 40). Schiller (2007) describes the privatization of collective or shared knowledge, as in the case, for example, of patent claims on traditional medicines, and the commodification of publicly subsidized or not-for-profit intellectual labor in the university. The expanded role of information in the era of "digital capitalism" has been met with what Schiller refers to as "elite programs of political-economic reconstruction" devoted to "enclosing the immensity of global communication and information provision . . . the paradigm for which was set via enclosure of common lands in England during the epochal transition to agrarian capitalism hundreds of years ago" (Schiller, 2007, p. 43).

The model of England's land enclosure movement is pivotal to critical accounts of capitalism because it illustrates the transformation of violent expropriation into a freely agreed-upon contractual arrangement. The forcible separation of workers from the means of production—a process that Marx (1992) describes as "primitive" accumulation, is, he argues, a necessary precondition for the institution of wage labor insofar as it creates a working class "freed" up to sell control over its labor power:

> . . . the theft of the common lands, the usurpation of feudal and clan property and its transformation into modern private property . . . all these things were just so many idyllic methods of primitive accumulation. They conquered the field for capitalist agriculture, incorporated the soil into capital, and created for the urban industries the necessary supplies of free and rightless proletarians. (p. 895)

As Kazanjian (2002) points out, freedom, in this context, is to be understood in a distinctly negative sense: "Writes Marx: "The free workers are therefore free from, unencumbered by, any means of production of their own" (p. 170). This form of freedom from the means of securing their own sustenance underlies a second form of so-called freedom: that of "freely" agreeing to enter into a labor contract under terms advantageous to employers and exploitative to workers (that is to say terms that workers wouldn't voluntarily agree to absent the coercion imposed by the expropriation of the commons).

Free acquiescence to the surrender of control over one's own productive activity is secured by depriving workers of any other option for sustenance—this is the version of freedom that underlies capitalist exchange relations. It is a form of freedom that is, in turn, reliant upon a spatial reconfiguration: workers must be *separated* from the land so that their access to it can be contractually regulated. With the advent of industrialization, entry into a labor contract also meant entry into a physical space operated and controlled by its owners. As Kazanjian puts it, Marx interprets enclosure as "one of the systems that . . . manufactures capitalists and wage-laborers" (2002, p. 172). The spatial correlative of the emergence of a "free" working class in the capitalist era is the formation of clearly bounded, privately owned, and operated enclosures to which worker access is strictly monitored and regulated.

However, the notion of *primitive* accumulation can be misleading insofar as it implies enclosure is a temporally discrete and prior process—one that takes place only in particular periods of capitalist or precapitalist development—rather than an ongoing process. A more satisfactory account—and one that bears closely on the process of digital enclosure—is provided by De Angelis (1998), who notes that the enclosure process, "is an inherent and continuous element of modern societies and its range of action extends to the entire world" (p. 3). In addition to the everyday process of wage labor and market exchange, capitalism is characterized by ongoing struggles over so-called "primitive" accumulation: attempts, for example, to privatize the national parks and transfer control over their resources to private control, the forcible expulsion of indigenous populations in Africa and Latin America from mineral or oil-rich homelands, and the eviction of farmers from communal lands in Nigeria, "to make way for plantations owned and managed by the World Bank" (Midnight Notes Collective, 2001, p. 2).

As a crucially important productive resource, land plays an important rule in accounts of enclosure—continuous, contemporary, and otherwise—not least because of the central role of agriculture during the early transition to capitalism. However, as De Angelis points out, land enclosure is but one example of the more general form of "primitive accumulation," understood as "an accumulation of capital claims—of titles to existing assets which are accumulated primarily for speculative reasons" (1998, p. 4). Once resources are recognized to be actually or potentially productive, they become subject to attempts to subsume them to capitalist social relations through an appropriation process that—and this is the core of "primitive accumulation" according to De Angelis—results in the "*separation between producers and means of production*" (1998, p. 5). As a strategy for providing capitalism with the basis for accumulation (both the private ownership of resources and a "free" workforce compelled to sell access to its labor) and for reproducing (and expanding) the forms of separation it relies upon, primitive accumulation in turn depends upon a "working class which by education, tradition and habit looks upon the requirements of that mode of production as self-evident laws" (Karl Marx, as quoted in De Angelis, 1998, p. 15). Thus, one of the triumphs of the enclosure movement and a crowning ideological achievement of capitalism has been its ability to win popular consent to, and the consequent naturalization of, the distribution of property crucial to the exploitation of waged labor. Much the same might be said of the emerging information economy, in which privatization of networks and databases and, therefore, of control over both the means of interaction and the information it generates has become the norm, despite the publicly subsidized character of the original Internet.

As conceptualized in this essay, the process of digital enclosure combines the spatial characteristics of land enclosure with the metaphorical process of information enclosure described by Schiller (2007), Boyle (2003), and Benkler (2006). As information commodities become increasingly valuable resources in the era of digital capitalism (Schiller, 1999), the construction of privately owned and operated interactive enclosures serves to separate users from the means of interaction, transaction, communication, and expression. This process of separation is what the resurgent model of server-client computing envisioned by the Internet cloud achieves. Constant connectivity in the contradictory world of contemporary capital, relies on the separation of users from their data. To the extent that information generated by consumers as they interact with one another, surf the Web, shop online and off, and interact with networks throughout the course of the day becomes economically valuable, the creation of interactive spaces facilitates its capture. Thus, the construction of privatized infrastructures for ubiquitous computing has become one of the economic drivers of investment in the digital media industries. According to the chief of research at computer-chip manufacturer Intel, the company has devoted most of its $4 billion annual research and development budget to products that anticipate the advent of an era of ubiquitous and "proactive" computing (Intel, 2005). In South Korea, a consortium of private developers in partnership with the tech company LG CNS, plan to raise $25 billion to build New Songdo City—the first comprehensive urban digital enclosure in which wireless computing will be ubiquitous (O'Connell, 2005). In the U.S. and Western Europe, mobile telephone companies are spending billions of dollars to develop "third-generation" wireless networks that will enable cell phones to serve as mobile Internet connections and data storage devices.

Investment in the construction of such interactive enclosures is testimony to the anticipated productivity of what Hardt and Negri (2000) describe as "immaterial labor" and Terranova (2000) calls "free labor"— or at least the subset of such labor that I have elsewhere described as "the work of being watched" (Andrejevic, 2004): willing or unknowing submission to monitoring practices that generate economic value in the form of information commodities. The value of transactionally generated information about the use of information technologies derives in large part from its anticipated uses in rationalizing the marketing process through the customization of goods, services, and advertising. In anticipation of the value of such labor, the proprietary claim made by private companies upon transactionally and interactionally generated information might be considered a form of accumulation of "titles to existing [and anticipated] assets . . . for speculative reasons" (De Angelis, 1998, p. 4). Consider, for example, the patent filed by Google, proposing to custom tailor advertising to online computer game players based on detailed observation of their style of play. According to the patent proposal, both player dialogue and play preferences will be analyzed "to characterise the user (e.g., cautious, risk-taker, aggressive, non-confrontational, stealthy, honest, cooperative, uncooperative, etc.)" (Bantick, 2007). The goal is to use this information to provide in-game ads, in real time, customized to fit the player's psychographic profile. Google's wager is that interactively generated game-player data will have economic value—value that may well increase when it is combined with other information captured by its various services (e-mail content, time-space path, search engine requests, and so on). The more ubiquitous access is to video games, the more comprehensive will be the data gathered by Google, and the harder consumers will be working as they play.

Microsoft has patented a similar plan to customize advertising to users based on the applications and data running on their personal computers. It is an ambitious plan to enclose information not by having it stored on centralized servers, but by inserting a layer of networked interactivity between users and the data on their own machine. In the scenario envisioned by the patent, in order to access our documents and run our applications, we will need to rely upon an operating system that communicates with the network and serves ads based on the information portrait we craft out of our own data: "the software is like adware that figures out what ads to display based on files on the hard drive and what's being displayed on the screen at a given moment" (Hoover, 2007). It is an ambitious plan to go Google one better by offloading even the data storage function onto users: "the software could conceivably gather information on every file on a user's hard drive and send it to advertisers, and the application does little to assuage security and privacy concerns" (Hoover, 2007). Users will still be separated from their data not by physical space but by the software they use to access it, which will stipulate monitoring as one of the terms of access. Even this model depends on the extension of the reach of a physical interactive enclosure: for it to work, just as in the case of the DVD that would not play in Australia, the computer has to be networked.

The process of digital enclosure differs from land enclosure, at least for the moment, to the extent that it does not take place under the threat of force. It does, of course, presuppose the property rights regime of the contemporary market economy—that is to say, it builds upon, extends, and reproduces the social relations secured by so-called primitive accumulation (land enclosure): "Once the separation is given, the production process can only produce it anew, reproduce it, and reproduce it on an expanded scale (Marx, 1973, p. 462). In other words, it is testimony to the naturalization process that the notion of a nonprivatized enclosure sounds vaguely outlandish—who would provide us with e-mail and Wi-Fi if not Google, EarthLink, et alia? Thanks to the legacy of private control over productive resources, it seems to pass without any serious challenge that the content we provide to companies like Google becomes their property. We think of our e-mail, for example, as our own creation—personal missives that we compose for our own use and that of selected correspondents. But by virtue of composing our letters online, these become the property of the entities that own and control the data enclosure in which our correspondence is stored. A close read of Gmail's privacy policy, for example, reveals that even when users delete messages from their Gmail accounts, Google reserves the right to retain copies indefinitely: "Residual copies of deleted messages and accounts may take up to 60 days to be deleted from our active servers and may remain in our offline backup systems" (Google, 2005). Given that Google's business model is based on accumulating as much information as possible, and the company is engaged in an ongoing expansion of its database resources to do so, we should not count on the company purging its back-up systems anytime soon.

This is not to deny that attempts to reinforce and secure relations of separation remain part of the ongoing process of struggle identified by Schiller (2007). There are still some municipalities in the U.S. working on public or nonprofit schemes for universal Wi-Fi access, but the telecommunications companies have been lobbying hard to restrict and even, in some quarters, to ban such initiatives. The lobbying efforts have resulted in restrictive state legislation and in the proposal of federal legislation to limit municipal Wi-Fi programs, including, for example, the "Preserving Innovation in Telecom Act" and the "Broadband Investment and Consumer Choice Act," both proposed by conservative, business-friendly congressional Republicans (Gnatek, 2006). Louisiana's state ban on free municipal Wi-Fi gained national notoriety when Bell South invoked the law in an attempt to shut down a Wi-Fi service that New Orleans residents relied upon during the devastation caused by Hurricane Katrina. Such efforts indicate that telecommunication companies understand much is at stake in preserving the privatized character of digital information enclosures. When it comes to other information services, such as e-mail and data storage, there is little in the way of proposed alternatives to a privatized commercial model—except, perhaps, in the educational and government research sectors associated with the preprivatized version of the internet.

In the face of the current commercialization of the Web, it is easy to forget that the original digital enclosure of information—its migration into digital storage and its transmission via digital networks—was a publicly subsidized one, a noncommercial, publicly funded network designed to facilitate access to and sharing of information. This historical fact should serve as a much-needed reminder that the convenience associated with digitized forms of data storage, sorting, and transmission is not inherently linked to commercialization or privatization, and that alternative information architectures are possible. Ownership matters, space matters, and materiality, as it were, still matters.

It is in this regard that enclosure is to be understood not simply as a metaphor but as a geographic process involving the reconfiguration of physical space in ways that structure relations of control over access to information of all kinds. As Henri Lefebvre observed, the production of space goes hand-in-hand with that of social relations: "Space is at once result and cause, product and producer; it is also a stake, the locus of projects and actions deployed as part of specific strategies, and hence also the object of wagers on the future" (1991, p. 143). Viewed through this lens, the land enclosure movement, for example, served as a palpably spatial strategy for shaping relations of production in an emerging capitalist economy. Separating workers from the land they cultivated was a necessary precondition for restructuring the terms of their access to productive resources. Against the background of restructured property relations, workers had little choice but to enter "freely" into exploitative wage labor agreements.

As in the case of land enclosure, digital enclosure facilitates control over resources so as to structure the terms of access. Private property is a precondition for the economic logic of digital enclosure which, in its commercial form, provides physical space with an interactive overlay (or multiple overlays) which facilitate the capture and control of data that can be resold in the form of cybernetic commodities. We might think of the expansion of such enclosures as a way of completing the process of spatial dedifferentiation inaugurated by broadcasting. If TV and radio signals were able to overcome the boundaries between sites of leisure and domesticity alike, bringing the messages of advertisers into spaces of recreation, domesticity and consumption, internet connections, cellular phone networks, and digital cable complete the circle by allowing marketers to extract information back from these same sites.

The physical process of enclosure—the creation of ubiquitous, always on networked spaces—becomes a precondition for the rapid expansion of information enclosure. Collecting increasingly fine-grained information about consumers, viewers, and citizens requires building interactive networks that make the collection process automatic and cost-efficient. When, for example, a supermarket "smart cart" tracks both the items placed in it (via radio frequency identification tags) and the location of the user in the shop, it can gather information that would have been prohibitively costly to collect accurately by either customer surveys or direct human monitoring. Searching out items in a large supermarket, an activity that once took effort but remained economically unproductive, can become value-generating labor when folded into the monitoring embrace of a digital enclosure.

The same might be said of a growing range of activities, transactions, and communication activities that are being encompassed by digital networks. When we make the move from snail mail to Gmail, for example, we make it possible for Google to store, search, and sort the contents of every message, noting when it was sent, received, and responded to. When we switch from analog to digital cable TV, we enable a quantum leap in the ability to track viewer behavior, thanks in part to DVRs that monitor not just which shows are stored and when they are viewed, but which segments are paused, rewound, or fast-forwarded. When we switch from terrestrial to cellular phone communications, we enable service providers to monitor not just our calling activity, but its relation to our time-space path throughout the course of the day. Already some municipalities, including the city of Baltimore, are using cellphone data as a traffic management tool, monitoring the movement of cellphones from one cell to the next to keep track of traffic flow and congestion (Dresser, 2005). As long as the phone is turned on, it serves as a passport into a monitored electromagnetic enclosure.

There is a self-stimulating character to the data-capture capability of digital enclosures—the more ubiquitous they are, the more likely they are to be used in a variety of locations for an increasing range of applications that generate an ever-more fine-grained portrait of users. The more ubiquitous such enclosures are, the more willing users will be to store an increasing range and quantity of personal data on them, from personal correspondence, to online journals and multi-media files. At the same time, the more information users store on commercial servers, the more detailed the user data such sites will be able to collect—not just about what users search for online, or what they write about in their e-mails, but, for example, when, where, and how often they listen to their music, view their pictures, and modify their online files, whom they contact for voice, text, and video communications, when, and where. The list has the potential to expand indefinitely, up to the point of what Bill Gates (1996) has described as a totally documented life—one in which every detail of quotidian existence is redoubled in storable, searchable, digital form.

Gates, however, imagined this data would be captured and controlled by the user rather than by overlapping layers of increasingly coordinated private data collection systems whose activities remain, for the most part, invisible to users. The frenetically productive information and communication environment envisioned by the engineers of such enclosures traces the productive spiral outlined by Lefebvre (1991) as a "sequence of operations" that, "implies a productive consumption: the consumption of a space . . . that is doubly productive . . . What actually happens is that a vicious circle is set in train which for all its circularity is an invasive force serving dominant economic interests" (p. 374). The more ubiquitous such applications become, the more likely users are to use them and thus to generate an expanding range of information commodities.

In its abstract form of ubiquitous computing, a digital enclosure describes a space of universalized recognition and communication in which the places through which we move and the objects they contain recognize individuals and communicate with them (via portable devices). It is a space within which cars know their location and can rapidly access information about their surroundings, one in which supermarket shelves know when they need to be stocked and when they are being approached by someone likely to buy a particular product. In more concrete terms, the infrastructure of the digital enclosure is rapidly becoming a privatized, commercial one—fueled by large investments in wireless technology and ubiquitous computing. As in the case of some of the most ambitious physical enclosures of the 20th century, including the giant shopping malls, the digital enclosures will be commercial ones. In this respect, the digitization of the enclosures—their ability to span sites of labor, leisure, and domesticity—does not merely dedifferentiate the public from the private; in but doing it, privileges commercial information gathering over personal control of information. It allows, in other words, for the privatization of public space to broaden its reach even as such enclosures reprivatize personal information as commercial property. The result is not the end of privacy but its repurposing in commercial form.

The privatization process relies not just on the construction of electromagnetic enclosures, but also on facilities to store the tremendous amounts of data captured by interactive networks. On the one hand, we are confronted by the overlay of physical space with interactive capabilities—space as interface: the grafting of the interactivity associated with the virtual enclosure of the Internet onto the physical spaces of daily life. On the other, we are witnesses to the unprecedented construction of giant data centers around the globe. Rather than a "cloud," the spatial formations associated with digital enclosure are vast data repositories—so-called "server farms"—sprouting up in locations where land and electricity are relatively inexpensive: along the Columbia River Basin in Washington

State and Oregon, in Texas, North Carolina, and elsewhere. Google has reportedly budgeted some $1.5 billion in 2006 as part of a project to build "a worldwide string of data centers" nicknamed "Googleplex" (Markoff & Hansell, 2006) and its rivals Microsoft and Yahoo have embarked on similar data warehouse construction projects.

For a business that seems to have no tangible products, Google relies heavily on very real "bricks-and-mortar" facilities. As one analyst put it, "Google is as much about infrastructure as it is about the search engine . . . They are building an enormous computing resource on a scale that is almost unimaginable" (Markoff & Hansell 2006, p. 1). The physical corollary of computing as pervasive and invisible as air is the concrete condensation of information represented by the construction of such data enclosures on a giant scale—acres of "air-conditioned warehouses filled with thousands upon thousands of computer servers" (Harden, 2006). These loom on the landscape like depopulated afterimages of industrial-era factories, inhabited not by workers, inmates, or patients, but by the combined data doubles of all of them: enclosures not of people, but of information *about* people assembled for the purposes of both assisting them and managing them more effectively. As the interactive enclosures expand and thereby facilitate the convergence of spheres of social practice (we can, thanks to the network, labor from home or the corner coffee shop, stream video at work, and so on), they also gather their resources into the tightly guarded and privately controlled server farms where rapidly growing databases can be mined for profit—in the billions of dollars, based on the earnings of internet giants like Google, Yahoo, and Microsoft, and of database companies like Acxiom and ChoicePoint that are cashing in on post-9/11 Homeland Security contracts and the demand for both security screening and marketing data.

IMPLICATIONS

The emerging information economy that I have described is predicated not on the loss of privacy, but on its galloping expansion in the form of the private control not just of the means of information storage, communication, and retrieval—a long-standing trend, in many respects—but also of the interactively generated information associated with the proliferation of digital enclosures. For years, media ranging from telephony to broadcasting (in the U.S.) have been under private control—but these technologies generated a relatively minimal amount of information about how they were used (as evidenced by the ongoing attempts by broadcasters to monitor viewers and listeners). As they entered the digital realm and were supplemented by networked information and communication technologies, these media technologies helped constitute the means for a quantum leap in information gathering—a leap that included, in many cases, information that could not be captured previously.

The resurgent server-client model envisioned by the proponents of ubiquitous computing further extends the reach of this capture process: activities that used to take place beyond the reach of interactive monitoring are migrating into the rapidly growing databanks of Googleplex and similar information warehouses. As they do so, they enter private domains that come with new terms of entry. We can access the data we have turned over to them, but only in exchange for willing submission to, among other conditions, the forms of monitoring and control facilitated by the interactive infrastructure.

The goal of this essay is not to downplay the conveniences attendant upon mobile computing and associated forms of networked interactivity. Even forms of target marketing—such as those practiced by Amazon.com—can be useful. It would be wonderfully convenient to be able to access all the music one has ever purchased wherever one happens to be and to be able to share information, data files, and photos effortlessly with distant friends, family, and co-workers, or to retrieve the various documents one is working on without having to back them up incessantly on a proliferating array of storage devices. Indeed, the economic model I have been describing would be untenable if there were not real advantages to the ubiquitous interactivity and communicative capability of what I have been calling digital enclosures. It is, however, critically important to consider precisely what the cost of these conveniences might end up being, not just in economic terms, but in terms of control over information. These costs, and the social relations that underwrite them, are masked by the metaphors of unfettered digital freedom so frequently invoked in discussions of next generation interactive technologies. They are further obscured by the taken-for-granted character of the privatization of networks and databases. "Of course," we reason, "we have to give up some measure of control in exchange for free Wi-Fi access or, for two gigabytes of e-mail storage—if we are only giving up control of information about ourselves that is not of any use to us, why not?"

But perhaps we are giving up more than we realize—not least of which might be the possibility of alternative conceptions of how digital, interactive infrastructures could be developed and implemented. The private, market-driven model of the digital enclosure imposes some significant limits on the promise of the Internet, as the conservative blogger Andrew Sullivan (2002) put it (in a free-market parody of Marx), to allow those with internet access to "seize the means of production." Consider, for example, the case of the Chinese political blogger Zhao Jing who, when the government used its control over Internet routers to block his Web site, switched to the Microsoft Corporation's blogging tool, MSN Spaces.

After he criticized the firing of an editor from one of China's more independent newspapers and called for a boycott of the paper, his blog was shut down again, this time by Microsoft at the Chinese government's behest. As one press account put it, "What was most remarkable about this was that Microsoft's blogging service has no servers located in China; the company effectively allowed China's censors to reach across the ocean and erase data stored on American territory" (Thompson, 2006). Microsoft, with an eye to the lucrative potential of the Chinese market, helped take the activism out of interactivity, with the explanation that in order to do business in China it had to follow the laws that "require companies to make the internet safe for local users" (Spencer, 2006).

Suggestively, the company has also reportedly taken the democracy out of its blog service: "In China, Microsoft does not allow the word 'democracy' to be used in a subject heading for its MSN Spaces blog service" (*War of the Words*, 2006) The company is not alone in making concessions with an eye to the bottom line: "Google . . . restricted search results for the Tiananmen Square massacre; and Yahoo handed over private e-mail information to the conviction of two internet dissidents" (*War of the Words*, 2006). United States politicians have been critical of the actions of these companies abroad, even while some of them defended the Bush administration's Justice Department's request for information about millions of searches made on popular search engines including Google, AOL, MSN, and Yahoo. It is not hard to imagine why large Internet companies with an eye to government regulators might be all-too-willing to comply (although Google did put up some token resistance). These forms of recentralized control over information are facilitated by the processes of privatization and separation associated with digital enclosure. To the extent the resources for communication, expression, and interaction are encompassed by a privatized digital enclosure, access to these resources is subject to enhanced forms of monitoring and control.

Such developments suggest the potential costs associated with a reliance on private companies for an increasing array of communication and information functions that entail surrendering an expanding range of information to their control. On the one hand, the Internet might represent a very powerful tool for free expression even—or perhaps especially—under authoritarian regimes. On the other hand, to the extent that expression becomes increasingly reliant upon private corporations more committed to the realities of the bottom line than to abstract principles of civil liberties, the technology that facilitates the ability to challenge entrenched power could evolve into a breathtakingly efficient tool for monitoring, tracking, and filtering dissident expression. The anarchic version of online communication associated with the Internet may well be an artifact of an early stage in its development represented by the years of government subsidy and limited control. As the informational slack is eliminated from privatized digital enclosures, every message will become traceable, every interaction, monitorable and recordable. Moreover, as the recent attempts by the U.S. Justice Department to peruse private databases suggest, the digital enclosure facilitates function creep. Data that can be almost effortlessly collected and inexpensively stored and sorted becomes a tempting data mine for state officials, as privacy scruples give way to the political mobilization of the "war" on terror.

In somewhat more abstract terms, to the extent that markets in personal data have proven lucrative, we might also consider the value captured by the digital enclosure as a form of exploitation. Those who submit to increasingly pervasive and productive forms of data-gathering do so as part of an exchange that is structured by private control over the means of interaction. If publicly funded municipal or cooperative Wi-Fi networks or e-mail services were readily available, we might not be so quick to surrender control over our personal information or to submit to detailed forms of information-gathering. Additionally, the regulation of monitoring practices might more readily be seen as a legitimate public issue— rather than an abrogation of the property rights of private corporations. If the city of San Francisco controlled its own Wi-Fi service, residents would approach the decision of whether or not to track and record their own time-space paths as a public issue subject to citizen oversight and accountability.

Finally, enclosure raises the issue of asymmetrical control over personal information, and the ways in which this can be exercised as a strategy for managing or manipulating consumers. It is one thing to imagine marketers targeting ads to users based on general categories of information in which they have demonstrated an interest, but quite another to envision the possibility of marketers targeting specific individuals based on details about their online browsing habits, combined with the content of their e-mail messages, the shape of their time-space path throughout the course of the day, and any other details of their personal and professional lives that can be gleaned from an increasing array of overlapping digital enclosures. Even if details of users' private lives are not publicly disclosed, the very fact that they are aggregated to create personalized advertisements shatters the anonymity that buffered the onslaught of advertising in mass society. The implications for the marketing of certain types of products—from medical remedies to self-help books, and so on—are at best unsettling. As increasingly detailed databases merge and recombine, we may find ourselves facing much more sophisticated and personalized forms of customization—products and services targeted not only on the basis of past preferences, but on increasingly high-resolution data portraits that combine details about our personal lives with demographic, psychographic, and biometric information. Will those who currently adopt a sanguine attitude toward proliferating consumer surveillance find cause for concern when they learn that details of their love lives, combined with their Web surfing habits, the size of the clothes they buy, the search terms they have entered in search engines, the places they have traveled to, and their daily commuting habits are used in combination not just to inform them about products, but to manipulate them based on their anxieties and insecurities as well as their hopes and fantasies? At what point does the amount of information available to advertisers come to constitute a form of control over consumers—especially in a context wherein consumers have very little knowledge about what information marketers have collected and how they are using it? This might be considered an empirical question (if it were not for the pervasive framing of self-disclosure as a form of empowerment and self-expression): will consumers start to perceive marketing as both a form of intrusion and unfair leverage when ads are priced according to information about past purchasing patterns and individual wealth? What about when advertisers start to use biometric information to determine when consumers might be most inclined to respond to advertising appeals?

As issue is more than a highly variable, legally contested, and double-edged right to privacy: such examples raise the issues of asymmetrical access to information resources, databases, and processing power. At issue is also the question of control over the benefits that accrue to the use of information consumers generate about themselves. As in the case of the land enclosure movement, within the digital enclosure those who control the resources—in this case, information-gathering technologies and databases—can lay claim to the value generated by those who enter "freely" into the enclosure. When submission to monitoring becomes a condition of access not just to work, but to goods and services (from food to telephony), relations of unequal access to and control over resources structure the terms of entry. When all retail outlets implement forms of electronic surveillance and payment, the "freedom" to avoid monitoring becomes, in practice, a theoretical one. Consumers will be free not to divulge information about themselves as long as they do not consume.

For the time being, this submission to monitoring is being portrayed by those who own and operate digital enclosures as a form of participation. Those of us within the reach of the conveniences of the digital enclosure have become habituated to multiplying possibilities for such participation—in designing our shoes, customizing our news, voting on our TV shows, and so on. One of the unifying themes of this seeming multiplicity of practices is that to the extent that they contribute to the production of products for the database industry, they serve as participatory forms of economically productive *labor*. This labor is productive not least because it is a form of active participation in the processes of marketing to and policing oneself: a version of "self-expression" as an active form of submission that preserves and consolidates relations of power and property.

Labor of this kind has been described as "immaterial," to differentiate the production of information commodities and other forms of communicative capital from that of, say, refrigerators and cars. Immaterial labor, as Hardt and Negri note, can "be dispersed across the unbounded social terrain" and it can expand "to fill the entire time of life" (2000, p. 53). Within the digital enclosure, activities such as playing video games, wending one's way through the streets of San Francisco, and driving on the freeway with one's cellphone can be economically productive, insofar as they generate information commodities with a market value. However, the "immaterial" descriptor can be misleading to the extent that it suggests the valorization of this labor takes place independently of capital resources that make interaction, communication, and information-gathering possible. Digital enclosures are to these forms of immaterial labor what land enclosure was to agricultural and, eventually, industrial labor. The digital enclosure movement—the construction of a privatized architecture for rendering physical space interactive—serves to separate those who generate value from the tools that have rendered immaterial labor so powerful and efficient in the digital era—communication networks, information databases, and so on—and in doing so to structure the terms for accessing these resources. Absent an engagement with questions of ownership of and control over such resources, the process of digital enclosure promises little more than the reproduction of the social relations it purports to overcome. It is no longer enough to call for the cultivation of participation and the deployment of ubiquitous interactivity as an antidote to the undemocratic character of mass consumer culture. We have to consider the actual costs of the convenience on offer and start thinking—and communicating—outside the digital enclosure.

NOTE

1. As of this writing, Earthlink has pulled out of the plan to equip San Francisco with free Wi-Fi access, leaving Google to look for another partner.

REFERENCES

Andrejevic, M. (2004). *Reality TV: The work of being watched.* Lanham, MD: Rowman and Littlefield.

Bantick, M. (2007). Lookout: Google watches your gaming activity. *iWire*, 15 May. http://www.itwire.com.au/content/view/12152/1092/. Last accessed August 20, 2007.

Bard, A., & Söderqvist, J. (2002). *Netocracy: The new power elite and life after capitalism.* London: Pearson Education.

Benkler, Y. (2006). *The wealth of networks.* New Haven: Yale University Press.

Bond, P. (2003). ID tags make products talk. *The Atlanta Journal Constitution,* 29 July, p. A1.

Borges, J. L. (1999). Funes, his memory. In *Collected fictions* (pp. 128–132). New York: Penguin.

Boyle, J. (2003). The second enclosure movement and the construction of the public domain. *Law and Contemporary Problems, 66,* 147–178.

De Angelis, M. (1998). Marx and primitive accumulation: The continuous character of capital's enclosures. *The Commoner Web Journal,* No. 2. http://www.commoner. org.uk. Last accessed August 20, 2007.

Dresser, M. (2005). Cell phone data tracing traffic in Md; System "watches" vehicles, raises fears about privacy. *The Baltimore Sun,* 18 November, p. A1.

Dyson, E., Gilder, G., Keyworth G., & Toffler, A. (1996). Cyberspace and the American dream: A magna carta for the knowledge age. *The Information Society, 12,* 295–308.

Gates, B. (1996). *The road ahead.* New York: Penguin.

Gilder, G. (2006). The information factories. *Wired,* 14.10, October. http:// www.wired.com/wired/archive/14.10/cloudware.html. Last accessed August 18, 2007.

Gnatek, T. (2006). Services. *The New York Times,* May 3, p. G1.

Google (2005). Gmail privacy notice. *Google,* October 14. http://mail.google.com/mail/ help/privacy.html. Last accessed June 6, 2007.

Harden, B. (2006). Tech companies lured by cheap energy; Microsoft, Yahoo have plans to build servers fueled by Washington dams. *The Houston Chronicle,* July 9, p. A3.

Hardt, M., & Negri, A. (2000). *Empire.* Cambridge, MA: The Harvard University Press.

Holliday, J., & Wieners, B. (1999). The internet cloud. *The Industry Standard,* July 9. http://www.thestandard.com/article/0,1902,5466,00.html. Last accessed August 20, 2007.

Hoover, N. J. (2007). Microsoft patents may hint at the future of Windows. *Information Week,* July 16. http://www.informationweek.com/story/showArticle. jhtml?articleID= 201001485&cid=RSSfeed_IWK_News. Last accessed August 3, 2007.

Intel (2005). Research proactive computing. *Intel.* www.intel.com/research/exploratory/. Last accessed 2 August 2005.

Kazanjian, D. (2002). Mercantile exchanges, mercantilist enclosures: Racial capitalism in the black mariner narratives of Venture Smith and John Jea. *The New Centennial Review, 3,* 147–178.

Kopytoff, V. (2006). Wi-Fi plan stirs big brother concerns; log-on rule would allow Google to track users' whereabouts in S. F. *The San Francisco Chronicle,* April 8, p. C1.

Lefebvre, H. (1991). *The production of space.* Oxford: Blackwell Publishers.

Lessig, L. (2004). *Free culture.* New York: The Penguin Press.

Lessig, L. (1999). *Code and other laws of cyberspace.* New York: Basic Books.

Markoff, J., & Hansell, S. (2006). Hiding in plain sight. Google seeks an expansion of power. *The New York Times*, June 14, p. A1.

Marx, K. (1992). *Capital volume 1: A critical analysis of capitalist production*. New York: International Publishers.

Marx, K. (1973). *Grundrisse*. New York: Penguin Classics.

Midnight Notes Collective (2001). The new enclosures. *The Commoner Web Journal*, No. 2., September. www.commoner.org.uk/02midnight.pdf. Last accessed August 2, 2007.

MIT Project Oxygen (2004). Project overview. *Project Oxygen*. http://www.oxygen. lcs.mit.edu/Overview.html. Last accessed May 20, 2007.

Mosco, V. (2004). *The digital sublime: Myth, power, and cyberspace*. Cambridge, MA: MIT Press.

Mosco, V. (1989). *The pay-per society*. Toronto: Ablex.

O'Connell, P. L. (2005). Korea's high tech utopia, where everything is observed. *The New York Times*, October 5, 2005, p. A1.

Pearce, C. (1997). *The interactive book*. New York: Penguin.

Reiss, S. (2006). His space: Twilight of the media moguls? Not for this guy. *Wired*, 14.07, July. http://www.wired.com/wired/archive/14.07/murdoch.html. Last accessed August 7, 2007.

Schiller, D. (2007). *How to think about information*. Chicago: University of Illinois Press.

Schiller, D. (1999). *Digital capitalism: Networking the global market system*. Cambridge, MA: MIT Press.

Spencer, R. (2006). Microsoft pulls plug on China protest blog. *The Telegraph*, January 7. http://www.telegraph.co.uk/news/main.jhtml?xml=/news/2006/01/06/ wmicro06. hml&sSheet=/news/2006/01/06/ixworld.html. Last accessed June 2, 2007.

Sullivan, A. (2002). The blogging revolution: Weblogs are to words what Napster was to music," *Wired* 10.5, May. http://www.wired.com/wired/ archive/10.05/mustread.html? pg=2. Last accessed January 12, 2006.

Tanz, J. (2007). Desktop, R.I.P. *Wired*, 15.04, March. http://www.wired.com/wired/ archive/15.04/wired40_rip.html. Last accessed April 10, 2007.

Telecommunications Industry News (2006). Google seeking patent on location-based Wi-Fi advertising. March 26. http://www.teleclick.ca/2006/03/google-seekingpatent- on-location-based-wi-fi-advertising/. Last accessed August 20, 2007.

Terranova, T. (2000). Free labor: Producing culture for the digital economy. *Social Text 63*, 33–57.

Thompson, C. (2006). The great firewall of China. *The Advertiser* (Australia), April 29, p. W9.

Trippi, J. (2004). *The revolution will not be televised*. New York: Regan Books.

Virilio, P. (2005). *The original accident*. Cambridge: Polity Press.

"War of the words" (2006). *The Guardian* (London), February 20. Retrieved November 6, 2007 from http://www.guardian.co.uk/china/story/0,1713317,00.html.

Of Ziploc Bags and Black Holes: The Aesthetics of Transparency in the War on Terror

RACHEL HALL

When Italian philosopher Giorgio Agamben read about the new security measures being instituted at U.S. borders in January 2004, he promptly resigned his teaching post at NYU, cancelled his March course and wrote a column for *Le Monde* in which he explained his actions (*Artists Network of Refuse and Resist!, 2004*). Agamben was protesting the then new US-VISIT program, which requires that most foreign visitors to the United States be digitally photographed and fingerprinted at the border (BBC News, 2004).

In his column, Agamben argues that the new program is part of a larger development. He writes that the high-tech collection of information about the body's biological life crosses a new threshold in social control:

Electronic filing of finger and retina prints, subcutaneous tattooing, as well as other practices of the same type are elements that contribute towards defining this threshold. The security reasons that are invoked to justify these measures should not impress us: they have nothing to do with it. History teaches us how practices first reserved for foreigners find themselves applied later to the rest of the citizenry.

What is at stake here is nothing less than the new "normal" bio-political relationship between citizens and the state. This relation no longer has anything to do with free and active participation in the public sphere, but concerns the enrollment and the filing away of the most private and incommunicable aspect of subjectivity: I mean the body's biological life.

These technological devices that register and identify naked life correspond to the media devices that control and manipulate public speech: between these two extremes of a body without words and words without a body, the space we once upon a time called politics is ever more scaled-down and tiny. (2004)

At the inception of the US-VISIT program in 2004, Agamben protested the new "normal" bio-politics by maintaining the articulated, articulate body: first, by refusing to allow the U.S. government to capture more information on the life of his body without words, and second, by restoring his body to words through the act of writing his column.

In what follows, I consider two visual events, which mark, for me, the limits of "the space we once upon a time called politics." In the first part of the essay, I analyze a State Department video that instructs foreign visitors to the United States in the new biometric procedures, protested by Agamben in early 2004. In the second half of the essay, I look at how mainstream media coverage of Saddam Hussein's capture invites Americans to identify virtually with the U.S. military. These seemingly disparate events in the visual culture of the "war on terror" are connected by a common aesthetic strategy for producing docile global citizen-suspects, which I call the aesthetics of transparency. My work builds on Agamben's insights with a careful analysis of the technological, media, and mediation shifts that produce—to borrow his chiasmic formulation—the body without words and words without a body, respectively.

AESTHETICS OF TRANSPARENCY

The aesthetics of transparency belongs to a rationality of government that understands security in terms of visibility. The aesthetics of transparency is motivated by the desire to turn the world (the body) inside-out such that there would no longer be any secrets or interiors, human or geographical, in which our enemies (or the enemy within) might find refuge. This objection to interiority is both physical and psychological, referring as much to the desire to rid the warring world of pockets, caves, spider holes, and veils as it is concerned to ferret out all secrets and stop at nothing in its effort to produce actionable intelligence from detainees.

The aesthetics of transparency establishes a binary opposition between interiority and exteriority and privileges the external or visible surface over the suspect's word. The historical articulation between security and the aesthetics of transparency can be traced back to the early days of police photography. While a thief was often a good liar, a photograph of a thief—it was believed—could not lie. Early on, the promise of photography as a form of identification lay in the 19th-century belief that an individual's identity resided in the physical features of the head and face. Physical appearance was understood as a code for deciphering the moral righteousness or decrepitude of a person. In the United States, the spread of photography during the 1840s and 1850s was coincident with the spread of the popular sciences of phrenology and physiognomy.[1] Both interpretive systems were justified by the belief that the surface of the body could be read as a series of signs or codes expressing inner character (Henning 2001, p. 221).

But the relationship between photography and police work was never that simple. In fact, the mug shot had to be standardized precisely because of a crisis of faith in the truth of appearance. It was a crisis rooted in older religious concerns over the relationship between a person's interior and exterior, where truth was thought to be located on the inside. This tension was echoed in the division between visual appearances (empirical observation) and the untrustworthy, duplicitous voice of the criminal as a storyteller. Long associated with roving bands of performers, actors, and musicians, the rogue, it was believed, is an excessively good liar, and possessing his photograph does nothing to change that. "Contrary to the commonplace understanding of the 'mug shot' as the very exemplar of a powerful, artless, and wholly denotative visual empiricism," writes Allan Sekula, "early instrumental uses of photographic realism were systematized on the basis of an acute recognition of the *inadequacies* and limitations of ordinary visual empiricism" (p. 18).

The aesthetics of transparency can be defined, then, as an attempt by the state to force a correspondence between interiority and exteriority on the objects of the panoptic gaze or better yet, turn the object of surveillance inside-out, thereby doing away with the problem of correspondence altogether. When it is done in the name of Homeland Security, the aesthetics of transparency aims to produce a traveler whose body and belongings already resemble the pristine x-ray images that Transportation Security Administration officials study on computer monitors as travelers pass through the metal detectors. Conversely, when it is done in the name of the war on terror, the aesthetics of transparency aims to locate and reveal the hiding places of "Iraq's Most Wanted": to "smoke 'em out of their caves."[2]

The equation of security with an open field of vision is reflected, to an obsessive degree, in the new airport security measures, which aim to render the traveler's body and belongings ready-for-inspection. Traveler transparency is supposed to protect against the irruption of the unpredictable (i.e., terrorist attacks). Airports aim to produce a "vast hygienist utopia" that plays alternately on fear and security.[3] If the Panopticon is an ideal model of disciplinary power, the security checks installed in American airports since 2001 constitute instead what Michel Foucault would call compensatory heterotopias: "another real space, as perfect, as meticulous, as well arranged as ours is messy, ill constructed, and jumbled" (2001, p. 235).[4] The objects currently used to produce the visual effect of a perfectly ordered and transparent traveler, grey plastic bins and Ziploc bags, bespeak a hygienist's view of security where everything is separated, sorted, zipped, sealed, and evenly distributed in space. As an added bonus, the practice literally creates a rotating display of personal hygiene and grooming products.[5]

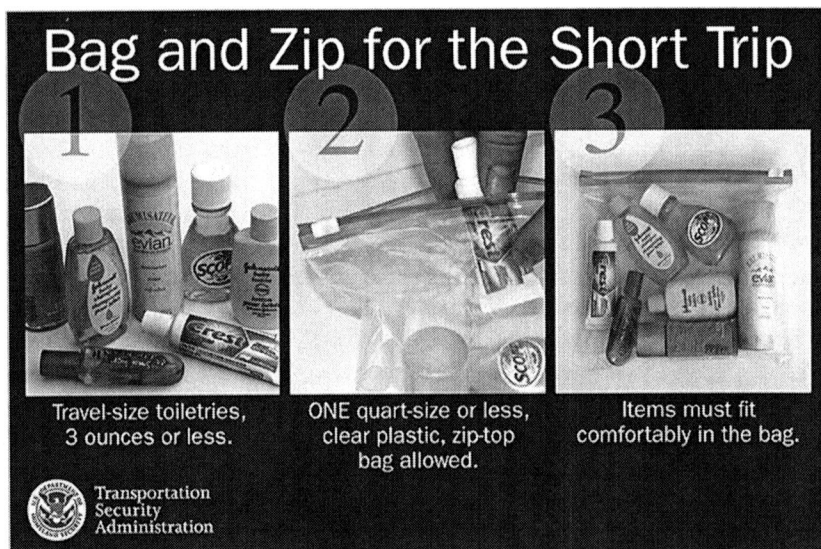

Figure 1. Bag Poster, Transportation Security Administration, US Department of Homeland Security, 2006.

Agamben argues that these so-called emergency measures effectively establish a new "normal" bio-political relationship between global citizens and the U.S. government. The crux of this relationship is transparency. The aesthetics of transparency aims to make "good" global citizens visible and legible to U.S. surveillance operatives within the new rationality of government: Homeland Security. Within the new global order, the ideal citizen-traveler is transparent or see-through. She has nothing to hide and is happy to show it by opening her bags to inspection, turning her pockets inside out, and in the case of many foreign visitors to the United States, agreeing to finger and retina scans.

The aesthetics of transparency asks the "good" global citizen to allow the U.S. government to translate her heterogeneous body into useful, visual information. First, the federal government puts on transparency in order to guard itself against the charges of domestic surveillance and racial profiling; second, images of transparency instruct global citizens in how to maneuver through purportedly transparent screening procedures and acts of image capture; third, images of transparency demonstrate "good" global citizenship and compel foreign visitors to the U.S. to become legible (i.e., transparent) security images.

Defined in these terms, the cost of security is dear. The aesthetics of transparency challenges human embodiment and poses significant risks to the ways in which human subjectivity is experienced and understood. Truth comes to reside not in the behavior or speech of bodies or in the assumption of one's body and the attendant social and political possibilities and responsibilities that embodiment entails. Rather, truth is to be found in the information encoded in iris scans and digital fingerprints, thereby doing away with the problem of the global citizen's agency altogether. Truth resides in the relationship between the scanned individual and the information held in U.S. databases. Just as the FBI's formation of a national fingerprint database rendered all fingerprinted citizens suspects of criminal or anti-American activity in the 20th century, the new security measures render every foreign visitor to the U.S. a suspected terrorist. The new procedures for extracting information from travelers do not require physical coercion or self-regulation. Instead, they involve the act of submitting to scanning procedures that require little to no physical contact with another person or even a machine. Information is quickly and painlessly extracted from the screened body so that it can potentially be used against the individual thus captured.

SCREENING VISITORS

"The US-VISIT program aims to create a 'virtual border' using computer networks, databases, fingerprints, and other biometric identifiers" (O'Harrow & Higham, 2004).[6] Approximately 24 million visitors to the

U.S. are entered into the program each year. The data collected through the US-VISIT program is used to check visitors against a national fingerprint database and terrorist watch lists (BBC News, 2004).[7] Officially named the "U.S. Visitor and Immigrant Status Indicator Technology," the program goes by a different name in promotional and informational materials aimed at laypersons: "US-VISIT: Keeping America's Doors Open and Our Nation Secure."

You can access the US-VISIT informational video from the State Department's website (http://www.dhs.gov/dhspublic/interapp/editorial/editorial_0435.xml). The opening segment of the video introduces the viewer to the main characters, highlights key moments of action, and establishes the setting in which the action will take place. Perhaps most importantly, the opening sequence familiarizes the viewer with the simulated world of the video in which a generic figure makes his way through customs.

While I am most interested in the video's visuals, I want to say a few words about its narration because it offers some important clues regarding the video's tone and mode of address. The voice of the narrator is pitched somewhere between the classic, male narrator of an educational film and the automated voice of a telephone answering service. The vocal quality of the narration enhances the viewer's sense of bureaucratic alienation. The speaker sounds like an attendant—someone who neither authored nor authorized the new program that he describes.

Figure 2. Screen capture from the US-Visit video, Department of Homeland Security.

The video not only sounds but also looks like an informational or safety video that you might have to sit through on a plane or a ship. It simulates camera work, offering the viewer level, overhead, and point-of-view shots on the action and equipment. Viewers of the video see most of the process from the visitor's perspective. For a brief period, viewers see things from the border official's perspective as he examines the finger scans and headshot he's taken on a computer screen and at another point, from the perspective of a mounted surveillance camera. The video also offers viewers close-ups on the left- and right-hand finger scanners. Periodically, nondiegetic, diagrammatic inserts interrupt the action much like they might in an educational video for schoolchildren.

The narrator kicks off the opening sequence: "At our points of entry, advanced technology is used to verify the documents of incoming visitors that are between the ages of 14–79." We watch a simulation of a foreign visitor and U.S. official interacting at customs. The border official stands in a grey cubical. A glass partition surrounds the official, separating him from the visitor, while still allowing the two to speak to one another and to pass documents back and forth over the top of the partition. They never touch.

The visitor places his left index finger on the scanner, which cuts to an overhead shot of the scanner. From this vantage point, we see the visitor swiftly remove his left finger and then place his right index finger on the scanner. Next, we return to the original shot of the official and visitor.

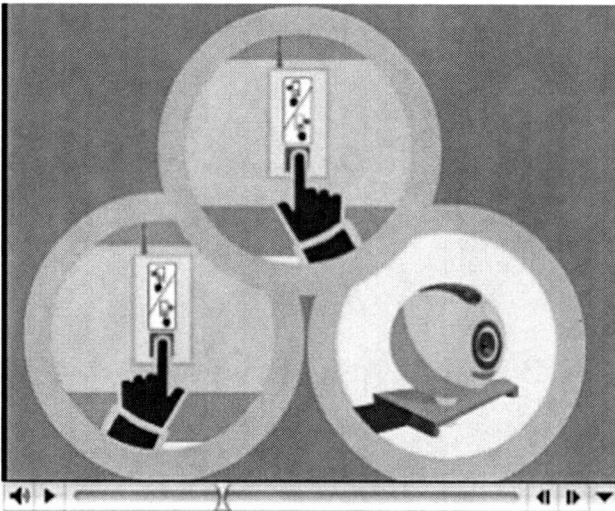

Figure 3. Screen capture from the US-Visit video.

The official pushes a small camera, shaped like a disembodied eyeball, across the counter and towards the visitor. Then the video cuts to a computer screen featuring the information that's just been captured: two fingerprints and a headshot.

The narrator informs the viewer: "This does not apply to United States citizens or its legal permanent residents. Using biometrics, US-VISIT enhances security while facilitating legitimate travel and trade." As the narrator says, "using biometrics," the video cuts to an overhead shot of two queues, as they might appear to a third official who monitors the action from a remote location via a surveillance camera. The next line is: "This does not apply to U.S. citizens." The corresponding shot shows the queue in which the visitor is standing and then pans over to a separate line where a second official waves the Americans past.

The video then moves through the following clips: a split screen featuring the visitor deboarding a plane on one side and a ship on the other, the visitor walking through the airport and the visitor approaching customs and interacting with an official. While these clips run, the announcer says: "These procedures, used both when entering the United States and when leaving, help us maintain our commitment to expedite travel for the millions of legitimate visitors we welcome each year and make them safer while in the United States by enhancing our ability to confirm identity."

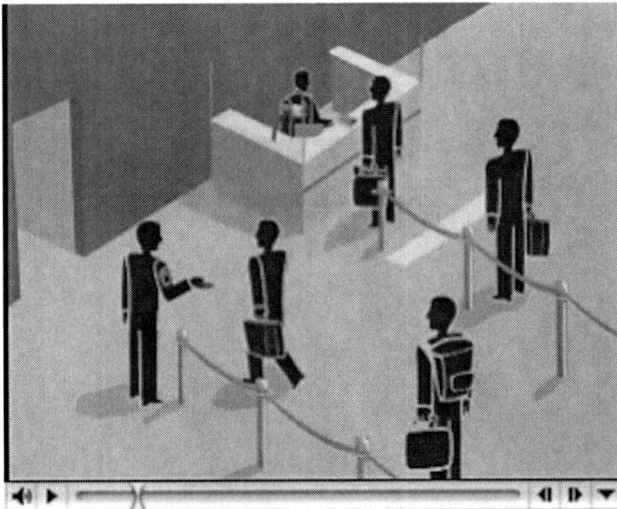

Figure 4. Screen captue from the US-Visit video.

TRANSNATIONAL SECURITY PEDAGOGY

In terms of the video's verbal and visual content, its function is pretty straightforward: the purpose of the video is to inform and educate U.S. citizens and foreign visitors about the new border security procedures. However, if we look at the video's formal aspects, particularly the visual form that it takes, there can be little doubt that its function is also to dematerialize the new border security procedures and de-emphasize the program's objective: the mass surveillance of travelers. The video employs the aesthetics of transparency to achieve these political goals.

The video is minimalist and uses a cool, neutral blue-grey monochromatic scheme throughout, with red and yellow accents framing the technology and its products. For instance, red frames the spot on the finger scanner where the visitor is supposed to put his index finger and yellow frames his headshot and fingertips as they appear on the official's computer screen. While the technology and the images it produces are highlighted by the contrast of warm red and yellow against cool blue and grey backgrounds, the "people" featured in the video are de-emphasized in terms of color. These figures are evaporated, weightless; they match the color of the screen when it is empty (before and after the video plays).

The State Department's vision of the border is communicated to viewers as a series of images without bodies. The actors in this video are cool blue outlines, which is why I am tempted to refer to the star of the video

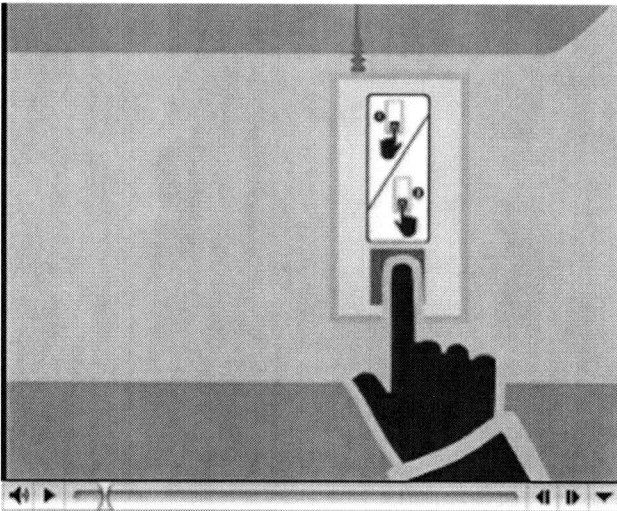

Figure 5. Screen capture from the US-Visit video.

as stick man. Actually, the best name for him might be blueprint man. He looks like a trace, a carbon copy of a slightly filled-out stick man drawn on another surface that we cannot see. There are no blueprint women in this video. There is one blueprint child, who appears briefly in the background of the exit procedure section.

The blueprint people are uniformly male, raceless, hairless, faceless, odorless, silent, disconnected, evenly distributed in space, unperturbed, unflappable, etc. While the blueprint people have lost most distinguishing characteristics, they retain nationality. Or to be more accurate, the video's narration and images reinforce the difference between insiders (Americans) and outsiders (the rest of the world). The video simultaneously instructs foreign visitors in the new procedures and reassures U.S. citizens that they will not be detained. Foreign visitors and Americans alike are offered images of swift movement and efficiency. There is no impatience, hunger, boredom, frustration, or anxiety in this airport. There are no petty officials or victims of discrimination and racial profiling: only blue outlines proceeding swiftly, but at an even pace, where they need to go.

The US-VISIT video's look communicates a difference between the new, cleaner and less invasive identification technologies and the older, messier identification technologies like film photography and ink-based fingerprinting. Writing about 19th century identification technologies, Tom Gunning describes fingerprinting and photography as bodily traces because of their indexical, that is, material relationship to the individual's body. In

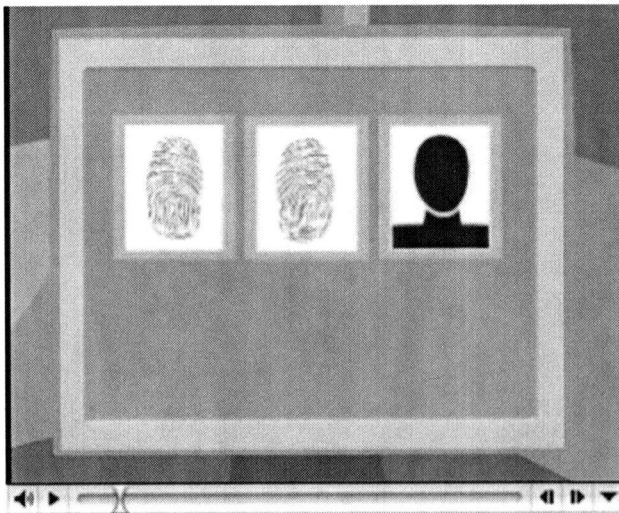

Figure 6. Screen capture from the US-Visit video.

this video, we are ushered into a new era in identification technologies where digital imaging severs the indexical relationship between the image and the referent. A visitor no longer has to dirty his fingers to be finger-printed. Screens and scanner beds mediate between eyes and bodies, bodies and eyes. One wonders if the US-VISIT procedures would have caused more of a stir if visitors were being fingerprinted using the ink method.

"Trace" no longer seems the appropriate term. Rather than bodily traces, the new identification technologies capture image sections of the body's surface. The video pictures this process with a simulation of a carbon copy. The blueprint man is like a carbon copy, only cleaner. There is no tracing involved, no pen to paper, no smudging, and no dirty hands for either the visitor or the official. This clean, blue-grey, and neutral space is all surfaces and outlines. There are no bodies to leave traces. In fact, a real fingerprint left on the surface of the small scanner bed inhibits the proper capture of a digital "print." Experts say the cleanliness of a finger scanner determines how effectively the technology works. The more often the official cleans the surface, the more likely he is to find a match (Braiker, 2004).

In the State Department video, transparency is not the only desired quality of the ideal visitor to the United States; it also serves as the State Department's alibi. The video's aesthetics of transparency defend the U.S. government against charges of racial profiling. Here transparency is transferred from the blueprint men to the blueprint border officials who scan them. The blue-grey monochromatic world of the ideal airport

Figure 7. Screen capture from the US-Visit video.

Figure 8. Screen capture from the US-Visit video.

diffuses tension and racism and by implication racial profiling through sameness: transparency is the great equalizer, the guarantor of justice. Hence, the video's aesthetic functions at once to project a more orderly traveler population to which its viewers should conform and defends the U.S. government against charges of discrimination.

Contrary to the video's image of democracy as a clean blue-grey field, the ACLU notes that US-VISIT was initially billed as a replacement program for the National Security Entry-Exit Registration System or NSEERS (a.k.a. the special registration program) instituted in the fall of 2002, which was widely criticized for racial profiling of Arab and Muslim men based on national origin (ACLU, 2004). The ACLU argues that US-VISIT is meant to supplement, not replace, the previous program and that racial profiling is likely to continue.

BLACK HOLES IN THE WAR ON TERROR

The aesthetics of transparency aims to expose potential hiding places and ferret out the terrorists who would take cover there. This is the unstated imperative of the new form of perpetual warfare instituted by the Bush Administration. In the visual culture of the war on terror, the State Department's blueprint men lie at the opposite end of the spectrum from the photographs of Saddam Hussein's capture. By this, I mean to say that the field of visual culture under exploration here is a network of visual relationships that

Figure 9. "Deposed Iraqi President Saddam Hussein Entered and left his underground hiding place near his home town of Tikrit through this small hole in the ground in Ad Dwar, Iraq, seen in this Dec. 15, 2003 file photo," Associated Press Images/Efrem Lukatsky.

Figure 10. "Captured former Iraqi leader Saddam Hussein undergoes medical examinations in Baghdad in this Dec. 14, 2003 file photo (in this image from television)," Associated Press Images.

extend from the mediation of foreign visitors to the U.S. (by the transnational pedagogy, screening techniques, and security technologies of Homeland Security) to the mediation of the war on terror for U.S. citizens (by American media corporations that invite consumers to participate virtually in neocolonialism).

The State Department video and mainstream media coverage of the manhunt for Saddam Hussein depict processes of capture. The first instructs global citizen-suspects in willful submission to biometric capture, and the second makes a consumer spectacle of Saddam Hussein's violent physical capture. The two image sets, respectively, picture compliant and noncompliant subjects in the visual culture of the war on terror.[8] The computer-generated imagery (CGI) video projects an airport world in which everything is externalized: the space of the ideal airport is merely a series of visible surfaces through which the camera and by extension the viewer moves with ease. By comparison, the photographs of Saddam Hussein's capture reflect an opaque, aging fugitive from justice and his grimy hideout.

Two images in particular visualize the enemy's opacity (interiority) or picture opacity as the true enemy in the War on Terror: photographs of Saddam's spider hole, taken from above, looking down into the darkness and images of his "medical examination," featuring the dark cavity of his mouth being pried open by an inspector. In the first image, the darkness of the spider hole signifies the limits of U.S. military vision and invites trespass. It shows the American audience an image of what was once an obstacle to transparency at the moment that the cover has been removed, allowing the light of day to break through. There is a strange doubling across the two images: the dark cavern in the first signifies U.S. mastery over the whole wide world; the dark cavern in the second signifies our dominance over an enemy of the state.

In the two images, U.S. mastery is revealed to be both visual and spatial: American soldiers can see in the dark and claim the enemy's body by refusing to recognize his corporeal boundaries. Darkness may be shown only once it has been defeated, at which point it signifies a victory rather than a challenge or threat. These images of darkness and interiority demonstrate to the American viewing public that it needs the military to do its seeing for it and that the visual payoff is being taken along for the ride. The black holes compensate for all of those other dark spaces that the U.S. military has not been able to master or penetrate.

In the image of Saddam's medical inspection, the body's full materiality must be revealed and surface scans will get you nowhere. His body clearly has an inside and an outside, which is held together by human flesh. Unlike all of those Saddam imposters that showed up in the news while he was in hiding, this body is real (really his body). In this case, the confirmation of identity requires more than digital scans of the surface. U.S. soldiers confirm the reality of his body by penetrating its surface. They go in through his mouth, visually demonstrating that his has become a body without words. We get to see the dark cavity of his mouth, extreme close-ups of his teeth. The medicalization of this encounter signifies Hussein's physical submission to U.S. authority, connotes his animality, and—to the American viewer—may suggest a benign version of U.S. imperialism, which has science, medicine, and the Enlightenment on its side. This painstakingly documented and widely circulated medical exam rehearses, therefore, what Ella Shohat and Robert Stam have called the "animalizing trope" of Empire or "the discursive figure by which the colonizing imaginary rendered the colonized beastlike and animalic" (1994, p. 19).

Whereas CGI gives us relatively empty environments through which to move, digital photographs like those of Saddam's medical inspection overwhelm us with the fullness of even one fragment of space and time. CGI is clean technology to photography's capture of messy bodies and places. Within this visual economy, CGI signifies the technological prowess and superiority of the West and the U.S. military in particular, whereas digital or remediated photography serves as evidence of the "primitive" Other: Saddam Hussein. We are told that the photographs and video made of Hussein's medical examination were circulated to prove to Iraqis that he had in fact been captured—as though Americans were beyond photography as a guarantee of anything—marking the cultural assumption of differential levels of technological sophistication between Americans and Iraqis.

For American viewers, Saddam Hussein's body must be revealed in all of its materiality and this materiality must be exaggerated because his body has to represent both himself and another, who is still missing (Osama Bin Laden). Saddam's body comes to stand in not only for Bin Laden, in the sense of a body double or substitution, but also potentially reads as a synecdoche of the Middle East—the region to be unilaterally "enlightened" and democratized by the U.S. military. If Iraq is to be forcibly democratized, the medical exam connotes the primary discursive statement of Operation: Iraqi Freedom: this is for your own good, Iraq. By extension and according to the neoconservative ideologies and American perceptions that promoted and produced the war, it is also for the good of the entire region of the Middle East as it is imagined and misunderstood by the U.S.

VIRTUAL WAR TOURS

For the privileged spectators of the war on terror, wartime surveillance provides discipline *and* entertainment or better yet, discipline-as-entertainment. At "home," the aesthetics of transparency produces American citizen-consumers as the see-through citizens who move through airports in an orderly fashion *and* the privileged subjects of the mobile and virtualized gaze of modern warfare.[9] "War is, then, the subject of these images," writes Nicholas Mirzoeff, "but it is also a means of creating subjects, visual subjects (2002, p. 5).[10]

Consider CNN's online Special Report, "Saddam Hussein: Captured." The online collection of hyperlinked texts and images is "news," and yet its celebratory tone and structuring of visual relations make it feel more like commemorative war propaganda. The site offers an interactive reenactment of Saddam's capture. Users may view slide shows composed from video footage of the press conference held when Hussein was captured. They may also view still photographs of the hideout or take virtual tours of Saddam's spider hole.

If the user clicks on the audio show entitled: "the raid," he or she will see the talking heads at the press conference interspersed with images of Saddam Hussein's medical examination: L. Paul Bremer, U.S. Civilian administrator in Iraq speaking: "Ladies and gentleman (pregnant pause), we got him." Cheers and applause can be heard from off-screen. Lt. Gen. Ricardo Sanchez speaking: "This is Saddam as he was being given his medical examination today." Again cheers and applause are heard from

Figure 11. Screen capture of the main page from CNN.com's online Special Report, "Saddam Hussein: CAPTURED."

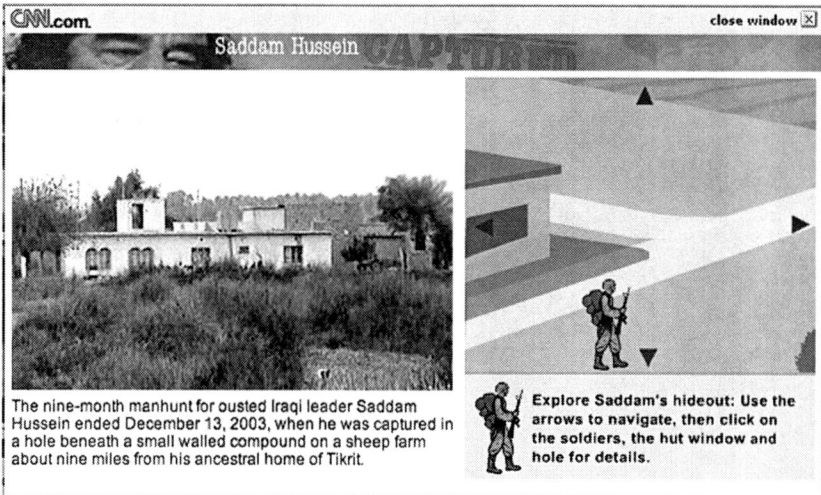

Figure 12. Screen capture of the interactive feature, "Explore Saddam's Hideout."

off-screen. Sanchez proceeds: "After uncovering the spider hole, a search was conducted and Saddam Hussein was found hiding at the bottom of the hole. The spider hole is about 6 to 8 feet deep and allows enough space for a person to lie down inside of it."

If the user clicks on the interactive feature provocatively titled, "Explore Saddam's Hideout," she gets a pop-up window with a documentary photograph of the compound on the left, duly captioned, and an interactive graphic on the right. The feature uses CGI to remake the hole—which signified the limits of vision, a space of mystery, and the unknown in the photograph—into the secret door of a virtual adventure for the user. The feature reenacts what actual journalists did when visiting the site: entered the hole for themselves and took a look around.

"Explore Saddam's Hideout" is a mix between the documentary conventions of reenactment and a video game. The user gets a bird's eye view of the hideout and a virtual tour of the spider hole. On the interactive map, the hole signifies the limits of U.S. military vision. It establishes a temporary boundary, which may be crossed by the user if she clicks on the black square that marks the hole. At first a boundary, the hole is made to reinforce technological transcendence of the barriers that stand in the way of mere mortals. No less than the Ziploc baggie, the hole serves the state aesthetics of transparency. The hole is something that American citizens want to see and virtually enter into.

Figure 13. Screen capture of the virtual tour of Saddam's "spider hole."

Because it is an online report, "Saddam Hussein: Captured," can be accessed over and over again by the same or different users. In its function as historical reenactment, the special report resembles mainstream media coverage of the first Gulf War.[11] The CNN Special Report differs from traditional documentary reenactments insofar as it pairs the pleasures of historical reenactment with the structure of consumer interactivity. Archived Internet "Special Reports" on the war in Iraq allow for shorter and more obsessive repetitions than filmic or televisual reenactments or docudramas. After a point, though, the user must pay to watch a particular video again. On CNN's site, this involves subscribing to CNN Pipeline, which gives the user unlimited access to its video archive.

NEODOCUMENTARY

Within the microcosm of CNN's Special Report, the transparency of the U.S. military and the Western media is communicated via CGI, whereas the opacity of the aging tyrant is pictured in photographs. Computer simulation offers the aesthetics of abstraction. The unrealistic look of the technology moralizes American foreign policy in Saddam's capture, much as it sold biopolitics in the State Department video. The unreal look of these images quietly pronounces: Cleanliness is godliness. Transparency is truth.

Within the story world of CNN's online Special Report, photography serves as evidence and proof of Saddam's capture in the same vein that

Figure 14. "A rudimentary kitchen is along one wall of the small hut where Saddam was captured" Associated Press Images/Efrem Lukatsky.

the postmortem photographs published of Saddam's sons proved their deaths and the professionally matted and gold-framed portrait of Abu Musab Al-Zarqawi proved his demise. As Saddam slips from spider to rat, the clean CGI images of the hole become the messy photographs of the hut's interior. If the user clicks on the photo gallery entitled, "Saddam

Figure 15. "Dirty dishes clutter the hut" Associated Press Images/Efrem Lukatsky.

caught 'like a rat' in a hole" and then a tab labeled, "the capture," she will see a series of still photographs taken inside the hut above-ground and adjacent to the spider hole. Accompanying the slides of the huts interior are moralizing captions.

At the risk of overstating the difference in what digital photography and CGI presently picture, it is a matter of time versus space. Photography can attest to the ravages of time: the beard, the grime, the scratches, and the dirty clothes, the accumulation of dirty dishes—all evidence of time spent underground. But CGI can animate the space of the spider hole. It takes us there, not in the sense of documentary, but rather in the terms of a cheesy mobile graphic that simulates a tourist attraction and lends a strange architectural, if not surgical, precision to U.S. military operations.[12]

In all, the Special Report serves two primary functions: it proves "we got him," and it offers American citizen-consumers a chance to tour his hideout. CNN mimics the conventions of true crime television, but it splices up the various elements that make up the report and creates hyperlinks between them. There is the reenactment, the charts and graphs and maps, the photographs, the captions, and the voiceover. But it is up to the user to decide which of these elements of the report to consume and in what order.

The visual relationship established between Saddam and the user enacts a neocolonialist politics between the Middle East and the West. Saddam Hussein's history of moral reprehensibility serves as an alibi for the Western media and by extension the Western consumer of the media or user of CNN's website. A neocolonialist vision is rehearsed in a manner that pretends to be only about a singularly evil individual. Again, the website sets photography against CGI in a compare-and-contrast game that equates the West with technological progress figured as the relatively empty look of computer graphics to the fullness of the photographs. Look, see the computer simulation of Saddam's spider hole. We have rendered it empty and clean and here are photographs taken of Saddam's hideout. They are so full and dirty.

The online Special Report departs from previous productions of the colonized, racialized body insofar as it makes the capture of the colonial subject into an interactive game of narrative reenactment. Saddam Hussein is figured as the stubborn, misbehaving outlaw, who must be physically, forcibly subdued. The scene of capture is akin to a scene from an early reality television program like *Cops* or some other true crime show. The "money shot" of this genre features cops violently subdueing animalized suspects. Such programs rehearse the drama of a predictable power dynamic between individuals coded as inferior based on their race, class, and lack of education, and the rational cops, who know how to "handle" them. While we don't get to see Saddam taken down, the images and video of his medical exam accomplish a similar spectacle of dominance and submission.

VIRTUAL SECURITY

In this essay, I have attempted to show how the body without words is no body at all. Or rather, it is a body without flesh—a virtual body. In the first part of the essay, I explored the virtual body desired of foreign visitors to the United States or what Agamben (2004) calls the biometric body without words. The federal government instills the aesthetics of transparency in the name of "Homeland" Security. In the second part of the essay, I examined the virtual body of the ideal American spectator of the war on terror. The aesthetics of transparency is also cultivated by the mainstream American media in cooperation with the U.S. military.

Even as the United States embraces a state aesthetics of transparency— opening every purse at home and turning over every rock abroad—it simultaneously creates "zones of darkness, zones established by the privilege of royal power or prerogatives of a corporation, zones of disorder" (Foucault, 1980, p. 152).[13] In the name of finding and exposing the terrorists, the Bush Administration has created nowhere places like Guantanamo, Abu Ghraib, and undisclosed secret prisons, where U.S. and international law neither apply nor are enforced. Terrorism requires U.S. legal exceptionalism, or the creation of "a threshold, a zone of indifference, where inside and outside [the law] do not exclude each other but blur with each other" (Agamben, 2004, p. 23). The zones of indifference created in the war on terror are seldom if ever made visible to the American public—they exist somewhere off-screen, belonging neither to the hypervisible surveillance technologies on display in airports, nor to the mundane visibility of mainstream war coverage readily available on home televisions and computer screens.[14]

In media coverage of the war on terror, the aesthetics of transparency invites American citizens to become virtual participants in the state of exception, but this is a ruse. The Western consumer's presumed virtual mobility, rather than his political power, guarantees and is proof of his privilege. A proof, Lisa Nakamura notes (2002), is often inversely proven by anachronistic images of frozen, still others. This dynamic is particularly acute in the special report's invitation to the viewer to tour Saddam's hideout: "Travel and tourism," writes Lisa Nakamura, "like networking technology, are commodities that define the privileged, industrialized first-world subject, and they situate him in the position of the one who looks, the one who has access, the one who communicates.

Microsoft's omnipresent slogan. 'Where do you want to go today?' rhetorically places the consumer in the position of the user with unlimited choices; access to Microsoft's technology and networks promises the consumer a 'world without limits' where he can possess an idealized mobility. . . . A sort of technologically enabled transnationality is evoked here, but one that directly addresses the first-world user, whose position on the network will allow him to metaphorically go wherever he likes" (p. 256).

In CNN's online Special Report, the citizen-consumer is invited to adopt the mobile and virtualized gaze of modern warfare. He is neither the flâneur nor the rubberneck.[15] He is more like a visitor to an interactive display at a museum of science and technology on the National Mall. The special report draws the user into a nationalist identification with the U.S. military under the guise of a democratic encounter with information made possible by new and improved media technologies. Interactivity offers us a model of the citizen-consumer who educates himself at his own will and chooses when and where he will consume war propaganda. Virtual imaging technologies enable his vicarious participation in the prosecution of the war as game, as entertainment, as celebration of the U.S. and proof that technology is on "our" side. For the foreign national, the same childlike condescension of CGI works toward different ends. If the CNN Special Report uses game-like interactivity to simulate pseudo-agentic users, who take visual pleasure in CNN's creative coverage of the war, the State Department video uses transnational pedagogy to simulate governmental transparency, even as it takes an authoritative and condescending tone with foreign nationals and renders them suspected terrorists.

What is perhaps most striking about the State Department video is its naïve look, especially when one considers that it is selling "advanced technology" as the answer to the problem of securing the U.S. against terrorist threats. While looks can be deceiving, they are not in this case. Assessments by investigators at the Justice Department, scientists at the National Institute of Standards and Technology, and researchers at Stanford University have found the program to be less than satisfactory. The biggest challenge is technological in nature. The U.S. government has already spent $1 billion for a program projected to cost up to $10 billion, which is "built on top of aging computer databases and software that government scientists concluded [three] years ago are out of date, poorly coordinated and ineffective" (O'Harrow & Higham, 2005). Networking and compatibility issues are also to blame. Investigators at the Justice Department concluded that the programs effectiveness has been compromised by chronic delays in the integration of the FBI fingerprint files with the databases used by border patrol officials ("Report," CNN.com). What is more, the US-VISIT program is not compatible with the border crossing cards issued to Mexican visitors and workers because the two systems were not designed to interact (O'Harrow & Higham, 2005).[16]

If US-VISIT has accomplished anything thus far, it has been to normalize the social spectacle of mandatory biometric data collection at U.S. airports and seaports—to create the expectation, if not the acceptance, of such encounters between foreign nationals and U.S. border officials. Even if the program is not effective in catching terrorists, it has effectively introduced the idea of virtually networking global criminal databases, terrorist watch-lists, and biometric data on travelers. The program has normalized the notion that it is the U.S. government's prerogative to collect, keep, and selectively share biometric information on innocent travelers.[17]

CONCLUSION

It is neither my intention nor my desire to reduce Agamben's provocative chiasmus of the body without words and words without a body to the colonial binarism. In the visual culture of the war on terror, the binary of the West and the rest becomes more subtle and diffuse. It is produced and maintained not so much through demonstrated, exaggerated, and exploited visual differences between Americans and "foreigners"— although these continue to play an important role. Rather, the neocolonial binarism is produced and maintained through the difference between a transnational, pedagogical, cinematic address directed at "visitors" to the "Homeland," in the first case, and a propagandistic, interactive address to cultural insiders and virtual political actors, in the second case. Both forms of address use the aesthetics of transparency to cultivate new forms of "good" global citizenship and provide U.S. imperialists with an alibi for the intensification of surveillance (at home and abroad) and the prosecution of perpetual warfare.

The colonial binarism is recast, therefore, in terms of the docile global citizen-suspects who willingly become transparent or turn themselves inside out, on the one hand, and the stubbornly opaque and animalistic enemies of the U.S.'s war on terror, on the other. One need not be a U.S. citizen to belong to the former category and the fact of U.S. citizenship by no means precludes one from belonging to the second category. The burden of proof is on the person who wishes to attain or keep good standing with the U.S. government and military as a "good" global citizen-suspect rather than an "evildoer" or enemy of "Homeland" Security. While these relations have become more diffuse and nuanced, it is still true that the burden of proof is not equally born by American citizens and non-Americans, or by Europeans and Asians, or by white and non-white Americans, for that matter. The racialized gaze continues to operate insofar as the perception of "Arabic features" (as if there were a uniform category) by

American border officials connotes opacity, as if the traveler in question were somehow automatically less transparent and therefore less trustworthy than a blonde suburban mother from Des Moines, Iowa. Or in the words of the narrator of Réda Bensmaïa's novel, *The Year of Passages*: "They've glued on us a face that looks like a mug shot" (quoted in Kumar, p. 42).

Transparency is a fantasy of U.S. imperial dominance and a strategy for producing docile global citizen-suspects. The desirability and safety of transparency is supported by periodic and spectacular returns to the undocile (i.e., opaque) enemy. These strategic spectacles of opacity rehearse older versions of the colonized and racialized body, as demonstrated by mainstream U.S. media coverage of Saddam Hussein's capture. Within the visual discourse of transparency, opacity invites violent punishment and death. Folded into the strategy of transparency, spectacular footage and still images of opaque enemies in the war on terror are meant to produce fear and xenophobia in Americans and other Eurocentric members of the viewing or reading audience. However, they do not necessarily or exclusively produce fear in "home" viewers. Images of opacity mark the limits of U.S. vision, power, dominance, and penetration. The black hole could just as easily signify the extraordinary ignorance and arrogance of U.S. foreign policy since 9/11.

And yet, it is difficult not to see the U.S. government and CNN as inviting, encouraging, even producing a spectator with neocolonial aspirations and identifications. Image events like these in the visual culture of the war on terror have established a global network of looking relations in which Americans are addressed as the privileged subjects of the new security screening procedures and sutured into virtual identification with the supposedly benign administrative state and the kick-ass macho American military and daring Western journalist. Foreign nationals attempting to enter the "Homeland" are addressed as suspect and potential terrorists. Both forms of address aim to produce the U.S. as metropole and translate American citizens and non-Americans alike into compliant subjects through processes of mediation that deprive individuals of embodiment and, therefore, political expression.

NOTES

1. Phrenology and physiognomy were pseudo-scientific projects motivated by a popular desire to classify bodies according to visual appearance. Phrenology was based on the idea that the topography of the skull could give clues to the mental functioning of the brain, while physiognomy claimed to read an individual's character through the classification of the features of the head and face (Henning, 2001, p. 221). In his essay, "The Body and the Archive," Allan Sekula points out

that these ways of seeing were linked to the explicitly racist pseudo science of eugenics in the work of Francis Galton.

2. The popular appeal of a large-scale military manhunt for "Iraq's Most Wanted" relies on an act of substitution: the one terrorist most wanted by the U.S. government, Osama Bin Laden, is replaced by 52 Iraqis, who are suddenly marked as terrorists and thereby made to belong to the same category as Osama Bin Laden. I am intentionally trying to recreate this ellipsis in the slippage from Iraq's Most Wanted to the caves of Afghanistan.

3. According to Robert Castel, "The modern ideologies of prevention are overarched by a grandiose technocratic rationalizing dream of absolute control over the accidental, understood as the irruption of the unpredictable." His description of this dream is particularly apt for border security: a "vast hygienist utopia" that plays alternately on fear and security (1991, p. 289).

4. Indeed, Foucault understands the compensatory heterotopia as an American phenomenon insofar as he holds up the Puritans of the New World as exemplary of this spatial order.

5. In the United States, the ideological articulation between hygiene and safety dates back to the social reforms begun in the late 19th century. John Tagg (1993) argues that police photography, along with the burgeoning sciences of criminology, psychiatry, comparative anatomy, germ theory, and sanitation, redefined the social as the object of their technical interventions in the late 19th and early 20th centuries (p. 5). These were bodies of knowledge and governmental practices motivated by a hygienic vision of a disease-free social space that would be open to vision and supervision—in short, orderly. It was this modern fantasy of order that motivated projects as diverse as missionary exploration, slum clearance, sanitary reform, health supervision, and constant, regularized policing (Tagg, 1993, p. 64).

6. The program is a direct result of federal legislation implemented after the terrorist attacks of September 11, 2001. The Patriot Act, the Enhanced Border and Visa Entry Reform Act, and the Aviation and Transportation Security Act all mandated some kind of biometric identifier to enhance public safety (Braiker, 2004).

7. The "virtual border" program involves "partnerships" between the federal government and private corporations. The U.S. government awarded the private firm, Accenture, a 10-year, $10 billion contract to create the US-VISIT program. In exchange, the company and its subcontractors promised to build a "virtual border" that would electronically screen foreign travelers to the U.S. (O'Harrow & Higham, 2005). More recently, the Bush administration announced plans to erect a virtual border between the U.S. and Mexico and has been experimenting with visas that transmit radio signals as a means of tracking travelers as they cross land borders (Lipton, 2006, 2005). President Bush has proposed biometric identification cards for Mexicans working in the U.S. on a temporary basis. And the Department of Homeland Security will soon accept bids for a border control system that will combine old and new technologies in a single integrated information system ("New Technology," *New York Times*). Boeing, Lockheed Martin, Northrop Grumman, Raytheon, Ericsson are expected to submit bids in the $20–55 billion range.

8. See the Capture/ "Saddam 'caught like a rat' in a hole" Gallery at http://www.cnn.com/SPECIALS/2003/saddam/)

9. Americans' virtual mobility: through cinema, television, video, and the Internet, is conditioned by their actual immobility. For arguments pertaining to immobility as a condition of spectatorship, see Anne Friedberg (2002).

10. "In the Gulf War strategy, the agency belonged to the "West," seen from the viewpoint of the weapons themselves. Pictures were transmitted showing their "view" of the targets right up until the moment of impact. This stunning representation of war seemed to suggest a new surgical precision of warfare, the endpoint of Walter Benjamin's famous comparison of the surgeon and the camera operator (2002). On September 11, the West discovered what it is like to be on the receiving end of tele-visual war . . . The globalization of culture turns out to be less predictable and far more dangerous than had been supposed" (Mirzoeff, 2002, p. 5).

11. Describing the 24-hour news coverage enabled by cable news, Sturken writes: "The knowledge that the 24-hour news cycles of cable television tend to produce is not cumulative, in part because each new moment literally cancels, without a trace, what we have just seen" (p. 126). Yet, Sturken argues, the essence of history on television is repetition, reenactment, and docudrama. Like the docudramas of the Vietnam War, television reenactments offer particular kinds of catharsis which in their mix of memory and fantasy produce forms of remembrance. The heavily choreographed coverage of the Gulf War made it already a docudrama (p. 136).

12. This form of military-technological spectatorship was first offered to U.S. citizen-consumers during the Gulf War. Marita Sturken argues that the two most iconic images of the Gulf War—bombs in the night sky over Baghdad and the POV approach of the "smart" bomb to its target—signified the myth of the war as one of clean technology (p. 129).

13. According to Foucault, modern disciplinary power inherited occularcentrism from the Enlightenment. The Panopticon drew inspiration from the Enlightenment dream of "a transparent society, visible and legible in each of its parts, the dream of there no longer existing zones of darkness, zones established by the privilege of royal power or prerogatives of a corporation, zones of disorder" (1980, p. 152). Defined as a clean field of vision, order is presumed to foster, if not guarantee, justice. In its treatment of the press, the international community, and the American public, as well as its attitudes toward science, the Bush Administration is staunchly anti-Enlightenment.

14. It is the creation of zones of darkness on the part of the U.S. government and military that makes the Enlightenment logic of exposure so compelling in stories like the Abu Ghraib prison scandal, which reignites the old democratic dream of the free press.

15. In the *Arcades Project*, Walter Benjamin distinguishes between two modern forms of visual subjectivity: "Let us not, however confuse the *flâneur* with the rubberneck: there is a subtle difference. . . . The average *flâneur* is always in full possession of his individuality, while that of the rubberneck disappears, absorbed by the external world, . . . which moves him to the point of intoxication and ecstasy. Under the influence of the spectacle, the rubberneck becomes an impersonal being. He is no longer a man—he is the public; he is the crowd" (2002, p. 429).

16. So far, the program has been most effective at catching foreign visitors with criminal records. As a means of stopping terrorists from entering the United States, the Americans' virtual mobility: through cinema, television, video, and the Internet,

program is less reliable. Rep. Jim Turner (D-Texas) wrote that a Stanford University study found that terrorists on the watch-list who alter their fingerprints with a film of rubber gum will be caught 53% of the time. Other critics of US-VISIT argue that the program will not catch terrorists, who are unlikely to have fingerprint records on file with the FBI. Former deputy director in the State Department's Office of Counterterrorism makes plain the incongruity between the program's stated goals and its practical outcomes: "The reality is the universe of fingerprints for terrorists is really small. There haven't been that many major terrorist attacks" (Gathright, Coile, & Hua, 2004). One federal official said: "If we ever catch a terrorist, we will only catch an extremely dumb terrorist" (Lipton, 2005).

17. Privacy International reports that the personal information collected under the program will be retained for 75 to 100 years and the system could encompass 1 billion people within 15 years (Privacy International, 2004). As the system grows, Privacy International argues that the opportunity for error will rise exponentially (Willan, 2004).

REFERENCES

ACLU says new border fingerprinting system likely to sow confusion, tracking of Arab and Muslims based on national origin will continue. (5 January 2004). American Civil Liberties Union. aclu.org <http://www.aclu.org/safefree/ general/16930prs20040105. html>. Last accessed 29 May 2006.

Agamben, G. (10 January 2004). Column for *Le Monde*, Italian prof resigns NYU, refuses fingerprinting at US border. (trans., Martin Rueff). The Artists Network of Refuse and Resist! <www.artistsnetwork.org/news11/news570.html>. Last accessed 29 May 2006.

Benjamin, W. (2002). *The Arcades project*, R. Tiedemann (Ed.). Cambridge: Belknap Press.

Border patrol fingerprint system identifies 30,000 criminal suspects attempting to enter the U.S. (22 February 2005). Govtech.net. Government technology. <http:// www.govtech. net/magazine/channel_story.php?channel=19&id=93149>. Last accessed 29 May 2006.

Braiker, B. (7 January 2004). "Very, very accurate": A biometrics consultant argues in favor of the technology used to fingerprint and photograph visitors to the United States. MSNBC.com. *Newsweek*. <http://www.msnbc.msn.com/id/3899039/>. Last accessed 29 May 2006.

Castel, Robert. From Dangerousness to Risk, in *The Foucault effect: studies in governmentality*, Edited by Graham Burchell, Colin Gordon, and Peter Miller. Chicago: University of Chicago Press, 1991.

Foucault, Michel. (2002). Of othering spaces, *The visual culture reader*, N. Mirzoeff, (Ed.). New York: Routledge.

Foucault, M. (1980). The eye of power. In: *Power/knowledge: Selected interviews and other writings 1972–1977*, C. Gordon (Ed.). New York: Pantheon.

Friedberg, A. (2002). The mobilized and virtual gaze in modernity. In *The visual culture reader*, N. Mirzoeff (Ed.). New York: Routledge.

Gathright, A., Coile, Z. & Hua, V. (6 January 2004). Photos, fingerprints taken at U.S. borders: Anti-terror program screens visitors at airports. *San Francisco Chronicle*, 6 January 2004. <http://www.sfgate.com/cgi-bin/article.cgi?f=/c/a/2004/01/06/MNGCR448EP1.DTL>. Last accessed 29 May 2006.

Henning, Michelle (2000). The subject as object: photography and the human body, in *Photography: A Critical Introduction*, 2nd Edition, Edited by Liz Wells. New York: Routledge, 217–250.

Kumar, Amitava (2000). *Passport Photos*. Berkeley: University of California Press.

Lipton, E. (18 May 2004). Seeking to control borders, Bush turns to big military contractors. *New York Times*.

Lipton, E. (11 August 2005). U.S. turns to science to protect its borders. *International Herald Tribune*. <http://www.iht.com/articles/2005/08/10/news/biometrics.php>. Last accessed 29 May 2006.

Mirzoeff, N. (2002). The subject of visual culture. In *The visual culture reader*, N. Mirzoeff (Ed.). New York: Routledge.

Nakamura, L. (2002). "Where do you want to go today?" Cybernetic tourism, the internet, and transnationality. In *The visual culture reader*, N. Mirzoeff (Ed.). New York: Routledge.

"New Technology on the Border." *New York Times* Graphic 17 May 2006. www.nytimes.com.

O'Harrow, R., & Higham, Jr. S. (19 October 2004). 2-fingerprint border ID system called inadequate. *Washington Post*. <http://www.washingtonpost.com/wp-dyn/articles/A43276-2004Oct18.html>. Last accessed 29 May 2006.

O'Harrow, R., & Higham, Jr. S. (23 May 2005). U.S. Border Security at a Crossroads. *Washington Post*. <http://www.washingtonpost.com/wp-dyn/content/article/2005/05/22/AR2005052200613.html>. Last accessed 29 May 2006.

PI raises alarm as U.S. starts mass fingerprinting. (27 September 2004). *Privacy International*. <http://www.privacyinternational.org/article.shtml?cmd%5B347%5D=x-347-182944>. Last accessed 29 May 2006.

"Report: U.S. border vulnerable," Associated Press/CNN.com. Last accessed May 29, 2006 <www.cnn.com/2004/US/03/02/border.security.ap/index.html.>

Sekula, Allan. The Body and the Archive, *October* 39 (Winter 1986): 3–64.

Shohat, E., & Stam, R. (1994). *Unthinking Eurocentrism: Multiculturalism and the media*. New York: Routledge.

Sturken, Marita (1997). *Tangled memories: The Vietnam War, the AIDS epidemic, and the politics of remembering*. Berkeley: University of California Press.

Tagg, John (1993). *The burden of representation: essays on photographies and histories*. Minneapolis: University of Minnesota Press.

US Fingerprints Foreign Visitors. (5 January 2004). *BBC News*. <http://news.bbc.co.uk/go/pr/fr/-/2/hi/americas/3367893.stm>. Last accessed 29 May 2006.

Willan, P. (1 October 2004). Human rights group blasts new U.S. border controls. *InfoWorld.com*. <http://www.infoworld.com/article/04/10/01/HNbordercontrol_1.html>. Last accessed 29 May 2006.

Monstrous Play in Negative Spaces: Illegible Bodies and the Cultural Construction of Biometric Technology

HEATHER MURRAY

INTRODUCTION: ILLEGIBLE BODIES IN NEGATIVE SPACES

"Our methods of measurement define who we are and what we value."

—Ken Alder, *The Measure of All Things* (2002, p. 2)

The word "biometric" links the prefix denoting "life; living organism" to a suffix meaning "of or related to measurement" (Dictionary.com, 2004). In the most general terms, a biometric device measures life, measures a body or body part. A textbook definition of biometric technology reads as follows: "the automated use of physiological or behavioral characteristics to determine or verify identity" (Nanavati, Thieme, & Nanavati, 2002, p. 9).[1] Interaction with physiological biometric technology involves a user enrolling in a database by placing a body part, such as a hand, eye, face, or finger, on or in front of a scanner that "reads" the hand, translates that information into a digital template, and brings up that template for a potential (and always approximate) match when the user attempts to access the technology at a later date.[2]

The U.S. government and the biometric industry have identified fingerprint scanning, iris and retinal scanning, and face recognition technology as essential tools in the fight against "terrorism."[3] Biometric technology installed at national border points is a key component in regulating the transnational flow of bodies in a global economy. Its growing presence in a number of social sectors in which it grants or denies access, allows or prevents mobility, and provides or withholds capital makes it an important focus for critical analysis. Michael J. Garcia, the U.S. Department of Homeland Security Assistant Secretary for Immigration and Customs Enforcement (ICE), has claimed biometric technology can "reveal the true identity underneath any alias" used by "criminals and others" (US, P. R., 2005). Such a statement assumes that there is a "true" form of identity that can be discovered through the readings of an ostensibly neutral machine, and that such readings are reliable because a body, also supposedly neutral, cannot lie, cannot support the aliases used by "criminals and others." These assumptions, by no means new to the history of technology or Western culture, deny the biases programmed into the technology that produce, in this case, illegible biometric bodies. Biometric technology struggles to read such bodies, failing to enroll them in a given database, failing to account for them in its digital archive of body parts. Irma van der Ploeg (2004, p. 582) has concluded that "biometrics generates a *readable* body: It transforms the body's surfaces into digital codes and ciphers to be read by a machine."[4] Although that is true in most cases, I would like to pluralize van der Ploeg's terminology to investigate the *bodies* produced by biometric technology.

This essay insists that biometric technology produces many identities, many bodies, and that in the case of the illegible biometric body, the Foucaultian logic of that production (*producing* what it claims "only" to represent) replicates that of the historical production of the category "monster." The second section of my article will trace the logic that informs biometric technology from Enlightenment notions of scientific visuality, through modernist films and photographs of criminals and so-called "savages," to biometric technology's production of illegible bodies. In the third section, I will focus on a particularly troubling confluence of human and animal attributes found in what is called the "biometric menagerie" as an example of the discriminatory logic behind what David Lyon (2003) has referred to as "social sorting". My argument concludes that rather than serving as evidence for the fixed legibility of all bodies, biometric technology, in its selective illiteracy, reveals bodies as emerging, as Judith Butler (1990, 1993) has argued, simultaneously through physical and discursive performance. Biometric technology is one example of the ways material experience always already coincides with discursive fields to inform our understanding of our bodies and their relationship with identity.

Biometric technology, then, cannot be defined solely according to the process of enrolling a particular user into the databank of a particular type of machine. In order to analyze the bodies produced by such technology, it is crucial to define it on a broader cultural level, acknowledging the sites competing for and contributing to its meaning. "Biometric technology," then, emerges at the intersection of philosophy, (colonial and postcolonial) politics, military strategy, law, (the history of) technology, film, and cyberpunk and science fiction—in short, to define biometric technology, one must look beyond the bounds of the physical product and into the cultural imagination, the modern social fantasy of the West.[5] Biometric technology cannot be separated from the socio-political, institutional, and material practices that co-constitute it, and are constituted by it.

"Technology" means to me not only some form of knowable, literal, scientific machine one can point to (as in a car battery or a telescope), but also in the sense that Donna Haraway or Michel Foucault have used it, respectively, as "ways of life, social orders, practices of visualization, . . . [and] skilled practices," or a series of complex rules and regulations that utilize social norms as control mechanisms regarding, for example, sex, criminality, and madness (Foucault, 1990; Haraway, 1991).[6] "Biometric technology" is a non-innocent[7] actor in that, as I will explain throughout this essay, it contributes to human understanding about identity, bodies, representation, measurement, and visuality. Given the above definition of technology, biometric technology is also a set of *practices* contributing to the very socio-cultural discourses that in turn construct "biometric technology." In other words, the technology is constituted by the practices involved in its use: the movement of one's body across a scanner and the role of the attendant instructing a user on the proper poses and gestures necessary for enrollment. The movement, the *performance* involved in a biometric scan is bound to *and produces* cultural understandings of gender, authority, and criminality, to name a few. These cultural understandings contribute to the development and use of biometric technology, and the technology, as it becomes part of the daily lives of travelers, ATM users, and government employees, among others, contributes to the meanings of the very cultural understandings that informed its development and use by putting things like gender, authority, and criminality in terms of the digital coding of body parts. Illegible bodies, just as much as ideal(ized) readable biometric bodies, are entangled in this complicated process. Illegible bodies are part of what I call the "negative space" archive of biometric technology.

Common to any introductory drawing class is the negative space drawing exercise. Such a drawing, of a chair, for example, develops not
through a focus on the chair, but on the space around and inside the chair
(between the legs and the slits in the back). The most well-known version
of a negative space drawing depicts either two faces in profile looking at
each other or a vase, depending on how one looks at it. Although "negative" space is described in relation to "positive" space (positive space is
the shape of the chair as opposed to the shape of the space around the
chair), a look at this type of drawing, at these types of spaces, makes clear
that making meaning of such a drawing depends on both spaces existing
at once. Therefore, you might say that whereas Michael J. Garcia understands biometric technology only by looking at its "positive space
archive," I intend in this essay to examine the "negative space archive."
Both are necessary for an understanding of biometric technology. Those
bodies that populate the "positive" spaces, those bodies that can be "read"
through the measurement of their parts, can only exist as evidence of an
objective or neutral reading if one denies the existence of those bodies
that populate the "negative" spaces. Like the positive space of the chair,
the "positive spaces" of biometric technology are those parts of its archive
someone like Michael J. Garcia is trained to see, those parts that individuals hoping for an infallible safeguard against "criminals and others" *want*
to see.

Once one is trained to see both negative space and positive space,
images become dynamic, in seemingly constant movement as the negative space changes from foreground to background, at times taking on the
dominance of the positive space. The image plays with a viewer's
attempts to read only the positive or only the negative space. An archive
developed through a focus on negative spaces, then, does not derive from
center/margin binaries, but is scattered throughout an image, a concept, or
a field. Illegible biometric bodies emerge around and between "readable"
bodies. It would be difficult to determine, in fact, which type of body constitutes biometric readability. Depending on how one looks at it, the technology is about illegible bodies or legible bodies; they both contribute to
its definition. The shift from one to the other happens unexpectedly, but
changes the picture dramatically. The negative space archive extends
beyond the outline, exceeds the limits but holds the shape of biometric
technology.

Most biometric technology textbooks[8] glance hesitantly at this archive.
At some point in their narrative, these texts acknowledge, "Certain ethnic
and demographic populations are more prone to high failure to enroll
(FTE) rates than others, a problem that can reduce deployability of biometrics in specific environments" (Nanavati et al., 2002, p. 35). More specifically, finger-scan technology struggles to read "elderly, construction

workers/artisans, and those of Pacific Rim/Asian descent . . . especially female users" because of faint fingerprint ridges, while facial scanning "may not be as adept at enrolling very dark-skinned users," and iris-scan technology strains to "locate distinctive features in very dark irises" (Nanavati et al., 2002, 35–37). In case studies (Woodward et al., 2001, p. 104), for example, "There is a problem with people who have small hands (e.g., Japanese flight attendants have been particularly problematic at LAX)." Other "problematic" populations include plumbers, carpenters, bricklayers, and health care workers.[9] Recommendations for studies of biometric technology (Jain, Bolle, & Pankanti, 1999, p. 58) include a specific description of the subject population, because a "study involving masons will have different statistical results than that involving white-collar workers whose hands are subject to less abuse. The age statistics should be described . . . The proportion of males and females should also be stated."

The class, gender, age, and race implications of such findings and recommendations reveal much about the cultural construction of biometric technology. The illegible bodies described above include those involved in physical labor, women (and specifically women of "Asian" descent), the "Asian" Pacific Rim population in general, dark-skinned and dark-eyed individuals, and the elderly. This illegibility results not from these bodies, of course, but from the technology that struggles to read them. One textbook (Nanavati et al., 2002, p. 37) admitted that unreadable skin color stems from "video cameras [in facial recognition technology] optimized for lighter-skinned users." Similarly, Jason Namkung, a representative for Jiris USA has pointed out that iris scanners in the U.S. cannot read dark irises simply because they were formatted for lighter eyes, whereas in Japan that problem did not exist.[10] As Shoshana Magnet (forthcoming 2008) has pointed out, this problem has occurred in countries other than the U.S.: "In the UK, biometric technologies have difficulty distinguishing 'Black' bodies. In Japan, one study posited that it would be most difficult for biometrics to identify 'non-Japanese' faces." The point is that the technology is gauged to the idealized bodies in a given culture, producing as "abnormal" those who do not correspond to the idealized model.

This is not unlike the "problem" of dark skin in film and photography. Richard Dyer (1997, p. 90) has made it clear that the "problem" is with the technology: "Stocks, cameras and lighting were developed taking the white face as the touchstone . . . photo and film apparatus have seemed to work better with light-skinned peoples, but that is because they were made that way, not because they could be no other way."[11] Biometric technology has been made, therefore, with a normative notion of "body" in mind; a culturally constructed notion of embodied identity exceeded, particularly in the U.S. and the U.K. by the bodies of women, ethnically

"Far Eastern" individuals, dark-skinned and dark-eyed individuals, blue collar workers, and the elderly. These bodies sketch out the limits of biometric technology. They are not, quite simply, light-skinned and light-eyed, young, white-collar men. This may seem a reversal of the modernist formula wherein certain white male bodies were rendered invisibly objective, while the weight and burden of embodiment rested with women and "people of color," but importantly, white male biometric bodies are mediated by technology as readable bodies, and the weight of embodiment still rests with illegible bodies, deemed too physically present for the transcoding from flesh to digits.[12] By depending on normative notions of bodies for readability, biometric technology produces "abnormal" bodies as excessive (too dark) or lacking (indistinct fingerprint ridges, small hands).

BIOMETRIC GENEALOGY AND MONSTROUS LOGIC

"To do their job, standards must operate as a set of shared assumptions, the unexamined background against which we strike agreements and make decisions. . . . Yet the use a society makes of its measures expresses its sense of fair dealing."

—Ken Alder, *The Measure of All Things* (2002, p. 2)

As I said above, the assumptions made by Michael J. Garcia are not new to Western culture. It is important to contextualize the assumptions behind biometric technology in order to comprehend the profound implications of its biases. I would like to start by placing biometrics in the trajectory of visualizing technologies common to the 19th–early 20th centuries in order to explore the complicated relationship between representation and ontology before moving on to the formulation shared by biometric technology and the historical production of monsters.

Rachel Hall's (2004) work on the wanted poster links productively to biometric technology in many ways. The wanted poster, according to Hall's analysis, serves as a form of surveillance and tracking, is an example of the "state's translation of the live body into text," suggests that anyone's face could adorn the poster, and, in conjunction with the outlaw's fingerprints, becomes "documentary evidence of his body's irreducible singularity" (Hall, 2004, pp. 22–23). Hall has looked beyond the instrumentality of the wanted poster to consider its function as a cultural performance. Its signification *as* evidence produces as a criminal the individual framed by the poster. As with biometric technology, what may seem to some a neutral "reading," a statement of "fact" lacking bias, performs in many ways to produce what it claims to identify as already established.

Allan Sekula (1992) has explored the complex relationship between photography, criminal science, eugenics, and physiognomic and phreno-logical practices at the end of the 19th century. Sekula's analysis of crimi-nal photographs reveals the relation of their subject matter to modernist notions of vision, prediction, risk assessment, and embodiment. The "pre-sumed denotative univocality of the legal image," the criminal photo-graph, led many to believe that aberrant behavior, or "moral insanity," could be read on the body and, in some cases, alleviated (Sekula, 1992, pp. 345, 349).[13] This type of logic, this investment in photographic truth[14] coinciding with the purported readability of the body, is rooted in attempts by the modern West to position itself as more highly evolved than the col-onized "Other," or by the modern Western bourgeoisie to position itself as more valuable than the modern Western working class. It sticks to con-temporary developments in biometric technology like a stubborn ancestor.

This genealogy is not rejected by the biometric industry. Julian Ash-bourn (2000), biometric technology systems designer, listed the same cast of players noted by Sekula, such as phrenologist Franz Joseph Gall, crim-inal archivist Alphonse Bertillon, mathematician Adolphe Quetelet, and criminal anthropologist Cesare Lombroso, as setting the 19th-century foundations for biometric technology. Ashbourn's reflection on such a family tree leads to this statement: "It seems that people continue to be fascinated by the possibility of aligning character traits with physical characteristics" (p. 5). Ashbourn's conclusion is an extreme example of the undertheorized status of the modernist influences on contemporary biometric technology, but the lingering modernist faith in observation as the means to empirical, objective evidence informs the confidence of many in the biometric industry.[15]

This lineage consists of technologies that, as I have already mentioned, claim "only" to represent what they, in fact, produce. Representation has been considered a way to read ontology. If someone "looked like" a crim-inal, s/he "was" a criminal. Similarly, biometric technology claims to be able to determine who someone "is" based on the appearance and mea-surement of his/her body parts. As the next section of this essay will explain, this logic continues in the figure of the monster, which, as Foucault has argued, is bound with the figure of the criminal: Previous to the 18th century, monstrosity "brought with it an indication of criminal-ity," whereas from the 19th century on, "the relationship is reversed and monstrosity is systematically suspected of being behind all criminality" (Foucault, 2003, p. 81). This relationship between visuality, criminality, and the production of "monsters" persists in the contemporary cultural production of biometric technology.

The word "monster" opens this essay up to a number of theoretical and historical discourses; its valences are innumerable; the word itself constitutes a monstrous hybrid. Monstrosity, as Zakiya Hanafi (2000, p. 55) has explained, "is redefined in different times and places . . . a monster is always an indication of transgression, of breakdown in hierarchy; it is quintessentially a symbol of crisis and undifferentiation. However, beyond these attributes a monster can take on any form." It is "not any particular *thing* . . . it is a category that becomes constituted in different ways according to different cultural and historical contexts" (Hanafi, p. 15). It is important, then, to look at Western constructions of monstrosity from the perspective of both historical and contemporary contexts in order to determine how it appears through biometric technology.

In order to explore my concern with the term "monster" and its history, I would like to examine the ways it shares with biometric technology a concern for vision, normativity, criminality, measurement, and taxonomy. The etymology of the word "monster" reveals a number of visual metaphors referring to a sign, omen, prediction, or display, and the birth of a child deemed monstrous was considered as far back as ancient Greece to be "bearing a sign of warning from the forces of the sacred" (Hanafi, 2000, p. 3). Rosi Braidotti (1996, p. 142) has pointed out not only that monsters have historically been put on display, but that they have constituted that which is foreign or "Other": "our culture has tended to represent the furthest away as the most monstrous—that is, the least civilized, the least democratic or law-abiding . . . from the geographical discourse of the Greeks to the concern for jurisprudence in the eighteenth century, down to evolutionary anthropology in the nineteenth." The production of such monsters as foreign coincides with and depends on the production of concepts of normativity defined as domestic and natural. Biometric technology is a visualizing technology, transcoding one's body into an image consisting of a binary digital code, and it is designed to flag particular users as dangerous; it predicts and assesses risk, and it does so through the measurement of a user's body part. Biometric technology, as is made clear through the illegible body, is gauged in the West for an image of normativity as a white, white-collar male; it delegates as "Other" those who do not meet this image.

Bodily measurement has historically been used in a number of ways, but it has also been a taxonomic enterprise essential to the cataloguing of bodies in Western colonial projects, often with the assistance of visualizing technologies such as photography and film. Fatimah Tobing Rony's *The Third Eye: Race, Cinema and Ethnographic Spectacle* (1996) examined the confluence of anthropology/ethnography, photography, film, the Western colonial project, and phrenology in the late 1800s. Noting the ways in which the camera has been considered neutral and unproblematic by anthropologists to this day, rendering for the filmmaker the "truth" of his/her subjects, Rony argued that the "Ethnographic becomes monstrous at the very moment of visual appropriation" and that the transformation of the ethnographic to the monstrous "was only an exaggeration of the common propensity to see native peoples as strange, bizarre, and abhorrent" (Tobing Rony, 1996, p. 161).

Ethnographic filmmakers such as Felix-Louis Regnault, fascinated by pathological and criminal anatomy, created films that served to demonstrate, through physical comparison, differences between Western Europeans and indigenous colonized peoples. This form of filmmaking was legitimized as scientific by its relation to anthropology, which "grew as the science of *reading* the human body" (Tobing Rony, 1996, p. 35).[16] The body was measured and weighed to produce an ideal Western body in contrast to the "monstrous" indigenous body. These ethnographic films created a catalogue, a taxonomy to demonstrate the ways in which the white European body was wholly "normal."

Much earlier than this, during the Renaissance, "'readings' of monstrous bodies . . . had precise propagandistic purposes . . . [they were] nothing less than an alternative political science" (Hanafi, 2000, p. 3). Today, in its application at national borders, biometric technology separates domestic from foreign, and produces an idealized, homogenized (U.S. and European) citizen. It is confounded by, even as it produces, the biometric noncitizen who migrates across borders, the refugee without origins, the foreign presence against whom the modern state claims to protect its citizens, and in general, the nonmember of Western national communities.

The historical uses of the category "monster" align in many ways with the purported functions of biometric technology, and the links of monstrosity to comparative anthropology, criminality, Western colonial projects, and an insistence on the inherent "truth" produced by visual technology inform the applications of biometric technology. Biometric technology, in the manner of the production of monstrosity, "shows the imbrication of genderized and racialized narratives and the role they play in constructing scientific discourses about the female body" (Braidotti, 1996, p. 149). Illegible biometric bodies, like those of the discourse on monsters, have been defined "in terms of *excess, lack*" (p. 138, italics original).[17] The logic of the production of "monsters" and its contemporary manifestation in biometric technology makes clear the dangers of accepting as fact the ability of biometric technology to determine someone's "true" identity, to reveal whom s/he "is."

Not only, then, does biometric technology inherit the modernist investment in visuality as empirical evidence and an understanding of the body's representation *as* its ontology, but it also bases its understanding of that body on longstanding formulas for normativity that inevitably produce varieties of the abnormal. Interrogating the failure of such formulas, the paucity of such investments allows for an understanding of biometric technology that supports rather than denies the unfixed nature of human bodies, readable or not.

THE BIOMETRIC MENAGERIE AS SOCIAL SORTING

"But the pursuit of precision, like all moral quests, is a hazardous affair."

—Ken Alder, *The Measure of All Things* (2002, p. 63)

The biometric industry has applied the term "goats" to human bodies that resist digital identification or, in industry terms, those who "fail" to enroll. Other such codes in what is called the "biometric menagerie" (Hicklin, Watson, & Ulery, 2005, p. 5) include "sheep," for those who are easy to match, "lambs," whose biometric readings are somehow susceptible to impersonation, and "wolves," who can easily impersonate others' biometric readings (Campbell, 1997; Doddington et al., 1998). The application of these animal terms might serve to fuel the flame of some Christians, who see biometric technology as producing the mark of the beast (Chandrasekaran, 1997; Davies, 1994). In the Book of Matthew (8:4), the last judgment is described as separating the sheep from the goats; the sheep [easy to read in biometric parlance] go to heaven, while the goats [difficult to read in biometric parlance] go to hell (New Jerusalem Bible). The idea of a wolf in sheep's clothing is also biblical, and also in the Book of Matthew (7:15), but prior to the writing of the bible this was also a phrase used in 6th century BCE Aesop's Fables. These cultural myths have moral connotations that make biometric labels such as "sheep" or "wolf" signify beyond the ways one interacts with a machine. Although I do not know the reasoning behind the choice of these appellations, it is certainly significant that in the biblical version the goats go to hell.

A 2005 (Hicklin et al.) study, entitled "The Myth of Goats," performed for the U.S. Department of Homeland Security by representatives of the non-profit organization Mitretek[18] and the National Institute of Standards and Technology tried to correct some of the earlier conclusions about illegible bodies. They claimed that for "frequent users of US-VISIT," "fingerprints that are hard to match *cannot* generally be attributed to intrinsic characteristics of a person's fingerprints, but should be attributed to collection problems or other characteristics of the specific fingerprints used" (p. 3). Nowhere in the report do the authors suggest that there is any problem with the technology in regard to establishing a norm, and the bulk of the argument revolves around clarifying that in any study, saying 2% of tested *fingerprints* were unreadable, does not mean 2% of the *population* is unreadable (p. 6).[19] Furthermore, they insisted that the original studies (also through NIST) that provided this percentage had tested a small number (about 100) of primarily "illegal immigrants under harsh conditions and not with high quality scanners" (p. 7). To rectify this, the authors claim they used a larger "general" population (p. 9). As the authors explain, their chosen "general" population is repeat users (10 or more times in a 6-month period) of the US-VISIT system. The US-VISIT system, according to the Department of Homeland Security website, "applies to all visitors (with limited exemptions) holding non-immigrant visas, regardless of country of origin."[20] The authors admit, however, that although their study group is "to some extent a cross-section of the world's population . . . [it is] primarily composed of flight crews and business travelers" (p. 10). A study set consisting primarily of flight crews and business travelers is no more representative of the "world's population" than the earlier study consisting of illegal immigrants. Despite their initial insistence, in fact, that their sample set proves that the 2% number was a misconception, they end with this caveat: "Different subject populations will not yield the same results. In particular, populations that have a greater proportion of manual laborers or elderly can be expected to have a greater proportion of hard-to-match fingerprints" (p. 23). Granted there were other problems with the earlier study, such as the "harsh conditions" and below-par scanners, but the make-up of the study population seems profoundly biased in *both* studies. A notable blind spot in the more recent study, as I have already suggested, is that it does not consider how the technology was originally gauged, and its concluding caveat returns blame to the bodies of the potential biometric users as "hard to match."

Rather than focusing on the meaning of 2% or the quality of scanners, we might consider the ways the division of biometric bodies into such animal categories is a form of what David Lyon (2003) calls "social sorting." Lyon has insisted that although humans have long depended on their ability to categorize those with whom they interact, the central aim of surveillance systems is "to classify people and populations according to varying criteria, to determine who should be targeted for special treatment, suspicion, eligibility, inclusion, access, and so on" (p. 20). The foundational assumptions of modernity have intensified the Western interest in classification, and they have also led to "data doubles," representations of individuals consisting of personal and coded data. Even when a data double is not produced, as in the case of illegible biometric bodies, interaction with digital surveillance such as biometric technology is, as Lyon put it, infused with "stereotypes or other prejudicial typing" (p. 22). Attempting to translate a body into computer code does not free it from the social codes that produce stereotypes. The same discriminatory codes that have historically produced the abnormal as "monstrous" have produced a number of biometric bodies. Biometric technology produces an image of "woman" and "Asian" and "elderly," as well as those in the healthcare industry, as soft and fragile, as lacking definition. Those with careers that require manual labor have "abused" hands (Jain et al., 1999); they develop through biometric technology as calloused and hardened, with no nuances or detail. Dark skin and eyes manifest as "problematic," fooling the computers that search for the particular contrast on the faces and within the pupils of idealized white bodies. The technology deems them *too dark, too much*; they exceed the limits of the technology's framework.

Taking into consideration the role biometric technology plays in assigning legality and criminality, citizenship and refugee status, and access and denial, the implications of the normative category of acceptable biometric bodies and the "problematic" illegible bodies such a notion produces are profound indeed. Giorgio Agamben (1998, p. 177) has insisted that a new understanding of human being, of person, of "people" has developed that is directly related to one's status as national citizen. In his articulation of a defining characteristic of modernism, that being the political existence of a being that can be killed but not sacrificed ("homo sacer"), rights "are attributed to man (or originate in him) solely to the extent that man is the immediately vanishing ground (who must never come to light as such) of the citizen" (p. 128).[21] If humans attain rights upon their categorization as citizen, then what of the status of someone who is established as neither citizen nor non-citizen, who is *illegible*? I agree with Louise Amoore (2006, p. 348), who argued that the "establishment of verifiable identity at the biometric border thus becomes a condition of being, in the sense of living within a particular society or way of life, if not indeed a condition of life itself." Furthermore, as Joseph Pugliese (2005, p. 14) stated specifically in regard to illegible biometric bodies, "not to produce a template is equivalent to having no legal ontology, to being a non-being; you are equivalent to subjects who cannot be represented and whose presence can only be inferred by their very failure to be represented." There is a sense in the work of both of these authors that the role biometric technology plays in Western societies could potentially affect our understanding of the category "human"; that the "failure to be represented" could result in "being a non-being." Simon G. Davies (1994) has considered the potential for "sub-cultures of outcasts . . . who choose not to participate in a general identification scheme." What kind of subculture of outcasts might be formed not by those who *choose* not to participate, but rather by those who are *prevented* from participating by the technology? What of those whose bodies are blamed when the fault, in fact, lies with technologically encoded cultural biases?

CONCLUSION: BIOMETRIC TECHNOLOGY AND SERIOUS PLAY

"Even our modern impersonal measures are the product of human ingenuity, human passion and the choices of particular people in particular times and places."

—Ken Alder, *The Measure of All Things* (2002, p. 370)

Ken Alder's historical narrative, *The Measure of All Things*, links the desire for a universal measurement system to politics, madness, and morals. It tells the story of the French savants, Delambre and Méchain, who set out on the eve of the French Revolution in hopes of completing an impossible task: to make measurement neutral and objective. They attempted to make unbiased the ways we represent difference and distance. They tried to use the shape of the earth to develop such a system, but discovered instead "that we live on a fallen planet—a world buckled, bent and warped" (p. 263). What in the end was an arbitrary unit of measure became the metric system, founded not on some objective distance derived from a perfectly spherical planet, but rather on the decision of specific men at a specific moment to cover up flaws in order to uphold the illusion of scientific precision.

If we are to use biometric technology, we cannot uphold the illusion of scientific precision. Biometric technology, in its current form, serves to categorize bodies with a dangerous discriminatory logic that cannot be touted as "true" or "objective." It proves not that bodies are fixable or always readable in equal manner, but instead that bodies signify through repeated performance and subjective interpretation. Biometric bodies exist through the discursive fields, the social codes that sort them into citizen or non-citizen, legible or illegible, "sheep" or "goat."

Even "sheep" must be trained to use biometric technology correctly, and many must scan their fingers several times for successful enrollment into a databank, but this does not mean that everyone is equally illegible. Like Haraway's cyborgs, biometric bodies do not call for a revolution in which humans blindly embrace their literal symbiosis with machines; rather, cyborgs allow for "*pleasure* in the confusion of boundaries and for *responsibility* in their construction" (1991, p. 150, italics original). Pleasure may be possible in heretofore-unimagined ways when humans interact or even merge with machines, blurring the boundary between the two, but illegible bodies are a warning about the importance of responsibility in the construction of boundaries. It is important to be able to identify when legitimacies are outlined and illegitimacies are produced. It is important to call out the drawing of irresponsible boundaries that sort humans into corrals of sheep and goats. It is especially important in this case to intervene in the understanding of a visualizing technology that claims to read and to produce fixable bodies. Bodies are not *fixable*. Biometric illegibility insists on a socially constructed body—an embodied, yet unfixable identity.

It is time for serious play with biometric technology. It is time to take seriously the historical trajectory I have aligned with biometric technology, a trajectory of technologies that produce as monstrous those bodies "Othered" by idealized, wealthy, young, white, male bodies. The word "play" in my title refers not to some type of happiness I associate with illegible bodies, for the production of such bodies does not call for celebration. Rather, serious play, calls on us to challenge the promises of biometric technology, to understand its logic and to question its motivation. It insists that we pay attention to the positive and negative spaces of biometric technology's archive, that we define it by the bodies it denies as much as by the bodies it promotes. Anyone who encounters the technology should know about its imprecisions even as government proponents make claims about its ability to discover "the truth."

Revealing the variety of biometric bodies makes clear the enormous stakes involved in defining biometric technology. If discourse about biometric technology opens this negative space archive, then what might seem an easy link between bodies and citizenship and criminality can blur and new boundaries will have to be constructed to account for, as Mary Layoun (1994, p. 69) put it, the "remarkable malleability of what is considered 'foreign,'" boundaries that keep in mind the inevitable, though unequal slippages of embodied identity. As discourses about biometric technology change, so too, can the workings of the machines themselves. The illegible bodies that are the subject of this article are only one of many types of bodies that will perplex biometric technology in its current form. How can the technology begin to consider "larger questions of displacement, travel, capital accumulation, and other transnational processes that affect large numbers of late twentieth-century subjects (who are geographically 'in place' and *displaced*)" (italics original) (Ong, 1999, p. 24)? We might consider from here the ways particular subjects are allowed to bypass customs and immigration checkpoints because of their socioeconomic status. Currently, frequent fliers registered through certain biometric systems can circumvent such checkpoints, walking through them rather than standing in line (Nanavati et al., 2002, p. 229). The technology encourages specific kinds of capital/subjects-with-capital to move freely while economically disadvantaged subjects encounter careful scrutiny.

The bottom line, perhaps, is that more than bodies cross borders. Borders are points of ideological movement just as much as they are locations to search and "identify" bodies. And ideologies cross bodies as well: "there can be no natural way of considering the body that does not involve at the same time the social dimension" (Douglas, 1973, p. 98). I have highlighted here the "social dimension" of biometric bodies, emphasizing the ways they are informed by the historical production of "monster," Christian myth, and the illusion of scientific precision. Biometric technology produces many bodies, unequally, and they emerge through both physical and discursive practice. They emerge to remind us that measurements tell us more about the culture that created them than about some objective distance. They measure not the truth, but instead, like all measurements, they "measure measuring means" (Cage, 1999).

NOTES

1. This article will focus on physiological biometrics, those which depend on the measurement of a body part, rather than behavioral biometrics, which depend on the measurement of bodily movement, such as keystroke or gait.

2. In fact, one of the ways fraud is detected in the use of biometric technology is if an exact match ever occurs. This is one of the primary reasons Corien Prins (1998, p. 163) insists that biometric scans *not* be used as evidence in a court of law. For a rigorous Derridian analysis of this aspect of biometric technology, see Joseph Pugliese's (2005) essay, "*In Silico* Race and the Heteronomy of Biometric Proxies: Biometrics in the Context of Civilian Life, Border Security and Counter-Terrorism Laws."

3. At the 2006 Biometric Consortium Conference, many of the presentations, including keynote addresses, focused on progress in the biometric industry since 9/11. Duane Blackburn, co-chair of the National Science and Technology Council (NSTC) Subcommittee on Biometrics, revealed in his presentation the details of the "National Biometrics Challenge." The NSTC is an executive branch committee chaired by the President and including the Vice President, Director of the Office of Science and Technology Policy, cabinet secretaries, agency heads and "other White House officials." The Challenge is for the purpose of communicating from the government to the biometric industry what should be the focus of biometric research to meet the needs of the nation as a whole. The top four concerns are listed in this order: National Security, Homeland Security and Law Enforcement, Enterprise and E-government Services, and Personal Information and Business Transactions. Of great interest in regard to the National Biometrics Challenge and to many presenters at the conference is the ability of biometric technology to identify individuals moving across national borders in moving vehicles. For more on the National Biometrics Challenge document, see http://www.biometrics.gov/NSTC/pubs/biochallengedoc.pdf.

4. Although the bulk of van der Ploeg's work addresses readable bodies, her more recent publications have directly addressed the fact that surveillance practices "produce infinitely better inhabitable identities for some people than for others" (2006, p. 193).

5. Although I will make reference to developments and uses of biometric technology outside of the United States, I am interested here in the influence of modernism on the technology as manifested in the West, and particularly the U.S.

6. Each of these notions of "technology" are bound to each author's understanding of science and power as non-innocent, invested, and biased, although Haraway's conception of science comes from a specifically anti-racist, feminist standpoint, whereas Foucault speaks in more abstract terms about presocial bodies upon which history is written by various technologies of power. In each case, however, technology represents a productive power, participating in the construction of social norms and ideologies.

7. I borrow this term from Donna Haraway's descriptions of epistemological positioning and scientific knowledge. She insists, as do many in science and technology studies, that technologies such as computers and lab equipment are agents or actors; they contribute knowledge and affect human understanding. Furthermore, she refuses the description of such technologies as "neutral," pointing out instead the ways they are "non-innocent" actors (1991, p. 191). Haraway defines "actors" as "entities which do things, have effects, build worlds in concatenation with other *unlike* actors" (1992, p. 311).

8. I am using the term "textbook" to refer to a variety of introductory books that describe themselves as available for many readers, often including students.

9. According to all of the texts who describe such workers as problematic, occupations such as bricklayers and plumbers result in a wearing down of the fingerprint to nearly smooth, while the repeated handwashing of healthcare workers also contributes to the erasure of fingerprints. These characteristics are exacerbated by the aging process.

10. Conversation with the author at the 2006 Biometric Consortium Conference. Namkung also claimed that iris scan technology that integrated infrared technology could overcome existing issues with eye color.

11. Joseph Pugliese (2005, p. 4, p. 14) has also noted, if only tangentially, the links of biometric technology with early uses of film and photography, but I argue here that those links are crucial in making clear the ways everyday uses of technology become depoliticized through the myth of neutrality.

12. I am grateful to Dr. Laura Kang for leading me to this important nuance.

13. As Sekula points out, Eliza Farnham used phrenological examination to support an argument against the death penalty and for the possibility of therapy and rehabilitation.

14. That biometric technology uses digital, and not photographic, technology is not insignificant; however, my point is that biometric technology and the forms of visualization described by Sekula share a faith in the evidentiary role of the visual, be that photographic and analogue or digital.

15. This is especially pervasive in biometric advertising. Consider the following advertisement text for biometric products: "Making Faces 'ID Ready'" (Animetrics "Forensica" Facial Image Enhancement System); "Know your enemy" (Identix Identity Solutions); "Knowing Who's Who When Security Really Counts" (Precise Biometrics). The advertisements referenced in this essay were made available to the author (and all attendees) by their respective companies at the 2006 Biometric Consortium Conference.

16. Also relevant to the history of bodily measurement for purposes of identity in the context of colonialism is the film *Mother Dao, the Turtle-like*, which edits together Dutch footage of the colonization of Indonesia with a soundtrack

consisting of Indonesian poetry. Several scenes depict Dutch representatives measuring the bodies of Indonesians as if cataloguing items in a museum (Monnikendam, 1995).

17. Braidotti referred here to the definition of monster from a 19th-century text by Geoffroy Saint-Hilaire.

18. Metretek Systems is now called Noblis. Their company information can be found at http://www.noblis.org.

19. Clarifying what 2% means is seriously debated in the biometrics industry. Others in the industry claim high FTE rates occur in a "small percentage of the population" or "2% of people" (Wing, 2006; Woodward et al., 2001, p. 12). 2% of the people in the United States measures in the millions.

20. Unless otherwise noted, any specific information about US-VISIT comes from the Department of Homeland Security, US-VISIT website at http://www.dhs.gov/xtrvlsec/programs/content_multi_image_0006.shtm. The "limited exemptions" include visitors admitted on particular visas, children under 14, persons over 79, and those the Secretary of State and the Secretary of Homeland Security or the CIA Director "jointly determine shall be exempt."

21. Unfortunately, Agamben does not acknowledge the place of slavery and colonialism in his formulation of "homo sacer." My thanks to Dr. Ranjana Khanna and the participants in her seminar at the 2007 Duke Women's Studies Workshop for pointing this out.

REFERENCES

Agamben, G. (1998). *Homo Sacer: Sovereign power and bare life*. Stanford: Stanford University Press.

Alder, K. (2002). *The measure of all things: The seven-year-odyssey that transformed the world*. London: Abacus.

Amoore, L. (2006). Biometric borders: Governing mobilities in the war on terror. *Political Geography, 25*, 336–351.

Ashbourn, J. (2000). *Biometrics: Advanced identity verification, the complete guide*. London: Springer.

Braidotti, R. (1996). Signs of wonder and traces of doubt: On teratology and embodied differences. In: N. Lykke & Rosi Braidotti (Eds.), *Between monsters, goddesses and cyborgs: Feminist confrontations with science, medicine and cyberspace* (pp. 135–152). London and Highlands, New Jersey: Zed Books.

Butler, J. (1990). *Gender trouble: Feminism and the subversion of identity*. New York and London: Routledge.

Butler, J. (1993). *Bodies that matter: On the discursive limits of "Sex."* New York and London: Routledge.

Cage, J. (1999). John Cage diary: How to improve the world (you will only make matters worse) [audio CD]. Wergo: Germany.

Campbell, J. P., Jr. (1997 September). *Speaker recognition: A tutorial*. Paper presented at the Proceedings of the IEEE vol. 85, no. 9 September 1997, p. 1437–1462.

Chandrasekaran, R. (1997 March 30). Brave New World–I.D. Systems using the human body are here, but privacy issues persist. *Washington Post*, p. H1.

Davies, S. G. (1994). Touching Big Brother: How biometric Technology will fuse flesh and machine [electronic version]. *Information Technology & People*, 7. http://www.privacy.org/pi/reports/biometric.html. Last accessed September 14, 2006.

Dictionary.com (Ed.) (2004). bio. (n.d.) The American Heritage Stedman's Medical Dictionary. Retrieved August 1, 2007 from Dictionary.com website: http://dictionary.reference.com/browse/bio; -metric. (n.d.) The American Heritage Dictionary of the English Language, Fourth Edition. Retrieved August 1, 2007 from

Dictionary.com website: http://dictionary.reference.com/browse/-metric. Doddington, G. Walter Liggett, Alvin Martin, Mark Przybocki, and Douglas Reynolds (1998). Sheep, goats, lambs and wolves: A statistical analysis of speaker performance in the NIST 1998 Speaker Recognition Evaluation [electronic version]. http://www.nist.gov/speech/publications/papersrc/icslp_98.pdf. Last accessed July 17, 2007.

Douglas, M. (1973). *Natural symbols: Explorations in cosmology*. London: Barrie & Jenkins.

Dyer, R. (1997). *White*. New York: Routledge.

Foucault, M. (1990). *The history of sexuality: An introduction*. New York: Vintage Books.

Foucault, M. (2003). *Abnormal: Lectures at the Collège de France, 1974–1975* (G. Burchell, trans.). New York: Picador.

Hall, R. (2004). *Danger and desire: Instrumental realism in the history of the wanted poster*. Unpublished dissertation, University of North Carolina, Chapel Hill, NC.

Hanafi, Z. (2000). *The monster in the machine: Magic, medicine, and the marvelous in the time of the scientific revolution*. Durham and London: Routledge.

Haraway, D. (1991). Situated knowledges: The science question in feminism and the privilege of partial perspective. In: *Simians, cyborgs, and women: The reinvention of nature* (pp. 183–202). New York and London: Routledge.

Haraway, D. (1992). The promises of monsters: A regenerative politics for inappropriate/d others. In: L. Grossberg, C. Nelson, and P. A. Treichler (Eds.), *Cultural studies* (pp. 295–337). New York and London: Routledge.

Hicklin, A., Watson, C., & Ulery, B. (2005). Myth of goats: How many people have fingerprints that are hard to match? [electronic version]. http://www.itl.nist.gov/iad/894.03/pact/ir_7271.pdf. Last accessed September 2006.

Jain, A., Bolle, R. & Pankanti, S. (Eds.). (1999). *Biometrics: Personal identification in networked society*. Boston: Kluwer Academic Publishers.

Layoun, M. (1994). The female body and "transnational" reproduction; or, rape by any other name? In: I. Grewal & Caren Kaplan (Eds.), *Scattered hegemonies: postmodernity and transnational feminist practice* (pp. 63–75). Minneapolis and London: University of Minnesota Press.

Lyon, D. (2003). Surveillance as social sorting: Computer codes and mobile bodies. In: D. Lyon (Ed.), *Surveillance as social sorting: Privacy, risk, and digital discrimination* (pp. 13–30). London and New York: Routledge.

Magnet, Shoshana. (2008) Using Biometrics to Re-Visualize the Canada-U.S. Border. In *On the Identity Trail: Anonymity and Authentication in a Networked Society*, edited by Ian Kerr, Valerie Stevens, and Carole Lucock. Cambridge: Cambridge University Press, Forthcoming 2008.

Monnikendam, V. (1995). *Mother Dao, the Turtle-like*. Netherlands: Nederlandse Programma Stichting.

Nanavati, S., Thieme, M., & Nanavati, R. (2002). *Biometrics: Identity verification in a networked world.* New York: John Wiley & Sons.

Ong, A. (1999). *Flexible citizenship: The cultural logics of transnationality.* Durham and London: Duke University Press.

Prins, C. (1998). Biometric technology law: Making our body identify for us: Legal implications of biometric technologies. *Computer Law & Security Report, 14,* 159–165.

Pugliese, J. (2005). *In Silico* race and the heteronomy of biometric proxies: Biometrics in the context of civilian life, border security and counter-terrorism laws. *Australian Feminist Law Journal, 23,* 1–32.

Sekula, A. (1992). The body and the archive. In: R. Bolton (Ed.), *The contest of meaning: Critical histories of photography* (pp. 343–379). Cambridge and London: MIT Press.

Tobing Rony, F. (1996). *The third eye: Race, cinema, and ethnographic spectacle.* Durham and London: Duke University Press.

US P. R. P. N. (2005, May 17). US-visit stops murderers, pedophiles and immigration violators from entering the United States through biometrics and international corporation. *PR Newswire Association LLC.* van der Ploeg, I. (2004). Written on the body: Biometrics and identity. In: R. A. Spinello & Herman T. Tavani (Eds.), *Readings in cyberethics* (2nd ed., pp. 571–584). Boston: Jones and Bartlett Publishers.

van der Ploeg, I. (2006). Borderline identities: The enrollment of bodies in the technological reconstruction of borders. In: T. Monahan (Ed.), *Surevillance and security: technological politics and power in everyday life.* New York and London: Routledge.

Wing, B. (2006). *Applications successes and failures.* Paper presented at the Biometric Consortium Conference Baltimore, MD.

Woodward, J. D., Webb, K. W., Newton, E. M., Bradley, M., & Rubenson, D. (2001). *Army biometric applications: Identifying and addressing sociocultural concerns.* Santa Monica, California: RAND.

"War Rooms" of the Street: Surveillance Practices in Transportation Control Centers

TORIN MONAHAN

Concerns over new surveillance technologies and security policies tend to focus on the most obvious systems or flagrant privacy breaches. These can include the proliferation of closed circuit television (CCTV) systems in urban areas, illegal government wiretapping programs, or liberal data sharing among private industries and government agencies. All the while, the rapid proliferation of digital technologies throughout everyday life creates affordances for surveillance capabilities that resist critical investigation or public awareness (Phillips, 2005; Gandy, 2006; Monahan, 2006c; Andrejevic, 2007; Lyon, 2007). This is true because of the ubiquity of the technologies, because their primary intended functions are not typically construed as being surveillance, and because the technologies are often embedded in infrastructures and thereby hidden from view (cf. Bowker & Star, 1999). Transportation infrastructures offer a case in point. Transportation flows are increasingly monitored and controlled with systems of diverse technologies, yet it is difficult to envision the data generated by traveling; how others might be interpreting, sharing, and responding to those data; and how mobilities or experiences might be altered based upon individual or automated reactions to those data.

In this article, I investigate the surveillance dimensions of "intelligent transportation systems" (ITS) in the United States, with a particular focus on the mediation of data by engineers in transportation control centers. Intelligent transportation systems are being—or have been—deployed, in some fashion, in most major cities around the world. A great deal of attention has been given to the rationalizing of transportation and tracking of passengers for purposes of efficiency, security, and commercial marketing (U.S. Department of Transportation, 1998; Accent Marketing and Research, 2004; BBC News, 2006). Especially for public transportation, global positioning systems (GPS) and "smart card" systems can be used to track the exact location of—and identity of each person on—trains and buses (Cameron, 2006). Similarly, radio frequency identification (RFID)-embedded smart cards allow for automated electronic toll collection for the use of highways and bridges (Reiman, 1995; Bennett, Raab, & Regan, 2003). License-plate recognition systems are deployed to minimize traffic congestion by limiting entry into cities (such as London) and assessing fines if entry time restrictions are violated (Glancy, 2004; Dodge & Kitchin, 2006). In-car systems such as black boxes, GPS units, or vehicle-to-vehicle communication technologies also open drivers up to increased scrutiny by insurance companies, marketers, rental car agencies, law enforcement, and potentially others (Vahidi & Eskandarian, 2003; Hay & Packer, 2004). Obviously, significant national and regional variation exists with ITS. It appears likely that the U.S. is prioritizing ITS for highways, roads, and bridges to maximize the throughput of vehicular traffic instead of—or as a supplement to—building additional roads or lanes, whereas other countries are prioritizing ITS for public transportation systems that have been operational for decades if not longer. The concentration in this article will be on publicly operated highway and road-based ITS in the U.S., and especially on the human mediation of these systems by control room operators in the southwestern U.S., where empirical research was conducted.

THEORETICAL ORIENTATION

Transportation resonates as both a means of and powerful metaphor for communication. As James Carey (1992) explains, prior to electronic communication, transportation served as the dominant mode for facilitating communication through the physical delivery of messages. As a metaphor, this transmission model of communication persists in the public imaginary and in much scholarship because of the ways in which it has been discursively conjoined with techno-scientific rationalities of progress, control, and efficiency. Additionally, the conquering of space and time made possible by both transportation and electronic communication is part of the mythology of the frontier; it is a mythology that privileges "enlightened," technological solutions to spatial and social problems, but often treats any concomitant externalities as mere unanticipated consequences or systems noise (Winner, 1977; Nye, 1996). As a partial corrective to this overreliance on transportation or transmission metaphors of communication, Carey (1992) encourages scholars to delve into the ritualistic sides of communication, to the analysis of symbols and everyday meaning-making practices in specific cultural contexts. Strange things happen, of course, with the artificial dichotomization of transmission and ritual, not the least of which is the eliding of conflict, power, and social exclusion, along with the troubling essentialization of communication rituals. Nonetheless, attention to the meaning-making practices and specific uses of communication systems is crucial to developing a deep understanding of emergent technological systems such as ITS.

The field of science and technology studies (STS) offers a complementary orientation for analyzing technological systems in their social and historical contexts. A starting premise is to understand technological systems as socially constructed. Rather than evolving in some unidirectional or predetermined way, technological systems are the result of complex negotiations among human actors, nonhuman "actants," and social institutions (Hughes, 1987; Law, 1987; Latour, 1992). They are shaped by technical and institutional constraints, inscribed with the dominant values of their origins, and modified by and given meaning through practice (Noble, 1977; Pfaffenberger, 1992; Eglash et al., 2004). In short, technologies are thoroughly social and contingent creations that acquire tenacity through their institutionalization and interlinking with other systems (Monahan, 2005). A second STS premise of relevance to the discussion of ITS is that of the "politics of artifacts." Langdon Winner (1986) coined this phrase to highlight the regulatory functions of technological systems, which exert (oftentimes silent, normalized, and unequal) control over people. Lawrence Lessig (1999) can be seen as offering a corollary argument with his compelling equation of computer "codes" with "laws" in his discussion of the constraints placed upon Internet activities. Although the idea that technologies embody values and control human behavior in nonneutral—or even discriminatory—ways strikes some STS scholars as being deterministic (e.g., Woolgar, 1991; Pinch, 1996; Joerges, 1999), urban studies researchers and philosophers (e.g., Jacobs, 1961; Lynch, 1984; Lefebvre, 1991) have long recognized the power of the built world over human action, be it intentional or accidental.

Concerning issues of mobility, communication scholars, geographers, and others have begun the project of theorizing transportation in general—and ITS in particular—as systems of governance and control. Jeremy Packer (2006a, 2006b) is one of the communication scholars at the forefront of this drive, showing how in the name of efficiency and safety, especially in the post-9/11 environment, the autonomy of the driver is increasingly delegated to automated systems, thereby reconstituting automobile individuals as controllable units whose threat to themselves and others must be minimized. Other scholars have laid the foundation for this type of analysis by calling attention to the increasing informatization and automated regulation of spaces and practices (e.g., Castells, 1996; Graham, 1998; Lianos & Douglas, 2000; Thrift & French, 2002; Hommels, 2005; Murakami Wood & Graham, 2006). Although surveillance is central to this project of vehicle and body control, the emphasis in recent scholarship is upon new articulations of governmentality, upon the automated management of resources and risks, rather than upon any overt form of disciplinary intervention (Hay & Packer, 2004; Dodge & Kitchin, 2006; Sheller, 2007).

ITS OVERVIEW

A heterogeneous network of technologies comprises ITS for highways and roads: video cameras, embedded or mounted traffic sensors, smart cards, smart card readers, GPS devices, license-plate readers, geographic information systems (GIS), computers, software, communications equipment, fiberoptic networks, wireless networks, electrical supplies, traffic signals, emergency vehicle detection devices, and so on. The most visible public interfaces for ITS are traffic signals, which regulate the flow of motorized vehicles, bicycles, and pedestrians on streets; "dynamic message signs," which can alert drivers to upcoming road conditions; and ramp meters, which regulate the flow of vehicles onto highways. Perhaps the most important ITS interfaces, however, are the one hidden from public view: traffic control centers, which monitor and respond to traffic conditions through remote manipulation of the system (and its data) as a whole. The hallmarks of these control centers are their impressive and oftentimes massive "video walls," which display road conditions in real-time, whether through a graphic representation of roads and signals, CCTV video feeds, or some combination of both (see Figure 1).

Typically speaking, departments of transportation for states, as well as for large cities, possess the most advanced ITS. In the U.S., a nationwide ITS program was established by the Intermodal Surface Transportation Efficiency Act of 1991 (U.S. DOT, 2006) and the government has invested over $1 billion in the systems over the past decade (Hay &

Figure 1. ITS Video Wall for State Department of Transportation

Packer, 2004). Although ITS is managed by the U.S. Department of Transportation, states and cities draw upon the ITS mission and protocols to implement their own systems, relying largely upon local resources to keep systems operational. For the region studied here, sensors are embedded every one-third of a mile on highways and are used to measure speed, volume, and density of traffic. Other nonvisual sensing systems include both sonar and radar detectors to fine-tune speed and volume readings. Installed every mile on the highways are high-end CCTV cameras equipped with pan, tilt, and zoom capabilities with a minimum range of half a mile. Local municipalities off of the highway system have less-developed but nonetheless impressive systems for their roads. These include sensors mounted at intersections for the detection of flow, speed, and density for each lane; sensors for the detection of emergency vehicle strobe lights, which when triggered will change traffic signals to give emergency vehicles "green" lights; and CCTV cameras at many, but definitely not all, intersections. The local ITS centers also receive information from the traffic signals throughout their cities and can alter signal times remotely and detect (and oftentimes fix) malfunctions. Finally, ITS operators at both the state and local levels routinely spot accidents and/or verify accident locations reported by others and then convey that information to public safety and emergency personnel. It is important to note, especially for the discussion of surveillance to follow, that almost all these systems are interoperable and interconnected. Thus, not only can local and state ITS operators monitor and control each other's systems, which they do frequently, but so can law enforcement agencies tap into these systems and their data at will.

The key to ITS is the translation of transportation flows into data that can be acted upon, preferably in real-time or in advance, through predictive modeling. The systems in the U.S. are currently geared toward the management of aggregate flows: to time traffic signals for optimal vehicular throughput or to update traffic signs to let drivers know of alternate routes for avoiding congestion or accidents, for example. As with other forms of mobile communication (Lyon, 2006), the technological trajectory, however, is toward the atomization of aggregate flows: to monitor individual vehicles with road sensors, GPS, RFID tags, license-plate readers, and so on (Cameron, 2006; Dodge & Kitchin, 2006).

Although ITS officials draw clear lines of demarcation between the functions of their systems and those of law enforcement, as this article will show, in practice these lines are quite blurred and likely the functions will continue to converge. Mainly, the systems are interlinked and accessible by personnel beyond the specific control center with jurisdiction, whether for traffic control or public safety purposes. Some operators also relate stories of listening to police radios while performing their traffic-management duties and assisting police officers in locating suspects. Finally, many ITS centers have been slated as "emergency operations centers" to manage evacuation procedures or coordinate response teams in the event of terrorist attacks or natural disasters. The systems are always, if latently, oriented toward national security, such that the operators routinely monitor "critical infrastructure," such as bridges and tunnels, for suspicious activity (White House, 2003).

The lines between the functions and interests of private industry and public agencies, on the other hand, are much less clear, even in principle. This is so because public-private "partnerships" are integral to the official ITS mission, whereby private companies are contracted to install and service equipment or to implement and manage entire subsystems, such as electronic oll collection (Bennett et al., 2003). Increasingly, state governments are selling to private companies the management rights for public highways that since their inception have been seen as essential public goods. Indiana, for instance, recently sold operating rights to all 157 miles of its primary interstate highway (I-90) to a consortium of foreign construction companies for $3.8 billion (Schulman & Ridgeway, 2007). The consortium stands to gain $11 billion in toll revenues over the 75-year life of the contract (Schulman & Ridgeway, 2007). Many other states and countries are following suite and embracing this neoliberal rationality, which is so clearly articulated by Indiana's governor, Mitch Daniels: "any businessperson will recognize our decision here as the freeing of trapped value from an underperforming asset, to be redeployed into a better use with higher returns" (cited in Schulman & Ridgeway, 2007, p. 52). With some of the management duties and individual transportation data in the hands of industry, privacy concerns may be amplified because companies have an interest in using or selling those data for the marketing of products and services (Regan, 1995; Zimmer, 2007).[1] Less obviously, social inequalities may be aggravated as companies restrict access to public highways through tiered toll-payment schemes or build private highways that are inaccessible to the general public, thereby constraining the mobility of the poor who cannot afford the added expense but often need to travel farther to work than do the relatively affluent (Press, 2000; Graham & Marvin, 2001; Patton, 2004).

Similarly, the management of abstract flows by ITS operates as a type of surveillance with unequal effects on the ground. I understand surveillance to be practices of identification, tracking, monitoring, or analysis that enforce degrees of social control.[2] The acknowledged goal of ITS operators is to collect and analyze data to manage transportation flows, or to manage the mobilities of others. The privacy of those individuals may not be at risk, as such, but they are nonetheless subjected to surveillance and their actions are influenced by it. This mode of surveillance may be more controlling than others because of its relative invisibility, as it is embedded in infrastructure and managed remotely, increasingly by automated computer software (Lianos & Douglas, 2000; Thrift & French, 2002; Murakami Wood & Graham, 2006). Furthermore, this surveillance may be more insidious because it is not seen as such by ITS operators; they perceive the systems as neutral even as the systems actively abstract complex social practices into discrete data for impersonal intervention.

Nonetheless, ITS and its operators engage in activities of social sorting (Lyon, 2007), valorizing certain mobilities over others, while normalizing unequal experiences of space. The control made possible with ITS should be seen as part of a larger transformation in the regulation of mobilities, spaces, and spatial experiences, from ideals of universal access to experiences of differential access based largely on socio-economic status (Caldeira, 2000; Low, 2003; Monahan, 2006a; Sheller & Urry, 2006; Adey, 2006). The dominant rationality of "flow" pervades the discourse and practice of ITS operators and infuses the systems with certain politics, which are enforced and felt on the level of bodies and materialities, even if they do not achieve representation in the systems.

METHODOLOGY

It is tempting to base one's analysis of ITS solely upon provocative industry reports, advertising campaigns, media proclamations, and political rhetoric about the highway systems of the future. No matter how critical one is of this content, however, the risk of relying on such intentionally produced documents is that the field of analysis will be circumscribed by the content available and that the hegemony of automobility will remain unchallenged. Put differently, there are many analytic blind spots in the media sources propelling ITS "solutions," so one needs to search for difference and disconnection in order to avoid reifying the automobile, the driver, or the process of automation as the primary units of analysis.

For example, ITS systems clearly operate (or can operate) as surveillance infrastructures, but they and their surveillance functions must be understood through social practices—or what James Carey (1992) might call communication "rituals." How such systems are designed, interpreted, and acted upon matters. Whereas the tendency in existing scholarship on social practices and software automation is to project the most extreme possible cases of control decoupled from human mediation and then to theorize the social or ethical implications of such automated worlds (e.g., Lianos & Douglas, 2000), this approach flirts too dangerously with technological determinism and may overlook, as a result, ever present degrees of human agency, whether in the design, use, navigation, or appropriation of such systems.

As a partial—and admittedly incomplete—corrective, this article draws primarily upon qualitative methods of ethnographic observation and interviews at ITS traffic control centers, attending to what traffic engineers do and say. This research was conducted from 2004–2005 in the southwestern United States. In addition to observational site visits and interviews, I reviewed government documents and industry reports on ITS goals and effectiveness. For the observational component, I made four site visits to city and state departments of transportation, where I observed demonstrations of street monitoring systems designed for the optimization of traffic flows. Traffic engineers or administrators walked me through the functions of their systems, showing me the systems' capabilities and limitations and relating to me their own—and others'—involvement in the monitoring processes. At every site, I took photographs of their elaborate video walls, computers, rooms for servers and routers (i.e., the hardware for receiving, sending, and processing data), and the monitoring facilities or spaces where they conduct their work. This served as an important data-collection method because it encouraged informants to relate candid stories to me about the development of the systems and the multiple uses to which the systems have been, or could be, put.

Eighteen semi-structured interviews were conducted, usually with small groups of traffic engineers or administrators each time. Interviewing people in groups instead of individually turned out to be propitious for data collection because in every case at least one person was extremely cautious and reserved, while another person was loquacious and candid, telling me stories that he—all of the operators were men—found to be of interest. This revealed both points of tension among interviewees and obvious negotiations of discourse, or of the "facts" that they wanted me to have. The second reason that interviewing more than one person at a time was especially effective was because it allowed interviewees to cue each other for stories that they thought I should know about, whereby they helped each other construct the narrative without too much prodding on my part. The average length for each interview was 90 minutes. The questions were crafted to elicit information about the uses of the systems, the management and cost of them, the potentials they envisioned for them, and the social contexts that might be affected by them.

Government documents and industry reports were reviewed to gain an understanding of the long-term objectives for ITS, the systems' development over time, the degree to which the systems were thought to be meeting those objectives, and the myriad technologies and processes that comprise ITS. It was especially helpful for this research project to perceive how certain assumptions about the problems of transportation (e.g., insufficient vehicular throughput) were codified in the official mission for ITS and then reproduced by the systems and their operators. Also interesting were the discrepancies between ITS documents, which do occasionally advocate for holistic (or even multimodal) solutions to transportation problems, and the dominant uses of ITS in the U.S., which prioritize the flow of cars and trucks over any public transportation option. The review of documents and reports provided essential background information for conducting site visits and interviews.

CULTURE OF SECRECY

It is more difficult than one might expect to obtain access to ITS control centers. Whereas news media occasionally run stories about control centers,[3] otherwise a culture of secrecy predominates. In most cases, operators or administrative personnel would speak with me or my research assistant when we first called but would quickly clam up when they discovered that we wanted to visit the control rooms and interview them. Many centers refused to return our phone calls or respond to our e-mails after the initial contact. Several sites agreed to participate in the research and then had a change of heart after talking with their "legal departments." The sites to which we did get access strung us along for some time while obtaining approval from their supervisors or legal staff. Given that these are publicly funded programs, the sites are in public buildings, the operators are government employees, and the researcher possessed some cultural credibility as a professor at a large public university, the obstacles to learning about ITS were inordinately high. Part of that may have to do with concerns over having insufficient time for an interview or the general "firewall culture" of government employees trying to avoid unnecessary scrutiny (Monahan, 2005, p. 151–154). It soon became apparent, however, that ITS operators knew that their centers had the look of surveillance and that they wanted to distance themselves from that characterization of their work.

Upon arriving at one city department of transportation, an engineer escorted me quickly to a small, drab conference room where another operator met with us for the scheduled interview. While my escort went to check the conference room schedule for any conflicts, I asked the other engineer if we would have time to see the control center as well, the sophistication of which I had heard about from engineers at another nearby city. He nervously vacillated, saying that things were probably too busy today, but that maybe I could view it through the glass of a secure door before I left. At that moment, the other person returned and informed us that there was a scheduling conflict in the conference room, so we would have to conduct the interview in the control room after all. The vast control center – referred to as the "war room" by the engineers—boasted the largest video wall I had seen apart from those at state-level DOT centers, which can be as large as movie screens. As we sat at the elegant control desk, with its embedded, flip-up monitors, another engineer emerged from a connected back office and joined the interview. Throughout the interview, one portion of the video wall displayed my interviewees and me sitting at the desk, while other portions displayed a map of the city's roads, CCTV feeds, computer video displays, and "Fox News" (see Figure 2).

Before the interview could begin, however, I needed to convince the engineers to sign informed consent forms, which were required for this project by my university's institutional review board for human subjects research. They were reluctant to sign because the forms indicated that I was conducting research on public surveillance systems. Even though government documents on ITS devote pages to describing the sensing and CCTV technologies as "surveillance" (U.S. DOT, 1998), the operators of the systems were loathe to see their technical work in that light. For them, surveillance implied the intention to monitor or spy on individuals, whereas all they cared about was rationalizing vehicular throughput in a completely disembodied and impersonal way. They did sign the forms after I explained that I was using surveillance as a generic term. Nonetheless,

Figure 2. ITS Video Wall for Local City.

their objections demonstrated worries about negative public attention. The objections and our discussion of them also revealed assumptions on their part that intentionality is required for "surveillance" to take place and that ITS is purely technical, not political or social in any way, and therefore should certainly not be seen as surveillance.

Because their systems rely upon CCTV cameras, which are conspicuous and increasingly ubiquitous on city streets, ITS engineers anticipate questions about privacy and have prepared software-based answers to them. As an example, when I was concluding the interview previously described, one engineer prompted one of the others saying, "You got to show him the little preset thing." It turns out that the "preset thing" was a programmed grey patch that could be applied to individual cameras so that operators could not view into people's houses or apartments. Once the software is running, if an operator zooms in too far, to the point where one might be able to view people in their private spaces, a grey box suddenly appears to block the view. The engineer explained:

> All I care [about] is the traffic there: is it moving, is it not moving, is it backed up, is it not backed up? And one of the issues you have is, you

put a camera on an intersection, and invariably people live near intersections. The biggest problem with cameras is a lot of times they'll lose
power to them, they'll swing over and go to a preset, a default preset,
and a lot of times it'll point right into somebody's house. Yeah and it's
like aaaaah I don't wanna see that! Yeah, the camera just, the camera
decided to be silly and got some capability. And a lot of the newer ones
[cameras] will allow you to program a preset on them, and our newest
ones will allow you to program areas that you can't even view.

It is interesting that by switching the privacy patch off and on at will, just
to demonstrate to me what "before" and "after" might look like, the engineers are tipping their hand, revealing that the software is indeed a façade.
They have complete control over whether to employ it, implying that its
main function is to prove to outsiders that they care about privacy, even if
everyone must trust them not to take advantage of the system's privacy-
violating capabilities. At the same time, it is fascinating to observe how
engineers discursively recognize the unpredictable agency of the systems,
whereby a camera "decided to be silly and got some capability." Because
the systems have acquired some agency, their surveillance modalities
must be mediated by the engineers or the systems must be further automated with corrective software patches. Related to this concern over surveillance is the mantra of all the interviewees that they do not record any
video footage. Yet interviewees confessed that it was technically easy to
do, if one so desired, and their digital systems are constantly "capturing"
data in any event.[4] Although I completely believed the engineers that they
had no interest in watching individual people, at least not as a daily practice, the systems possess vast potential for "function creep," meaning use
for purposes that were not originally intended.

EXCEPTIONS TO THE RULE

As ITS becomes ubiquitous, the primary rationales for the systems may
shift to accommodate secondary rationales of police or security functions,
or of commercial marketing. This was a point candidly acknowledged by
ITS operators: "I think that what you're seeing here is an infancy of
deployment of this type of equipment. I think once the equipment
becomes operational and there's a lot of it, then they'll find every kind of
use possible for it." Many of these potential uses are already extant. In
interviews, examples of obvious cases of surveillance accumulated
slowly, usually offered as anecdotal asides to the dominant message of
traffic management. Although the history of communication technologies
and transportation systems illustrates that the control properties of new
systems have often been taken advantage of for police purposes (Hay &

Packer, 2004, p. 220), for my informants, these capabilities emerge as serendipitous discoveries. As one traffic engineer recounted:

> I heard on the radio that somebody had assaulted a Circle K [convenience store] manager, and we had a camera at that location where we could see the Circle K. The gentleman came out of the Circle K and walked down the street and fit the description perfectly of what they were saying he was. I watched him come out and go into a bar around the corner, and the whole time I'm on the radio with the officer who responded. And I said "He's here; he's in the bar." And then he came out of the bar and got on the bus. And there was only one bus going westbound at the time. So, [the police] didn't have any problem. They pulled the bus over about a quarter mile down the road and hauled him off.

Here, one of the same traffic engineers who initially objected vociferously to me talking about ITS as "surveillance" described in detail how he tapped into the explicit surveillance functions of the system to assist the police. Whereas this surveillance occurred through real-time processing of information and active coordination of different communication media, other publicized cases of ITS lending itself to function creep are more retrospective and data-driven, as with Great Britain's recent admission of secretly spying on people by sorting through the data generated by individuals' "smart cards," which they use to access public transportation (BBC News, 2006).

The interoperability and interconnection of systems signal another obvious avenue for function creep. When I asked operators and administrators about the logistics of verifying accident locations for public safety, they admitted that public safety personnel often simply tap into the system to control the cameras without the need for ITS engineers to get involved. In fact, the design preference for all new control centers is to combine ITS and public safety departments within the same building so that access to the systems will be identical. In interviews with police, for a related research project, they admit that they occasionally use ITS for police purposes, even if it is less precise than surveillance that they would set up for specific investigations. One detective viewed ITS video cameras as important inoculation for the American public to become desensitized to public surveillance systems that the police would like to use. Barring any technical or legal safeguards (such as encryption for privacy protection or new laws governing ITS use, respectively), secondary uses of the systems will likely continue to grow without much public awareness or oversight.

National security concerns, especially in the post-9/11 context, provide another strong rationale for secondary ITS functions. In the years following September 11, 2001, most—if not all—U.S. government agencies have transformed their missions to prioritize national security and/or have incorporated security responsibilities (Monahan, 2006b). Departments of transportation are no exception. As might be expected, the monitoring of "critical infrastructures," such as bridges and tunnels, is part of the responsibility of many ITS control centers. Moreover, many control rooms are slated to become emergency operation centers in the event of terrorist attacks or natural disasters. As emergency operations centers, they could coordinate evacuation procedures and response teams, including police and fire departments, and possibly hazardous material teams or military units. An engineer for one city-level department of transportation center explained:

> Right now the State has its own state emergency operation center [EOC], so, if the Governor declares a state of emergency, it is the Division of Emergency Management that handles [the Governor's] directives . . . But actually our IT department and some other parts of our city have identified this facility as being an important facility that needs to keep running in case anything happens, and we're kind of worked into that whole process. Because we do have some of the backup systems and, so there is some recognition in the value of what we do here and keeping it live and well. We've only been here a year and the EOC is just really kinda getting off the ground, and over the next few years, I can just see a lot of growth in working out all those [coordination] issues . . . Yeah, and that would be, you know, kinda again one of those Homeland Security concepts, you got your police and your fire and if anything unpleasant were to happen, they've got their secured command center [the ITS center] to dispatch the resources that are needed.

The responsibilities for critical infrastructure monitoring and emergency operations management provide insight into the multi-dimensional character of ITS, whereby the analytic distinction between primary and secondary functions is too facile a characterization of the systems, even if it is an accurate description of the daily practices of engineers. Given the definition of surveillance offered above (as enacting forms of control), these security functions point to the inherent, and in this case intentional, surveillance capabilities of ITS.

These examples of function creep highlight to the lack of explicit protocols or collective conversations about the surveillance functions of these systems or the desirability of tapping into those functions. Instead the surveillance modalities are exploited because the systems allow them to be. The discourse of abstract control of flows at a distance illustrates an approach to the systems that denies the existence of these alternative uses, as well as social context (Monahan, forthcoming). Nonetheless these systems, along with their discourses and practices, actively shape the world and sort bodies in very biased ways. It is to this social sorting that I next turn.

THROUGHPUT RATIONALITY

Whereas the police and security applications of ITS may be the most visible instantiations of surveillance, the active management of people and their mobilities should also be considered as such. Both existing ITS and dominant throughput rationalities are coproductive and hegemonic, oftentimes to the detriment of other experiences of space or modes of transport. As one engineer put it:

> As the *cities mature,* and the right of way is used up, we lack the ability to add more pavement, add more lanes, add more capacity to the roadway. But with the ITS Smart Technology, we're moving towards a traffic control system that will make and manage the capacity more efficiently. And so you know, when you reach build-out, you know, there's nothing else you can do, save for using the capacity, *using the pipe* way more intelligently [emphasis added].

There are many assumptions embedded in such an articulation. First, "mature" cities are those that have reached a threshold with the number of vehicles its roads can carry and with the space available for the construction of new roads or lanes. The history of a city, its cultures, and institutions are subordinated to the development of its roadways in any evaluation of a city's evolution. Second, rather than question the automobile as the dominant form of transportation or criticize development patterns that lead to increasing distance between places of living and work, the logical solution advanced by ITS is to utilize existing infrastructures more "intelligently," meaning in a more efficient, informatized way. Finally, from this perspective, streets and highways are reduced to metaphorical "pipes," serving as conduit from one place to another, rather than as places in their own right.

Within this discursive framework, and within these "smart" infrastructures, alternative mobilities or experiences of space are often marginalized. The infrastructures themselves, once analytically reduced to "pipes," become intolerant of, or actively hostile to, difference. Of course, this is true of the history of road development more generally, especially in the U.S., but as the roads achieve greater throughput of vehicles, there is a corresponding diminishment of nonvehicular space, or gaps between vehicles (Patton, 2004). For instance, maximum throughput makes it much more difficult to back out of a driveway on a busy street, turn onto such a street, or cross streets, especially as a pedestrian.

The ways in which ITS traffic engineers speak of pedestrians illustrates the symbolic marginalization of difference, which is informed and reproduced by the systems. First, there is a sense of frustration with pedestrians for slowing down the traffic flow—or, more precisely, for forcing engineers to slow down traffic flow to ensure that signals will be "synced"[5] in the eventuality that a pedestrian pushes the "walk" button:

> If you have to accommodate a lot of ped time, it means the intersections are going to take a longer time to get around [i.e., for the signal lights to cycle from red to green to red], and the longer it takes an intersection to get around, typically, the slower the drive speed is, so then you end up with intersections where the speed limit's 45 miles an hour, and there's no way you can time it for that speed so you end up timing it for a lower speed.

This concern with limiting throughput in order to accommodate pedestrians compels some engineers to take shortcuts, timing intersections for a higher vehicle speed in the hopes that few pedestrians will cross the streets and that the signals will remain synced. Invariably, this approach fails, traffic gets backed up, and the signal times need to be recalibrated. A second approach is to limit the amount of time allotted for pedestrians to cross the street, forcing them to move quickly or face increased risk of being hit. In the cities I studied, pedestrians were assumed to walk at a rate of 4 feet per second, and the signals were timed accordingly. Obviously, the handicapped, elderly, and children may not be able to achieve the necessary speed to make it across streets, some of which are up to seven lanes wide. This is one very real danger introduced by a transportation system rationalized for vehicles and destinations, rather than people and places (Jain, 2004).

A final example, this time of a pedestrian getting hit by a car, reveals the tendency of ITS surveillance to objectify people and privilege vehicles as primary units of analysis. A control room operator related:

> Unfortunately, I watched a lady get hit by a car one day . . . A man made a right turn right in front of her, as she was walking across the street, and she literally walked into the van and got caught by it. I'm like, "how in the hell could that happen," and I was sitting here watching it the whole time, and I couldn't believe what I was watching.

In this instance, the operator who witnessed the accident strangely elects to fault the lady for somehow walking into a moving car, rather than saying that the person in the moving car violated the pedestrian's right-of-way by cutting across her path and hitting her. While it is common for most people to lend agency to vehicles by saying things such as "the car went through the light," when filtered through the lens of ITS, the operator takes this tendency a step further to blame the pedestrian who was in the right, at least according to the law. Given the sordid history of U.S. transportation systems and their tendency—or the tendency of engineers and planners—to divide neighborhoods, displace people, and discriminate against nondrivers in extremely racist and classist ways (Lewis, 1997; Bullard, Johnson, & Torres, 2004; Patton, 2004), ITS builds upon rather than replaces these previous biases. Similarly, the perspective of the engineer relating this story is undoubtedly shaped by the logics of the systems he oversees and his professional training. Intelligent transportation system present themselves, therefore, as a lens for perceiving the rearticulation of throughput rationalities in digital and increasingly automated forms.

In summary, as ITS is integrated into existing transportation infrastructures, it reproduces and modulates a rationality of maximum vehicular throughput at the expense of other experiences or values. It monitors and regulates flows retrospectively, in real time, and prospectively. Currently, this largely invisible and normalized form of social control occurs mostly at the level of aggregate data, but more and more it is individualized, with systems tracking and storing unique identifiers (from smart cards, GPS devices, license plates, etc.) for future scrutiny and intervention. As the examples in this article demonstrate, neither ITS nor the social orders established by it are value-neutral. They carve up the world in very particular ways according to the contexts within which they are applied, oftentimes reinforcing inequalities that are not represented by the transportation grids, flow diagrams, or software codes that define the parameters of the systems.

CONCLUSION

The proliferation of digital technologies throughout everyday life enables new modalities of surveillance. Whether the technologies are mobile phones, smart cards, GPS units, or video cameras, they tend to create and store data as a default, thereby lending themselves to surveillance uses. If the key to determining whether surveillance is occurring rests in the criterion of "control," as I have asserted, then one must look to the *social practices* surrounding such systems and analyze them in *spatial context* to see how control is or is not manifested. One must also attend to how various assemblages of digital technologies become embedded in infrastructure and hidden from view, such that certain rationalities of movement or spatial experience are normalized, depoliticized, and hidden from view. In this article, I have added to previous theorizations of ITS and software-based productions of space to highlight the surveillance dimensions of ITS, as seen through the discourse and practice of control center operators. While it is apparent that ITS performs at the level of infrastructure to control and sort people in nonneutral ways, much more empirical research needs to be done to better understand the physical and symbolic negotiations of ITS by people in other domains and across multiple mobilities.

The difficulty of obtaining information on the actual work of ITS engineers and the functions of the systems is itself revealing. Engineers understand that what they do can be perceived as surveillance, mostly because of dominant cultural meanings associated with video cameras. As a result, these government workers seek to insulate themselves from scrutiny by preventing access to their spaces. They articulate a pure, technical version of their activities (i.e., managing flows) that strips people from the equation entirely. Their implied rhetorical argument is that without people, or even representations of them beyond the unit of the car, surveillance cannot be occurring. This is true, from their viewpoint, because surveillance is perforce a social, intentional, and interested activity; what they do is technical, whereby any attention to individual people is unintentional and disinterested. This, of course, is a highly problematic distinction. Technical operations are always social and embodied practices (Haraway, 1997; Slack & Wise, 2005; Monahan & Wall, 2007). Moreover, surveillance can operate on the level of groups—or upon groups of mobilities, as the case may be—without any explicit intention or interestedness on the part of those running the systems (Fisher, 2006; Fisher & Monahan, forthcoming). Surveillance does not have to be intended to be felt.

Even if one were to accept engineers' initial description of ITS as rational traffic management, their narratives betray the polyvalence of ITS, which is also the case with all communication technologies. They proudly talk of listening to police radios and using the system to assist police with the apprehension of criminals. They admit that personnel from public safety control centers access and direct their systems at will, and while ITS engineers do not record any video footage, they cannot prevent others with access from doing so. Finally, many ITS centers serve a dual function of being emergency operations centers in the event of terrorist attacks or natural disasters. Given the fact that the interstate highway system, which ITS helps to regulate, was initially conceived of as a national security infrastructure, these security functions of ITS should not be that surprising—they are part of the historical trajectory of the U.S. highway system. On one hand, these secondary uses illustrate the function-creep potential of ITS. On the other, perhaps the differentiation between primary and secondary uses is dangerous; it may serve to inoculate such systems against critique because one could always say that any problematic uses are not the primary or intended ones. At the very least, these few examples do signify the valence of such systems toward explicit surveillance and security applications.

The social-sorting ramifications of ITS should not be overlooked, even if they are the most difficult to perceive. The dominant rationality of efficient vehicular throughput pervades American culture as a whole, dramatically affecting experiences of mobility, space, and place (Patton, 2004; Jain, 2006). When streets are perceived as conduit from one place to another, instead of as places in their own right, the imperative for speed subordinates that of sociality, or of a sense of collective responsibility for social well-being (Demerath & Levinger, 2003). In this way, ITS can be seen as sustaining ongoing neoliberal development patterns by emphasizing "pipes" over places, maximizing the flow of privately owned vehicles through those pipes, and facilitating the privatization of highways and industry (and state) profits through tiered toll schemes and the abrogation of public rights to access. Control manifests in the unequal privileging and (infra)structural support of certain mobilities over others: private over public transportation, driving over walking or bicycling. Control also manifests in the largely invisible governing of mobilities, directing where one can go, by what means, and under what conditions. Thinking about ITS in terms of surveillance can ground it analytically, opening it up for further critical investigation and intervention.

NOTES

1. Michael Zimmer (2005) expands upon the discussion of privacy threats introduced by such systems, arguing convincingly that such systems challenge the "contextual integrity" of personal data in public places.
2. It is important to note that not all surveillance should be viewed as negative. As David Lyon (2001) has argued, the control dimensions of surveillance can be interpreted as "care" or watching out for those in need, such as children, the elderly, or stranded motorists. Obviously, classifying surveillance practices along the control-care continuum is a highly subjective exercise, whereby even the most obvious examples of care-based surveillance can be viewed as paternalistic and controlling from the perspective of those scrutinized, or from the perspective of scholars studying the scrutiny, as the case may be.
3. Additionally, some news networks broadcast traffic reports from state-level ITS control centers. When they do so, they typically display CCTV feeds of traffic conditions, and not footage of the centers themselves.
4. The term *capture* is a loaded one that I use here in accordance with how the systems are described by my informants. Although it is common to refer to information systems as oriented toward data "capture" (e.g., Agre, 1994), it would be more accurate to focus on the act of data "creation" that occurs with such

systems. They restructure social practices and categories in an active way that is elided by the somewhat positivistic term *capture*.

5. The system for emergency vehicle preemption (where green lights are triggered for emergency vehicles) is perceived similarly as a threat to the synchronization of traffic signals.

REFERENCES

Accent Marketing and Research. (2004). *Town Centres Survey 2003–4: Summary report*. London.

Adey, P. (2006). "Divided we move": The dromologics of airport security and surveillance. In T. Monahan (Ed.), *Surveillance and security: Technological politics and power in everyday life* (pp. 195–208). New York: Routledge.

Agre, P. E. (1994). Surveillance and capture: Two models of privacy. *The Information Society, 10*, 101–127.

Andrejevic, M. (2007). *iSpy: Surveillance and power in the interactive era*. Lawrence, KS: University Press of Kansas.

BBC News. (2006, March 13). Oyster data is "new police tool." *BBC News*.

Bennett, C., Raab, C., & Regan, P. (2003). People and place: Patterns of individual identification within intelligent transportation systems. In D. Lyon (Ed.), *Surveillance as social sorting: Privacy, risk, and digital discrimination* (pp. 153–175). New York: Routledge.

Bowker, G. C., & Star, S. L. (1999). *Sorting things out: Classification and its consequences*.

Cambridge, MA: MIT Press.

Bullard, R. D., Johnson, G. S., & Torres, A. O. (2004). *Highway robbery: Transportation racism & New routes to equity*. Cambridge, MA: South End Press.

Caldeira, T. P. R. (2000). *City of walls: Crime, segregation, and citizenship in São Paulo*. Berkeley: University of California Press.

Cameron, H. (2006). Using intelligent transport systems to track buses and passengers. In T. Monahan (Ed.), *Surveillance and security: Technological politics and power in everyday life* (pp. 225–241). New York: Routledge.

Carey, J. W. (1992). *Communication as culture: Essays on media and society*. New York: Routledge.

Castells, M. (1996). *The Rise of the Network Society*. Cambridge, MA: Blackwell Publishers.

Demerath, L., & Levinger, D. (2003). The social qualities of being on foot: A theoretical analysis of pedestrian activity, community, and culture. *City and Community, 2*, 217–237.

Dodge, M., & Kitchin, R. (2006). *Code, vehicles and governmentality: The automatic production of driving spaces* (No. 29). Maynooth, Ireland: NIRSA Working Papers Series, No. 29 (March).

Eglash, R., Croissant, J. L., Di Chiro, G., & Fouché, R. (2004). *Appropriating technology: Vernacular science and social power*. Minneapolis: University of Minnesota Press.

Fisher, J. A. (2006). Indoor positioning and digital management: Emerging surveillance regimes in hospitals. In T. Monahan (Ed.), *Surveillance and security: Technological politics and power in everyday life* (pp. 77–88). New York: Routledge.

Fisher, J. A., & Monahan, T. (forthcoming). Tracking the social dimensions of RFID systems in hospitals. *International Journal of Medical Informatics.*

Gandy, Jr., O. (2006). Data mining, surveillance, and discrimination in the post-9/11 environment. In K. D. Haggerty & R. V. Ericson (Eds.), *The new politics of surveillance and visibility* (pp. 363–384). Toronto: University of Toronto Press.

Glancy, D. J. (2004). Whereabouts privacy. *STS Nexus,* Spring.

Graham, S. (1998). Spaces of surveillant simulation: New technologies, digital representations, and material geographies. *Environment and planning D: Society and space, 16,* 483–504.

Graham, S., & Marvin, S. (2001). *Splintering urbanism: Networked infrastructures, technological mobilities and the urban condition.* New York: Routledge.

Haraway, D. J. (1997). *Modest_witness@second_millennium.femaleman_meets_ oncomouse: Feminism and technoscience.* New York: Routledge.

Hay, J., & Packer, J. (2004). Crossing the media(-n): Auto-mobility, the transported self and technologies of freedom. In N. Couldry & A. McCarthy (Eds.), *Mediaspace: Place, scale and culture in a media age* (pp. 209–232). New York: Routledge.

Hommels, A. (2005). Studying obduracy in the city: Toward a productive fusion between technology studies and urban studies. *Science, Technology, and Human Values, 30,* 323–351.

Hughes, T. P. (1987). The evolution of large technological systems. In W. E. Bijker, T. P. Hughes, & T. Pinch (Eds.), *The social construction of technological systems: New directions in the sociology and history of technology.* Cambridge, MA: The MIT Press.

Jacobs, J. (1961). *The death and life of great American cities* (2002 ed.). New York: Random House.

Jain, S. (2006). Urban violence: Luxury in made space. In M. Sheller & J. Urry (Eds.), *Mobile technologies of the city* (pp. 61–76). New York: Routledge.

Jain, S. S. (2004). "Dangerous instrumentality": The bystander as subject in automobility. *Cultural Anthropology, 19,* 61–94.

Joerges, B. (1999). Do politics have artefacts? *Social Studies of Science, 29,* 411–431.

Latour, B. (1992). Where are the missing masses? The sociology of a few mundane artifacts. In W. E. Bijker, & J. Law (Eds.), *Shaping technology/building society: Studies in sociotechnical change* (pp. 225–258). Cambridge, MA: The MIT Press.

Law, J. (1987). Technology and heterogeneous engineering: The case of Portuguese expansion. In W. E. Bijker, T. P. Hughes, & T. Pinch (Eds.), *The social construction of technological systems: New directions in the sociology and history of technology.* Cambridge, MA: The MIT Press.

Lefebvre, H. (1991). *The production of space* (D. Nicholson-Smith, trans.). Cambridge, MA: Blackwell.

Lessig, L. (1999). *Code: And other laws of cyberspace.* New York: Basic Books.

Lewis, T. (1997). *Divided highways: Building the interstate highways, transforming American life.* New York: Viking.

Lianos, M., & Douglas, M. (2000). Dangerization and the end of deviance. *British Journal of Criminology, 40,* 261–278.

Low, S. M. (2003). *Behind the gates: Life, security and the pursuit of happiness in fortress America.* New York: Routledge.

Lynch, K. (1984). *Good city form.* Cambridge, MA: MIT Press.

Lyon, D. (2001). *Surveillance society: Monitoring everyday life*. Buckingham UK: Open University.

Lyon, D. (2006). Why where you are matters: Mundane mobilities, transparent technologies, and digital discrimination. In T. Monahan (Ed.), *Surveillance and security: Technological politics and power in everyday life* (pp. 209–224). New York: Routledge.

Lyon, D. (2007). *Surveillance studies: An overview*. Cambridge: Polity Press.

Monahan, T. (2005). *Globalization, technological change, and public education*. New York: Routledge.

Monahan, T. (2006a). Electronic fortification in Phoenix: Surveillance technologies and social regulation in residential communities. *Urban Affairs Review, 42*, 169–192.

Monahan, T. (2006b). Securing the homeland: Torture, preparedness, and the right to let die. *Social Justice, 33*, 95–105.

Monahan, T. (Ed.). (2006c). *Surveillance and security: Technological politics and power in everyday life*. New York: Routledge.

Monahan, T. (forthcoming). Dreams of control at a distance: Gender, surveillance, and social control. *Cultural Studies < = > Critical Methodologies, 8*(4).

Monahan, T., & Wall, T. (2007). Somatic surveillance: Corporeal control through information networks. *Surveillance & Society, 4*, 154–173.

Murakami Wood, D., & Graham, S. (2006). Permeable boundaries in the softwaresorted society: Surveillance and differentiations of mobility. In M. Sheller & J. Urry (Eds.), *Mobile technologies of the city* (pp. 177–191). New York: Routledge.

Noble, D. F. (1977). *America by design: Science, technology, and the rise of corporate capitalism*. New York: Oxford University Press.

Nye, D. (1996). *American technological sublime*. Cambridge, MA: MIT Press.

Packer, J. (2006a). Becoming bombs: Mobilizing mobility in the war of terror. *Cultural Studies, 20*, 378–399.

Packer, J. (2006b). Rethinking dependency: New relations of transportation and communication. In J. Packer & C. Robertson (Eds.), *Thinking with James Carey: Essays on communications, transportation, history*. New York: Peter Lang.

Patton, J. W. (2004). *Transportation worlds: Designing infrastructure and forms of urban life*. Unpublished doctoral dissertation, Rensselaer Polytechnic Institute, Troy, NY.

Pfaffenberger, B. (1992). Technological dramas. *Science, Technology, and Human Values, 17*, 282–312.

Phillips, D. J. (2005). From privacy to visibility. Context, identity, and power in ubiquitous computing environments. *Social Text, 23*, 95–108.

Pinch, T. (1996). The social construction of technology: A review. In R. Fox (Ed.), *Technological change: Methods and themes in the history of technology* (pp. 17–35). Amsterdam: Harwood Academic Publishers.

Press, J. E. (2000). Spatial mismatch or more of a mishmash? Multiple jeopardy and the journey to work. In L. D. Bobo, M. L. Oliver, J. H. Johnson Jr., & A. Valenzuela (Eds.), *Prismatic metropolis : Inequality in Los Angeles* (pp. 453–488). New York: Russell Sage Foundation.

Regan, P. M. (1995). *Legislating privacy: Technology, social values, and public policy*. Chapel Hill: University of North Carolina Press.

Reiman, J. H. (1995). Driving to the panopticon: Philosophical exploration of the risks to privacy posed by the highway technology of the future. *Santa Clara Computer and High Technology Law Journal, 11*, 27–44.

Schulman, D., & Ridgeway, J. (2007). The highwaymen. *Mother Jones, 32*, 48–55, 84.

Sheller, M. (2007). Bodies, cybercars and the mundane incorporation of automated mobilities. *Social & Cultural Geography, 8*, 175–197.

Sheller, M., & Urry, J. (2006). *Mobile technologies of the city.* New York: Routledge.

Slack, J. D., & Wise, J. M. (2005). *Culture + technology: A primer.* New York: Peter Lang.

The White House. (2003). *National strategy for the physical protection of critical infrastructures and key assets.* Washington, DC.

Thrift, N., & French, S. (2002). The automatic production of space. *Transactions of the Institute of British Geographers, 27*, 309–335.

U.S. Department of Transportation. (1998). *Developing traffic signal control systems using the national ITS architecture* (No. FHWA-JPO-98–026). Washington, DC: U.S. Department of Transportation.

U.S. Department of Transportation. (2006, November 7). Frequently Asked Questions: Intelligent Transportation Systems. http://www.its.dot.gov/faqs.htm. Last accessed January 9, 2007.

Vahidi, A., & Eskandarian, A. (2003). Research advances in intelligent collision avoidance and adaptive cruise control. *IEEE Transactions on Intelligent Transportation Systems, 4*, 143–153.

Winner, L. (1977). *Autonomous technology: Technics-out-of-control as a theme in political thought.* Cambridge, MA: MIT Press.

Winner, L. (1986). *The whale and the reactor: A search for limits in an age of high technology.* Chicago: University of Chicago Press.

Woolgar, S. (1991). The turn to technology in social studies of science. *Science, Technology, & Human Values, 16*, 20–50.

Zimmer, M. (2005). Surveillance, privacy and the ethics of vehicle safety communication technologies. *Ethics and Information Technology, 7*, 201–210.

Zimmer, M. (2007). *The quest for the perfect search engine: Values, technical design, and the flow of personal information in spheres of mobility.* Unpublished doctoral dissertation, New York University, New York.

Getting Carded: Border Control and the Politics of Canada's Permanent Resident Card

SIMONE BROWNE

New technologies of surveillance and mobility regimes are turning individuals into data by digitizing body parts. The growing privatization of such security arrangements marks the prominence of an identity industrial complex that is increasingly aligned with the security imperatives of the United States and the European Union. The rationale behind these (pre-existing) security imperatives is often purported as the consequence of the events of 11 September 2001 and the subsequent "war on terror". More alibi for heightened securitization than rationale, these events brought with them a refashioning of the conditionality of the status of those produced as "outsiders", and in the case examined in this article the conditionality of the status of the Canadian permanent resident. Within such security regimes, the body comes to function as text, or as document (Lyon, 2001). My concern in this article is in learning how documentary procedures, particularly Canada's Permanent Resident Card (PRC) and important events surrounding its introduction, turn people and bodies into differentiated and identifiable state subjects and data. My intention here is to make the links between the ways in which modern power makes up populations and individuals and allows for practices of identification to emerge through visual and visualizing regimes that inscribe some individuals as "subjects", while marking others as "bodies". The PRC, while part of the bureaucratic governance of permanent residents as a population, is also part of the productive effort to create the unmarked Canadian citizen.

This article is organized as follows. In the first section, I provide a brief introduction to the PRC and what I see as its role in the transnational regime of border control. The second section outlines concepts that I employ, such as "border control" and "nationalization", and the term "economies of bodies". In the last section, I examine three key moments surrounding the PRC: excerpts from a parliamentary committee public hearing; the first PRC prototype to be released into the public domain; and using various Canadian print news media sources, I take a look at the experiences of some permanent residents, questioning the ways in which the management of transnational movement and access to the nation-state were meted out by way of the PRC. With identity documents serving as a key technology in the management of mobility, an examination of the bureaucratic production of the PRC as a state issued status document could provide insight into the processes of this particular aspect of state- and nation- formation. I am suggesting that the identification and classification achieved through the PRC help to write the nation on the body, and shape our individual and collective imaginings about citizenship and belonging to the nation.

SECTION ONE

The Permanent Resident Card

Canada's Permanent Resident Card was introduced with the *Immigration and Refugee Protection Act* (*IRP Act*), first tabled in the House of Commons in February 2001 and enacted 28 June 2002. The PRC is a proof-of-status document that replaces the paper IMM 1000 *Record of Landing* document. New immigrants to Canada are issued a card upon arrival. For those already situated in Canada, application for the card is voluntary, but the PRC is required for re-entry by commercial carrier into Canada for Canadian permanent residents as "secure proof" of their status. Interestingly, this re-entry rule has not always been equally enforced, as I will discuss in more detail below. In March 2004, Citizenship and Immigration Canada (CIC) reached the one million mark for cards issued. Approximately 1.5 million permanent residents live in Canada. As a more sophisticated technology than the contemporary Canadian passport, the PRC provides a laser engraved photo and lists the holder's date of birth, nationality, gender, eye colour, client identification number, and other eye-readable non-secure data. Other "personal information" is encrypted in an optical stripe and is said to be available only for the purview of authorized officials. Made from multilayer polycarbonate, the PRC holds 1.1 megabytes of digital data stored in a 16 mm optical memory stripe. In capacity, this is the equivalent of about 500 pages of data. Polycarbonate is a lightweight, durable plastic used in commercial applications. Visible on the optical memory stripe is an Embedded Hologram™ of the cardholder's picture, along with eye-readable data such as date of birth, country code of the cardholder's nationality, and the phrases "Property of the Government of Canada" and "Propriété du Gouvernement du Canada". Developed by LaserCard Corporation, the Embedded Hologram™ is said to be an anti-counterfeiting security device.[1] Digital files that are machine-readable are encoded on the optical stripe, so that the optical stripe includes all information from the IMM1000 *Record of Landing* or *Confirmation of Permanent Residence*. Biometric data could be encoded within the card at a later date. Perhaps the most likely biometric technologies to be digitally encoded could be facial data and fingerprint data since the *IRP Act* requires that refugee claimants, who may later become permanent residents, be fingerprinted upon arrival in Canada.[2]

Some assumptions are made here. First, it is my assertion that claims to "legitimate" or normative citizenship are understood through the "bordering" of those depicted as potential threat to these citizenship claims and the rights to mobility and stability that come with them. In fact, according to CIC, the *IRP Act* is "tough on those who pose a threat to Canadian security".[3] However, my interest lies with the mutually constitutive relationship between citizenship and those state subjecthoods that are considered "not so threatening", card-carrying members of the state, in this case the category of the "permanent resident". Second, I situate the PRC as part of a larger effort in the production of insecurity by a transnational regime of border control. The PRC is the world's first International Civil Aviation Organization (ICAO) standard compliant optical memory card. As well, the International Card Manufacturers Association awarded the PRC the 2002 *Elan Award for Technical Achievement*. Clearly, the transnational regime of border control is dependent upon the triangulated operations of private enterprise, states, and non-governmental organizations, such as the ICAO. Furthermore, there is a mutually emergent and equally important player in the transnational regime of border control: the emotions of citizens, including fears, anxieties and imaginings. Third, in my view, identity documents such as the PRC "nationalize" immigrant bodies by codifying place of birth and country code. Seemingly, identity documents are one of the technologies that organize and function as the symbolic and material representations of how nationalization is delineated, and how categories of state subjecthood such as "citizen" and "permanent resident" are produced. I use the term "bodies" rather than people or individuals here not to deny ontological validity to those categorized as "permanent resident", but to point to the ways that the PRC fragments individuals and reduces them to bodies and body parts (sex, height, colour of eyes; and technology that could digitize permanent physical features, such as a fingerprint) for the purposes of what David Lyon terms "biosurveillance" (2001).

According to Anthony Richmond, "passports and visas no longer facilitate movement between countries but are instruments of exclusion" (2002, p. 716). For Richmond, these documents, as instruments of exclusion, work in conjunction with increasingly invasive surveillance technologies as part of "a formidable armoury of control devices" (p. 716). While agreeing with Richmond that technological advances dealing with the monitoring of mobility and population control often encroach on human rights, I am suggesting that these state issued status documents in general, and the PRC in particular, simultaneously function as instruments of inclusion and exclusion. This is an inclusion for citizens that is predicated on the exclusion of, often interchangeable, "others", in this case those categorized as "permanent residents" and undocumented "illegal migrants". To better understand how this apparent interchange operates, I look to Didier Bigo's model of a "stock exchange of security" where, as he put it:

> if each security service uses the word immigrant as a sign of danger, a consensus is possible—because such a word can designate a foreigner as an Algerian (a member of an ethnic minority that may already have citizenship) or as other kinds of

foreigner. Each country can then sell its fear to the other country (hence, Algerians come under surveillance in Britain and Germany, and Kurds in France and Britain). (2002, p. 71)

In such a model, "immigrant" is a signifier of danger or at least potential danger. Further, the fear of this presumed danger is commodified, marketed and used to propel what Bigo terms "the main technique of securitization". In Bigo's own words, this technique operates

> to transform structural difficulties and transformations into elements permitting specific groups to be blamed, even before they have done anything, simply by categorizing them, anticipating profiles of risk from previous trends, and projecting them by generalization upon the potential behaviour of each individual pertaining to the risk category. (p. 81)

The point here is that, given this logic, a presumed danger can subsume an entire group through its categorization as such. Could this logic have prevailed during the parliamentary processes surrounding the creation of the PRC? Was the PRC the outcome of a "technique of securitization" where structural difficulties—in this case the need for "measures for preventing counterfeiting, forgery or fraudulent use of identity papers and travel documents"[4]—were transformed by producing some as "risky bodies" needing mobility/identity documents to regulate them and to produce certain truths about them?

Much of the research on the functioning of mobility documents situates passports as markers of the bearer's allegiance to the issuing state, for example, Torpey (1998), O'Byrne (2001), and Adey (2004). Darren O'Byrne, for example, sees one of the functions of the passport as being that of a "political tool because it allows an administrative body to discriminate in terms of who can and cannot travel in its name" (2001, p. 403). For me, the PRC is a political tool in O'Byrne's sense. However, it is not about allegiance to the state but about calling the allegiance of the permanent resident into question. A look at the application procedure reveals how this questioning of allegiance is made possible.

The Application

In completing the PRC application (IMM 5444) the applicant must provide "ADDRESS, WORK AND EDUCATIONAL HISTORY" for the past five years. Each month must be accounted for. Sections cannot be left blank, as doing so could delay the processing of the application; instead "N/A" must be recorded where applicable, for example, during a time of unemployment. Since permanent residents are required to be physically present in Canada for a minimum of 730 days within each five-year period in order to fulfil residency requirements, the applicant must provide a detailed account of any absences from Canada, including vacations. The information booklet that accompanies the application notes that considerations may be made on compassionate and humanitarian grounds for those who have not fulfilled their residency obligations, inferring here that one's status can be revoked if the residency requirements are not met. The application document also requires the applicant to reveal "PERSONAL DETAILS" such as height, eye colour (six possible colours to choose from, as well as a box marked "other"), date of birth, marital status, country of citizenship, and given and family names. Interestingly, the information booklet notes that family names over 20 characters and given names over 15 characters will be automatically shortened due to space restraints. The application must be accompanied by a *Supplementary Identification Form* (IMM 5455) upon which must be affixed a 35 × 45 mm photograph of the applicant. False hairpieces can be worn, as long as they do not disguise, what the application booklet terms the "natural appearance of the bearer" (IMM 5445E, Citizenship and Immigration Canada, 2004, p. 13). Tinted prescription glasses may be worn, but not sunglasses. Hats and hair coverings or "anything that interferes with the photo's value in providing a means of identifying the isuee for the benefit of travelling control, are not acceptable" (IMM 5445E, Citizenship and Immigration Canada, 2002, p. 11). However, exceptions are made for religious headgear.[5] Unlike the requirements for the Canadian passport photograph, the "no smile rule" is not in effect.

Given the above requirements and specifications, the process of filling out the IMM 5444 requires the applicant to produce a dossier of evidence, or a body of data, to substantiate her claims. Such a dossier comes to stand for the applicant, as a textualized representation of the subject that, along with the applicant's body data, once encoded on the optical stripe of the card, becomes the digitized intellectual property of the state. I term this intellectual property as belonging to the state because the application states that "the Permanent Resident Card issued by Citizenship and Immigration Canada remains at all times the property of the Government of Canada and must be returned to Citizenship and Immigration Canada at its request" (Application, 2004, p. 3). As such, through the completion of the application procedure, the applicant produces herself as a "responsible immigrant", a responsible immigrant being one who can account for her employment, residences, comings and goings, and who can provide a guarantor to verify her claims. Importantly, this concept of a guarantor, a Canadian citizen who can vouch for the applicant, is a key subject in this making of the responsible immigrant. Without suitable details, the applicant's allegiance to the state is questioned, with the possibility of undergoing a special review through the *Quality Assurance Program*. This calling of allegiance into question that is achieved by way of the application process is significant as it points to rights to mobility and stability and the distinct relation of these rights to power, self-government and the making of the responsible immigrant. Here the restriction of mobility is an effect of power. As well, the application process points to the conditionality of this particular immigrant status, a status that requires accountability. Conditional in that the card is only valid for five years, this is a type of inclusion that is dependent on fulfilling particular responsibilities and that requires the repetitive production of the applicant as responsible and accountable. Given this, the application is one technology that *allows* permanent residents to produce themselves as "responsible immigrants". Through this processing, from application to the finished personalized card, the body of data and the body data become a commodity that brings together both the subject and the body. I use the term commodity here as these data are surrendered and exchanged for mobility rights and access to movement. The card accounts for the subject, and with the possible addition of biometrics, the card could produce an ontological and scientific "truth" of its holder. If the production of the responsible immigrant takes place through the application procedure and the production of the card, it can also be said that this process, with its organizing, managing and serializing of the permanent resident, also produces the citizen, as an unmarked Canadian with less restrictive mobility rights.

SECTION TWO

Border Control and Economies of Bodies

In examining the discourses and practices of border control and how they were put into effect in the production of the PRC, it is important to focus on the particularization of bodies within the nation-state. Particularization, for the purposes of this paper, occurs by way of the categorization and investment of gendered and racialized meanings to certain bodies. Through the process of particularization, some groups and individuals are apparently fixed and made known as being within the Canadian nation-state. My concern here is with those individuals and groups that come to occupy the position of outsider-within status in the nation-state, and the ways in which this outsider-within status shapes how citizenship and other forms of state subjecthood are constituted. The term "state subjecthood" encompasses a variety of subject positions, including citizens, immigrants, migrant workers, refugees, temporary visitors, visa holders, as well as the undocumented. Also, the notion of "bordering" as articulated by Sunera Thobani (2000) is an important concept to understand. Bordering occurs through the situating of particular bodies as "outsiders" that symbolically demarcate the nation and who belongs to it. This differentiating of bodies takes symbolic, discursive and material forms with the aim of achieving particular kinds of subjects, often in gendered, racialized and sexually specific ways. As such, I situate bordering as one of the key disciplinary practices of the nation-state, with classificatory identity/mobility documents playing an important role. These documents not only regulate mobility and access to space, but they do the organizing work of "fixing" identities. This "fixing" is one element of border control. While the greater imperative of border control is the security of both geopolitical and financial space, the term also signals the operational dynamics by which the state regulates mobility and sometimes confines some bodies within the state, while deterring other bodies outside of the state from entry. It is a process that is not singular, but one that shifts according to the historical moment. These operational dynamics have both material and ideological implications. In this way, "border control" suggests the bordering of particular individuals, groups and bodies, referred to above, that at once situates these bodies as outsider-within the nation-state with the function of determining how the citizen comes to know itself as "citizen". A useful way to think about citizenship here is that it does the work of bordering "members of a polity from another as well as members of a polity from non-members" (Isin & Wood, 1999, p. 20).

The state, through its policy-making, administrative practices, judicial system and other regulatory practices, helps to shape the nation and to give it the appearance of order. By way of but not solely through this shaping, ideologies and imaginings of the "nation" are made possible. Some individuals and groups are bordered, racialized, de-racialized and nationalized as members of the nation-state, while others are ascribed an outsider or outsider-within status along with the penalties that come with this status. The practice of nationalization, or of "being nationalized", is understood here as the fixing of particular individuals as *belonging* to Canada's geopolitical space, while other individuals are fixed as *belonging* to other geopolitical spaces, even though such individuals may be located in Canada. In this practice, the individual is inscribed with a certain subjectivity, nationalizing her as she is differentiated from others. Following Radhika Mongia (1999), nationalizing can be understood as a practice of racialization, where individuals are particularized in totalizing groupings and attributed essential racial meanings. I am suggesting that identity documents, such as the PRC, are one of the technologies that organize and serve as the symbolic and material representations of how nationalization is delineated. For more insight on the working of nationalization, I turn to Orvar Löfgren's (1999) suggestion that the anxiety that comes with the passport regime is one that is accompanied by the "nationalizing gaze" cast by border control and customs officials. To this understanding I would add the disembodied nationalizing gaze cast by surveillance technologies, such as verification machines, that read passports and other identity documents for the purpose of sorting their bearers. Similarly, Peter Adey (2004) suggests that passports make a person "legible" to the state as they are markers of the holder's identity and of the limits, or limitlessness, to the holder's spatial mobility. Is such legibility encoded in the PRC? Perhaps the nationalizing gaze, cast by customs officials and verification machines, is also achieved by the PRC's marking of country code representing its holder's place of birth. Here, the nationalizing gaze is part of the making of a "PRC identity" where the body functions as text and one is compelled to live up to this identity, in order to re-enter Canada from travel abroad, and increasingly for access to other benefits from the state.[6]

The term "economies of bodies and body parts" signals a system whereby body data is digitized by way of disciplinary mechanisms to, borrowing from Michel Foucault, "work the body retail" (1979, p. 137) for the production of normalized, docile bodies. Here "retail" signals individualizing processes. Within this system, the body, and increasingly digitized parts and pieces of the body are not only worked retail, but are also worked wholesale in databases (criminal databases, soccer "hooligan" databases, permanent resident databases, "suspect terrorist" databases). These parts and pieces are circulated through transnational spaces, traded (as suggested by Bigo's "stock exchange of security"; Bigo, 2002), commodified by private corporations that market some populations as "risky" and who develop security technologies capable of making some permanent physical features and behavioural traits, or body data, into digitized intellectual property. Also, there exists the possibility of identity documents capturing counterfeited body data. That being said, the term points to a set of interrelated activities where bodies are both produced and consumed. Below, I outline key concepts that lend clarity to the term "economies of bodies". I suggest we can find these concepts in Michel Foucault's discussions on reason of state and disciplinary society.

In "The political technology of individuals" (1988) Foucault poses the following question:

> Which kind of political techniques, which technology of government, has been put to work and used and developed in the general framework of the reason of state in order to make of the individual a significant element for the state? (p. 153)

This question is important for in its answer lies the means through which we come, as Foucault notes, "to recognise ourselves as a society, as part of a social entity, as part of a nation or state" (p. 146). In this work, Foucault sets out to explain "reason of state" and he deals with the seventeenth century emergence of the modern political subject. Foucault's concern, in this work and others, was with a subject that was strictly bourgeois, European and male (1990a, 1990b). For Foucault, reason of state is "a technique conforming to certain rules" within which "the art of governing people is rationale on the condition that it observes the nature of what is governed, that is the state itself" (1988, p. 149). In other words, the ways in which a population is governed by the state are contingent upon that state's own preservation. For Foucault, the means and techniques through which the modern state achieves its goal of population management are dependant upon the modern state acting on the interest of the population "at the level of the consciousness of each individual who goes to make up the population, and interest considered as the interest of the population regardless of what the particular interests and aspirations may be of the individuals who compose it" (p. 100). For Foucault, this particular art of governing is tied with the emergence of what he calls "political arithmetic" where statistics deal not with probability, but with the "knowledge of the state", its strength, and that of other states' respective powers (p. 151). In this way, states were conceived of as continually having to preserve themselves through correct governance. How so? The form that this correct governance assumes and the rationale behind it is linked to one "idea" that Foucault develops from reason of state, which is that under the conditions where the state is continually concerned with its preservation, "the individual becomes pertinent for the state insofar as he can do something for the strength of the state" (p. 152). With this idea, Foucault raises the question of the individual's political utility:

> The individual exists insofar as what he does is able to introduce even a minimal change in the strength of the state, either in a positive or in a negative direction. It is only insofar as an individual is able to introduce this change that the state has to do with him. And sometimes what he has to do for the state is to live, to work, to produce, to consume; and sometimes what he has to do is to die. (p. 152)

At the heart of this is the suggestion that reason of state is concerned with what Foucault terms the "happiness" of individuals. This is a happiness where the police see to making people into, and sustaining them as, useful state subjects.[7] We can interpret from the above quote that individuals, living as part of a population within the environment as a social body, and their experience of "happiness" on which the state depends, can be done away with as this is a political rationality under which the strength of the state must be preserved. In this case, the question of political utility arises. If the individual only exists to the extent that she can introduce a change in the strength of the state, then discipline is the thing that determines her utility.

Foucault opines that the political rationality of our time is one where the processes of the integration of individuals into the political totality are characterized by a constant correlation between an increasing individualization and the reinforcement of this totality (pp. 161–162). With such a rationality, techniques of reason of state are employed to bring about the docility of individuals. Here the state is concerned with the "happiness" of individuals, as well as with its own preservation. In other words, the state is concerned simultaneously with technologies of the self and with disciplinary technologies. These are technologies that reinforce each other, in an effort to *know* the individual, have the individual *know* herself in order to facilitate self-government, and to submit her to certain practices for the production of a docile body. As such, this is an effort at working the body retail by way of disciplinary techniques. Through these techniques, what Foucault terms "simple instruments"—techniques of identification, registration, hierarchical observation, normalizing judgment, correct training—the individual is made known as a subject. Although disciplinary power is individualizing, through normalizing judgment individual actions are referred "to a whole that is at once a field of comparison, a space of differentiation and the principle of a rule to be followed" (1979, p. 182). Here the examination is important as it orders and "establishes over individuals a visibility through which one differentiates them and judges them" (p. 184). Foucault argues that

> the examination that places individuals in a field of surveillance also situates them in a network of writing; it engages them in a whole mass of documents that capture and fix them. The procedures of examination were accompanied at the same time by a system of intense registration and of documentary accumulation. A "power of writing" was constituted as an essential part in the mechanisms of discipline. (p. 189)

Further, Foucault notes that disciplinary power is "exercised through its invisibility", while imposing a "compulsory visibility" on its targets (p. 187). So disciplinary power can be said to operate, at times, as a visual and visualizing regime where "documentary accumulation" and "a network of writing" are put into practice to produce a scrutinizing surveillance that individuals are at once subjected to, and that produces them as subjects. It is with this understanding of the operational dynamics of visual regimes in disciplinary society that I wish to situate my query of how identity documents function to nationalize individuals through the individualizing and essentializing processes of particularization. These documents by way of a visual and visualizing regime facilitate the state's ability to serialize and "fix" individuals and sometimes control their transnational movements, or at least what the state defines as legitimate movement.

SECTION THREE

In November 2002, then immigration minister Denis Coderre put forward a recommendation for a national debate on the issue of identity cards for all Canadians. Proposing that such a card would be similar to the PRC, Coderre noted that "identity has taken on new prominence" since the events of 11 September 2001. He also suggested that debating an identity card would provide the opportunity "to clarify what it means to be a citizen, a Canadian" (Coderre, 2003). Coderre's call led to the *Biometrics: Implications and Applications for Citizenship and Immigration* forum held by CIC in October 2003. Government officials, participants from the private sector and other "experts" attended this by-invitation-only forum. Coderre's suggestion of a national identity card was met with critique. The former Privacy Commissioner of Canada in his Overview of the *Annual Report to Parliament* declared, among other things, that a national identity card would create "Big Brother dossiers" that could "open the way to being stopped in the streets by police and required to identify ourselves on demand" (Radwanski, 2003, p. 3). The national identity card did not move beyond debate, however Coderre's recommendation was not the first instance of such a call. One occasion in particular had certain elements in common with Coderre's, namely, the suggestion that the card would thwart terrorists. A *Notice of Motion* was filed in October 1971 in the House of Commons considering the "Compulsory Carrying of Identification Cards" for Canadian citizens and immigrants. Filed by Member of Parliament Fernand Leblanc, this motion was in response to the 1970 events known as the October Crisis involving the Front de Libération du Québec (FLQ), the kidnapping and killing of Quebec Justice Minister Pierre Laporte, the kidnapping of British Trade Commissioner James Cross and the invoking of the *War Measures Act* by the federal government. Leblanc noted that "such a card could ensure the protection of the community in case of riots and terrorist acts", while one MP argued that the motion be "examined from every angle with very long tongs, and then dropped into a furnace and burned" (Leblanc, 1971).

Parliament as a Site of Discursive Production

Why parliamentary processes as a site for analysis? To briefly answer this I turn to Benedict Anderson's suggestion that "individually, legislators represent particular interests, localities, and prejudices; collectively and anonymously, as Parliament, Diet, or Congress, they represent a unitary nation or sovereignty" (1994, p. 319). By examining the procedures through which Members of Parliament legitimize the idea that they represent a unitary nation, such a presumed anonymity can be challenged. As well, examining select parliamentary processes can point to the conditions that made the PRC possible and can uncover documentary evidence of the methods of bureaucratic decision-making in the policy-formation process. I suggest that by examining the parliamentary discursive practices that shaped policy-formation and legitimized the creation of the PRC, we can learn how the categorization of some as "permanent residents" shapes understandings of Canadian citizenship and the borders of the nation. Along with press releases, policy papers, speeches from the throne, and press conferences, Standing Committee meetings are parliamentary processes of truth-making and knowledge production. What follows are verbatim excerpts from the Standing Committee on Citizenship and Immigration meeting on 9 February 2000. During this meeting, the Standing Committee conducted hearings on the refugee determination system and "illegal" migrants. Representatives from non-governmental organizations presented to the Committee after their submission of consultative documents.

> Mr. Warren Everson (Vice-President, Policy and Strategic Planning, Air Transport Association of Canada): /.../One particularly frustrating and expensive problem that is getting worse by the day is the fraudulent use of genuine Canadian IMM 1000 resident cards by illegal migrants. The cards are notorious for their vulnerability to fraudulent use. There is no photo ID on the document. The IMM 1000 incorporates no modern validation techniques. In short, it's an open invitation to manipulation by professional movers of illegal migrants. It's impossible for airline personnel to detect when a genuine Canadian IMM 1000 is fraudulently used in combination with a genuine foreign passport. CIC nevertheless subjects our carriers to financial penalties when that card is used by arriving passengers who are subsequently identified as inadmissible.

> ... So if there is a single recommendation that we think this committee could make that would help the airlines reduce the fraudulent use of the Canadian document, it would be to insist on a replacement of the card with a document that uses currently available technology.

Here it is made known through "expert" testimony that the imperatives of ATAC, a non-governmental organization, regarding border control and the deterring of illegal migration to Canada are aligned with those of the state. The borders of the state are represented as particularly porous, due to the "problems" caused by the easily forged IMM 1000 that are exploited by "professional movers of illegal migrants". With the suggestion that new technologies be employed to control the flow of illegal migrants, we can understand this Standing Committee meeting as a social event where, what I referred to earlier as, the triangulated operations of states, non-governmental organizations and private enterprise in the transnational regime of border control are put into practice.

Mr. Leon Benoit (Director, Government and Industry Affairs; Legal Counsel, Air Transat, Air Transport Association of Canada): ... I might remind you, as we mentioned before, that airport authorities in other countries aren't always very willing to listen to our problems in terms of what we have to do under Canadian legislation.

There is a fundamental issue in some countries—I won't name them—where clearly the country in question has absolutely no interest in helping you stop that person from getting on your flight, leaving their territory and going to Canada, because basically they have just eliminated another problem for themselves. We operate in that sort of environment. So I think we are making that effort.

On this issue of a scanner, I would like to know what you think this thing could do. I am just asking how this would work. Would this be something—

The Chair (Mr. Joe Fontana (London North Centre, Liberal)): Scan their eyeballs.

Mr. George Petsikas (Director, Government and Industry Affairs; Legal Counsel, Air Transat, Air Transport Association of Canada): As long as it doesn't induce blindness, that's fine.

Mr. Steve Mahoney (Mississauga West, Liberal): That's not what it would do, Mr. Chairman.

From this excerpt, we can begin to see that blame for the "problem" of the undocumented is placed both on "unnamed countries" that wish to "unload" their problems, and on the restrictions produced through Canadian legislation that could be understood here as seeming "too lenient". Also, there is the suggestion that such "problems" could be regulated through the use of a visualizing regime that employs surveillance technologies, such as the PRC and like practices, that rely on the notion that the body will reveal the "truth" about a person's identity despite the subject's claims.

The Chair: ... With most of the people who come to Canada wanting to claim refugee status, if they're coming directly by plane and landing in our airports or perhaps coming via the United States or wherever, obviously you ask these people for their proper documentation to make sure they can board the plane. That's notwithstanding the fact that you said some nations may very well be wanting to get rid of their problems and therefore they're prepared to do whatever.

Ms. Jean Augustine (Etobicoke—Lakeshore, Lib.): There is one curiosity I have. With the stowaways, what is the profile? What is the age, sex? Could you give me the profile of a stowaway?

Ms. Sonia Simard (Manager, Policy and Government Affairs, Shipping Federation of Canada): What we have seen in recent years are mainly stowaways coming from Romania. More than 70% of our stowaways are coming from Romania and they are males under the age of 25. So we do see a profile there.

In the above excerpts two important assumptions are revealed. First, the undocumented are produced as problems that sending nations wish to get rid of, and that are arriving at "our" airports. The use of "our" signals a sense of ownership and belonging to the nation and the citizenship rights that this belonging entails, as well it points to the fears and anxieties surrounding the idea of porous borders. In this way, certain bodies are understood as unlawfully invading social spaces that *belong* to citizens and other documented state subjects. Second, a profile of the recent stowaway is made known, the majority of who are gendered and nationalized as Romanian males. This nationalization of the stowaway is not a static process but one where the nation is interchangeable, as other "expert" testimonies that took place before the Standing Committee that same day centred on a discussion of Tamil asylum seekers. Seemingly mundane at first glance, Standing Committee meetings reveal a particular type of truth-making where testimony and opinions of "expert" witnesses are often produced as fact. In this particular meeting, the suggestion that the IMM 1000 be replaced with a more secure document marks the beginning of the remaking of the category "permanent resident", where the permanent resident is remade, through the PRC, in relation to the anticipated security "threats" attributed to illegal migrants.

12 October 2001

When former Citizenship and Immigration Minister Elinor Caplan first announced the PRC during a press conference held at the Canada-US border at Niagara Falls in October 2001, she stated that "we are not going to allow this border crossing, or any other, to be held economic hostage by terrorists" (Thompson, 2001). During this press conference, Caplan produced a prototype of the PRC that depicted a blonde-haired, most likely white woman listed as 17 years of age. The name on the card was listed as Ponnuthaureuithirai Jagatheswary, whose nationality was identified as LKA. LKA is the country code for Sri Lanka. A link can be made here between anxieties around imagined threats to national security, Caplan's narrative of the need for protection of the borders from terrorists (especially those said to pose a threat to the economy), and those who the state assigns suspect, or potential threat status to, expressed through country code. With this particular prototype and the announcement made during this press conference, Ponnuthaureuithirai Jagatheswary (whether a "real" individual or not) in particular, and Sri Lankan nationals in general, were bordered as threat to the nation and its economic relations with the United States. Here race is codified as nationality, revealed by the country code. Clearly, this is an example of nation profiling. Interestingly, the prototype now used in the promotional material for the PRC shows a racially ambiguous Kiki Latesa from the Bahamas, a seemingly more "benign" state than Sri Lanka with no viable secessionist movements.

Travel Agency

In order to address how access to the nation space is sometimes demarcated based on national origin, it is useful to examine how the PRC was first put into practice. Midnight 31 December 2003 marked the deadline when permanent residents would need a PRC to re-enter Canada by way of commercial carrier. Without a PRC or a temporary travel document issued at a Canadian visa office, permanent residents would be denied re-entry. Getting a temporary travel document could prove difficult. If one were in Albania, for example, the closest Canadian visa office where one could apply for a temporary travel document is in Rome, Italy. In December 2003, an email from an official at CIC sent to travel agents and tour operators was leaked to the news media (Thompson, 2003). Stating, "I am pleased to confirm that persons holding visa-exempt passports will not require a PR card and may board return flights in the normal way", this email revealed information in contrast to the official information available on the CIC website and through the PRC advertising campaign. These exempt countries included Australia, Japan, most European nations, and Britain. Holders of valid US green cards would be exempt also.[8] In contrast, citizens of countries such as Algeria, Jamaica, Pakistan and Syria would be subject to the re-entry requirements. This restriction of mobility, in effect, bordered some and created two categories of permanent residents to which different practices were applied.

In a January 2004 interview with the *Toronto Star*, then immigration minister Judy Sgro reported that 82 people had been denied re-entry for not having a PRC (Frasier, 2004a). Sgro also credited the PRC for barring a Jamaican citizen, previously deported from Canada, who attempted to return using an allegedly fraudulent *Record of Landing* on 1 January 2004. Some newspapers and the online message board at www.settlement.org reported that enforcement of the re-entry rule was not equally meted out. Those reports noted that nationals from India, Poland, Hong Kong, and Taiwan scheduled on return flights to Canada were prohibited from boarding the aircrafts due to lack of a PRC, while certain others were allowed to board planes without the PRC after the 31 December deadline. The enforcement of the re-entry rule by airline officials demonstrates how agencies outside of the state serve as border control due to the obligation set out in the *IRP Act* that airlines and other commercial carriers must ensure that their passengers are properly documented. Some permanent residents found the requirement of the PRC, given a backlog in application processing, an unreasonable limit on their movement and were able to do something about it. For example, a university instructor wishing to attend the premiere of his opera in Pittsburgh, Pennsylvania was able to have his application processed in a manner quicker than most with the help of the Canadian Consulate in Buffalo and the constituency office of his Member of Parliament (Morris, 2004). In another case, the owner of a manufacturing company in Belleville, Ontario who had business to attend to in Germany and Italy expressed to the *Toronto Star* that "I have created jobs here, I have paid millions of dollars in taxes", and that he would take his chances using his German passport and *Record of Landing* (Frasier, 2004b). Also, many people were able to get around the re-entry rule by entering Canada by private vehicle at Canada-US border crossings. Given this apparent loophole, if the PRC is meant as a technology to "protect the borders", the process is definitely flawed.

CONCLUSION

The "PRC identity" could be understood as one where the marking of "permanence" that the PRC achieves is rather temporary as the card is valid for five years, and points to a unique form of card-carrying, state subjecthood where the holder is not completely of the nation, but the possibility of membership is alluded to, and sometimes deferred.[9] Capturing and fixing through "a network of writing" and a visualizing regime, the PRC does the organizing work of bordering immigrant bodies, in relation to citizens and undocumented peoples. Given this, borders and bordering can provide narratives of how citizenship is understood in the nation. This notion of bordering opens up the concept of the border from a fixed place to a verb or a process. As such, bordering does not only occur at the territorial boundaries of the nation-state, it can also be internal to it. Although fear, suspicion, anxiety and complacency are some of the emotional reactions to our present moment, spaces are continually being created where people question and sometimes resist "techniques of securitization" and the conversion of bodies into data.[10] Such activities point to the shaping of alternate imaginings of our investment in and belonging to the nation.

NOTES

[1] The manufacturers of the PRC are the Canadian Bank Note Company, Limited (CBN) subcontracted with California based LaserCard Corporation, in partnership with Anteon Corporation. Also subcontracted is Information Spectrum Incorporated. The five-year subcontract with LaserCard Corporation was awarded with Canadian Bank Note in 2002. CBN prints and distributes the card from its facility in Ottawa, Canada.

[2] *Immigration and Refugee Protection Act* c.16 (2) (a). According to a document released under the *Access to Information Act* request, *Biometrics: CIC Business Requirements*, the CIC intends to have two biometric identifiers in the card, with facial data as the primary one and fingerprint templates as the secondary identifier. In this way, the PRC would be similar in function to the US Department of State's Laser Visa Border Crossing Card, a multiple entry visa used by Mexican citizens to enter the US. This card, also produced by LaserCard Corporation, is used to biometrically verify the cardholder's identity through a one-to-one identification process between the cardholder and the encoded fingerprint data.

[3] "Immigration and Refugee Protection Act", Citizenship and Immigration Canada website, available at: www.cic.gc.ca/english/irpa (accessed 5 December 2003).

[4] United Nations Security Council Resolution 1373, September 2001.

[5] In practice, this was not always the case. In July 2004 the Prime Minister announced that religious headscarves were acceptable after complaints that women were being forced to remove their religious headscarves to be photographed for their PRC upon arrival at Pierre Elliot Trudeau Airport in Dorval, Quebec (Hustak, 2004; Stanstna, 2004). Hair and ears are not considered "facial features".

[6] Although the PRC was introduced as a mobility document, Social Development Canada now requires a PRC in order for permanent residents whose Records of Landing were issued before 28 June 1973 and after 27 June 2002 to obtain a Social Insurance Number (SIN) or to replace a damaged or lost SIN Card. Given this, the PRC can be understood as a measure of the Canadian state's imperative to not only manage access to geopolitical space of the nation, but increasingly to the nation's financial space as well. This is especially the case for homeless and underhoused persons, as SIN cards are needed to apply for numerous government benefits. The difficulties faced by homeless and underhoused peoples in accessing the PRC are many. These include accessing the application form by Internet or by mail to a fixed address; payment of the application fee; accounting for employment and residence histories; securing a guarantor; and care of the application and photograph, which could be rejected if torn, bent or otherwise flawed.

[7] See Foucault's discussion of Nicolas Delamare's *Traité de la police* (1705) (Foucault, 1988, pp. 153–157) where the police are said to "see to everything regulating society" and "everything pertaining to

men's happiness" (p. 157) where through the technique of the police the "integration of individuals in the state's utility is achieved" (p. 153). In a development on Delamare's work of systematizing French administrative practices, Foucault suggests that this is a project that through its classification of needs attempts to determine "the correlation between the utility scale for individuals and the utility scale for the state" (p. 157). For Foucault, reviewing Delamare's manual is instructive because in it Delamare positions human happiness as a political object (p. 158). Or as Foucault put it: "Now happiness is not only a simple effect. Happiness of individuals is a requirement for the survival and development of the state. It is a condition, it is an instrument, and not simply a consequence. People's happiness becomes an element of state strength" (p. 158).

[8] A complete list of exempt countries and those whose nationals require visas can be found at: http://www.cic.gc.ca/english/visit/visas.html

[9] In a survey conducted with permanent residents, some respondents said that they would not apply for the PRC within the first two years of its introduction (Environics Research Group, 2003).

[10] A class action lawsuit involving 46 permanent residents was filed on 18 December 2003 claiming that the CIC engaged in systematic discrimination of permanent residents based on their nationalities (*The Province*, 2004). The application was dismissed in April 2004.

REFERENCES

Adey, P. (2004) Secured and sorted mobilities: examples from the airport, *Surveillance & Society*, 1(4), pp. 500–519.

Anderson, B. (1991) *Imagined Communities* (London: Verso).

Anderson, B. (1994) Exodus, *Critical Inquiry*, 20, pp. 314–327.

Bigo, D. (2002) Security and immigration: toward a critique of the governmentality of unease, *Alternatives: Global, Local Political*, 27(1), pp. 63–92.

Canada (2002) House of Commons debates (*Hansard*), Number 026, 18 November.

Citizenship and Immigration Canada (2002) Applying for a Permanent Resident Card form IMM 5445E.

Citizenship and Immigration Canada (2004) Applying for a Permanent Resident Card form IMM 5445E.

Coderre, D. (2003) Why discuss a national identity card?, Minister's speech, appearance before the Standing Committee on Citizenship and Immigration, 6 February 2003.

Environics Research Group (2003) *Permanent Resident Card Advertisement Recall: Final Report* (Ottawa: Environics Research Group).

Foucault, M. (1979) *Discipline and Punish: The Birth of the Prison* (New York: Vintage Books).

Foucault, M. (1988) The political technology of individuals, in: L. H. Martin *et al.* (Eds) *Technologies of the Self: A Seminar with Michel Foucault* (Amherst: University of Massachusetts Press).

Foucault, M. (1990a) *The History of Sexuality: An Introduction—Volume One* (New York: Vintage Books).

Foucault, M. (1990b) *The Use of Pleasure: The History of Sexuality—Volume Two* (New York: Vintage Books).

Frasier, G. (2004a) Controversial card keeps out criminal; deportee was barred from flight to Canada Sgro cites success of permanent resident ID, *The Toronto Star*, 19 January, p. A14.

Frasier, G. (2004b) Man to take his chances with no card, *The Toronto Star*, 26 January, p. A6.

Hustak, A. (2004) Muslim women arriving in Canada need not remove hijab at security check, PM says, *National Post*, 14 August, p. A5.

Isin, E. F. & Wood, P. K. (1999) *Citizenship & Identity* (London: Sage).

LaserCard (2004) LaserCard wire: newsletter, available at: www.lasercard.com/downloads/wire/013_April_2004_pdf(accessed 20 September 2004).

Leblanc, F. (1971), Canada. House of Commons debates (*Hansard*), 8 October, pp. 8572–8578.

Löfgren, O. (1999) Crossing borders: the nationalization of anxiety, *Ethnologia Scandinavica: A Journal for Nordic Ethnology*, 29, pp. 5–27.

Lyon, D. (2001) Under my skin: from identification papers to body surveillance, in: J. Caplan & J. Torpey (Eds) *Documenting Individual Identity: The Development of State Practices in the Modern World* (Princeton, NJ: Princeton University Press).

Mongia, R. (1999) Race, nationality, mobility: a history of the passport, *Public Culture*, 11(3), pp. 527–555.

Morris, M. (2004) Have card, will travel, *The Globe and Mail*, 10 January, p. A19.

O'Byrne, D. (2001) On passports and border controls, *Annals of Tourism Research*, 28(2), pp. 399–416.

Province, The (2004) Airline passengers without new travel card denied re-entry into Canada, 2 January, p. A14.

Radwanski, G. (2003) Commissioner's overview, in: *Annual Report to Parliament 2001–2002* (Ottawa: Privacy Commissioner of Canada).

Richmond, A. H. (2002) Globalization: implications for immigrants and refugees, *Ethnic and Racial Studies*, 25(5), pp. 707–727.

Standing Committee on Citizenship and Immigration (2000) Evidence 36th Parliament, 2nd Session, 9 February.

Stastna, K. (2004) Hijab hassle haunts airport, *The Gazette*, 26 June p. A7.

Thobani, S. (2000) Nationalizing Canadians: bordering immigrant women in the late twentieth century, *Canadian Journal of Women and the Law*, 12(2), pp. 279–312.

Thompson, A. (2001) Immigrant ID reflects "changed world", *Toronto Star*, 13 October p. A1.

Thompson, A. (2003) Resident rules eased: official, *Toronto Star*, 14 December p. A1.

Torpey, J. (1998) Coming and going: on the state monopolization of the legitimate "means of movement", *Sociological Theory*, 16(3), pp. 239–259.

United Nations (2001) Security Council unanimously adopts wide-ranging anti-terrorism resolution; calls for suppressing financing, improving international cooperation, Press Release SC/7158, available at: http://www.un.org/News/Press/docs/2001/sc7158.doc.htm (accessed 8 August 2002).

Therapeutics of the Self

Surveillance in the Service of the Therapeutic[1]

RACHEL E. DUBROFSKY

At the onset of the twenty-first century, contemporary reality-based television programming[2] has captured the attention of TV viewers in the United States. Scholarship on television has responded in kind to the reality-based TV phenomenon with a surge in publications on the topic (Andrejevic 2002, 2004; Brenton and Cohen 2003; Corner 2002; Couldry 2002; Dovey 2000; Glynn 2000; Hill 2002; Kilborn 2003; McGrath 2004; Murray and Ouellette 2004; Palmer 2002; Pecora 2002; Ross and Moorti 2004a, 2004b; Scannell 2002; White 2002). This article examines the coupling of surveillance and the therapeutic in the reality-based shows *The Bachelor* and *The Bachelorette*.

Reality-based shows often bring together key conventional elements of the therapeutic: self-reflexive comments in displays of the self and an emphasis on talk and confession. On the shows, these activities are carried out under surveillance: viewers watch participants talk directly to the camera about their experiences and what these have taught them about themselves. The combining of surveillance and conventional therapeutic rituals make reality-based television an interesting site to examine emerging trends in therapeutic culture in the United States. In this article, I ask: How is it that the therapeutic comes to rely on surveillance in reality-based television? How are conventional notions of the therapeutic transformed through the use of surveillance?

THE BACHELOR INDUSTRY

The Bachelor is particularly interesting because it is one of the first of the reality-based romance shows and has proven the most enduring in a genre characterized by short-lived programming.[3] The first season of *The Bachelor* started a financially successful series that set the stage for a virtual "Bachelor Industry" (BI), a phrase I use to describe the larger televisual-mediated event that includes twelve seasons of *The Bachelor*, four seasons of *The Bachelorette*, and many related program specials in the United States. I use the term *industry* to gesture beyond the economic success of the shows: so successful have been *The Bachelor* and *The Bachelorette* that an industry is needed to support and bolster its imperatives and put into operation its ideals. Hence, although the BI shows are financially successful, they are also part of an industry that produces, sustains, and technologizes specific ideas and dynamics. This article focuses on the mechanisms used by the BI to perpetuate ideas about the therapeutic.

The Bachelor allows a man (a different one each season) to select from among twenty-five eligible women, over an eight-week period, one woman to be his potential wife. The main action revolves around the bachelor whittling down the pool of twenty-five eligible women to his final selection. At the end of each episode, there is a rose ceremony in which the bachelor offers a rose to each of the participants he wants to remain on the show. Between rose ceremonies, participants go on group dates with the bachelor, and a lucky few go on individual dates. On *The Bachelorette*, the format is the same, except the star of the series is a woman, and she picks one man, out of twenty-five eligible bachelors, to be her potential husband. Of course, at the rose ceremonies, the bachelorette offers the men rose boutonnières instead of long-stemmed roses.

The BI has proven a ratings success. The first season of *The Bachelor* aired in March 2002 and the September 7–13, 2002 issue of *TV Guide* declared that "if television were the World Series, *The Bachelor* would be voted ABC's Most Valuable Player" (P. 36). Over its first five seasons, *The Bachelor* "averaged 11.3 million to 16.7 million viewers" (Oldenburg 2004). The premiere of the first season of *The Bachelorette* in January 2003 pulled in 17.44 million viewers, beating an original episode of *The West Wing*, which drew 13.96 million viewers (Rogers 2003). In spring 2004, *The Bachelor* was ABC's top-ranked show, with the exception of *Monday Night Football* (Rogers 2004). The ratings success of the BI shows translates into sizeable monetary gains for the network. According to an article on *Forbes* online, *The Bachelor* and *The Bachelorette* are among the top five most profitable U.S. reality-based shows, with *The Bachelor* pulling in a network profit of $38.2 million for the fourth season (with a price tag of $231,400 per thirty-second advertising spot) and *The Bachelorette* pulling in a network profit of $27.7 million for the second season (with a price tag of $178,000 per thirty-second advertising spot) (Patsuris 2004). *The Bachelorette*, however, suffered a decline in ratings for both the second and third seasons (Lisotta 2005, 10–11), but nonetheless aired a fourth season in spring 2008. Although there was a decline in viewers for the fifth, sixth, and seventh seasons of *The Bachelor* (Azote 2006), viewership increased for the eighth season (Azote 2006). And while ratings for for the ninth season were lower, they were high enough for ABC to renew the show for a tenth season (Rogers 2006). The season finale of the tenth season averaged 12.7 million viewers, winning its time slot (Rocchio and Rogers 2007). ABC aired an eleventh season of *The Bachelor* in fall 2007, a twelfth in spring 2008, and has plans for a thirteenth in January 2009. TV analyst John Rash suggests that "while the 'Bachelor' may never be the cultural phenomenon it was in its first few iterations, its ratings have stabilized and it remains a strategic component of ABC's schedule"(Azote 2006).

REALITY-BASED PROGRAMMING

As I have written elsewhere (Dubrofsky 2006, 4), the term *reality-based* refers to TV shows that are unscripted, though most have a very specific structure (with set tasks and events for each episode). The term implies that the shows are based on reality without suggesting that they are reality—emphasizing the constructedness not only of reality-based programming but also of TV representations more generally. My analysis assumes that what occurs on reality-based shows is a constructed fiction, like the action on scripted shows, with the twist that real people create the fiction of the series. In other words, reality-based shows use footage of "real" people in "real" situations to create a fictional text, while scripted shows use a script to create the action. What happens on reality-based shows is not, of course, a representation of what "really" happened (if this can ever be accessed). The narrative is constructed by TV workers, sometimes using a tiny percentage of footage actually shot. The production and editing process involved in creating a reality-based series is integral to the story that will be told on a reality-based show. My use of the term *reality* assumes that reality is contingent on a given context: it is contextually based. I do not believe there is an essential "real" that can be accessed but rather that there are versions of reality based on the logic arising from a given context.

THE THERAPEUTIC AND TELEVISION

Few scholars discuss the therapeutic on television (with the exception of Cloud 1998; Peck 1995; Shattuc 1997; White 1992, 2002), and almost none discuss the intersection of the therapeutic and contemporary reality-based shows (with the exception of Andrejevic 2004). In addition, neither the scholarship on television and the therapeutic nor scholarship on the therapeutic in contemporary Western culture[4] fully account for one of the particular ways that participants on reality-based shows articulate the therapeutic: the process of affirming a consistent (unchanged) self across disparate social spaces, verified by surveillance. I label this process the "therapeutics of the self".

Traditional models of the therapeutic assume a desire to change the self alongside the imperative to accept or affirm the self; self-acceptance or affirmation is never the only or the main goal. In the Alcoholics Anonymous (AA) model of the therapeutic, for example, although the process involves accepting the self, it is also, most importantly, about being vigilant to change the self and not act on one's essential identity as an alcoholic.[5] Scholarship on therapeutic culture in the West notes that therapeutic discourse emphasizes solving social, political, and structural problems by focusing on changing the self (Cloud 1998; Peck 1995; Shattuc 1997; White 1992, 2002). For instance, Dana Cloud (1998) writes that the therapeutic has transformed political and cultural discourses using the language of psychotherapy, what she calls "the conservative language of healing, coping, adaptation, and restoration of a previously existing order" (P. xiv). Cloud's definition of the therapeutic is in line, very generally, with that used by many scholars studying the therapeutic in Western culture. Specifically, the work one must perform on the self involves healing, coping, and adapting. Cloud cites an example in which, "in response to what Susan Faludi has called an antifeminist backlash in popular culture and politics, feminist activist Gloria Steinem came out with a new plan for a 'revolution from within' based on self-esteem" (P. xii).[6] In essence, to cure our culture of antifeminism, we need to work on feeling better about ourselves, on bolstering our self-esteem. Hence, social, political, and economic problems are turned into personal problems that can be solved by an individual who is willing to work on him- or herself.

THERAPEUTICS OF THE SELF

The "therapeutics of the self" traces a subtle shift from conventional models of the therapeutic. People enacting the "therapeutics of the self" are not, as they are in therapeutic models, admitting something "bad" about the self to change this "bad" part (as in the AA model) or responding to larger social or political problems by focusing on changing the self (as in the Steinem example), but rather, they admit something "good" about the self and embrace it or admit that one's "true" and "authentic" self is good (no matter what that self is like). While in the BI there are instances of people admitting "bad" things about themselves and the need to change these, there are also many instances in which people embrace who they are no matter how "good" or "bad"—these two things can coexist, but the focus of this article is on the latter, as it has yet to be discussed by scholars.

In reality-based shows, surveillance plays a key role in the therapeutic process I outline. According to Mark Andrejevic (2004), surveillance is often twinned with self-expression and the therapeutic in contemporary popular culture to prove self-knowledge. Andrejevic looks at this phenomena through the example of Jennifer Ringley, who put herself on display on the world wide web via a web camera named the "Jennicam" and provided commentary on her experiences with the Jennicam. This example helps illustrate the trend in therapeutic culture I am outlining. Andrejevic writes:

> Ringley sees herself as an advertisement for the personal benefits of self-disclosure: "I think most of what people go into private to hide—their bodies, their silly habits, their insecurities—is only doing more harm than good by being hidden. . . . I'm not doing Jennicam to show the world my details necessarily, but hopefully to show generally that owning up to these things isn't a bad thing, it's great!" Voluntary submission to comprehensive surveillance becomes a therapeutic experience. (P. 86)

There are some striking assertions made by Ringley that suggest a notion of the therapeutic that is counterintuitive. Her comments point to remarkable slippages between a therapeutically transformed self and an unchanged self. Implicitly, she affirms that not changing the self provides a therapeutic good. Framed in the language of therapy ("insecurities," "owning up to things"), Ringley's articulation of the benefits of putting herself under surveillance is not about how exposing her private self has transformed or changed her self for the better. For Ringley, the benefits are that she has exposed her "real" (private, "true") self, that she has not changed or modified this self under surveillance, that she will proudly display who she "really" is (who she is in private as well as in public),[7] and that recognition of herself as consistent is therapeutic.

An improved self, what a therapeutic experience generally signifies, is not the value of the experience Ringley claims. Rather, the importance is in the act of exposure and in the display of self-consistency across disparate social spaces. Surveillance comes to play a key role in Ringley's therapeutic experience. In fact, surveillance is here subservient to the therapeutic, which is a common trend in the BI and many reality-based shows.

What I term the "therapeutics of the self" builds on the popular trend in therapeutic culture in which subjects are constantly incited to work on (change) the self, but adds a layer in that the impetus is to assert a consistent (unchanged) self as therapeutic. I use the term *therapeutics* because the assertion of the self is often made using paradigms and terms from therapy, implicitly suggesting that the affirmation of a consistent self will yield the rewards of a therapeutic transformation. This use of the discourse of therapy, I argue, requires an expansion of current scholarship on the therapeutic to account for the implications of this trend, a trend that promotes stasis. Current scholarship argues that therapeutic discourse encourages individuals to focus on changing the self rather than cast a critical eye on larger social structures. My analysis adds to this the idea of being content with the self—not changing the self. The affirmation of self-consistency works in a therapeutic capacity because it is framed as a therapeutic transformation. Now therapeutic subjects can be content with who they are *and* with the state of the world around them. There is no impetus to change anything, but rather, people are invited to learn to become comfortable with things as they are.

Although this article uses the reality-based romance[8] shows *The Bachelor* and *The Bachelorette* as a lens through which to discuss the "therapeutics of the self," arguably this trend can be seen in many other reality-based shows. I chose these shows because they are among the most successful and longest running in the reality-based genre. As well, because the focus of the shows is on romantic relationships, there is an explicit emphasis on people's feelings and emotions, which are often expressed using therapeutic language and paradigms. But most importantly, structuring the argument within the framework of *The Bachelor* and *The Bachelorette* allows me to develop a nuanced, focused, and detailed analysis of the mechanics of the "therapeutics of the self."

THE SPECIAL: "THE WOMEN TELL ALL," "THE MEN TELL ALL," AND "AFTER THE FINAL ROSE"

I focus primarily on statements made during the specials "The Women Tell All," "The Men Tell All," and "After the Final Rose" because this is where participants articulate an assessment of their actions on the series.[9] The series frames this assessment as influenced by the insight afforded by a period of reflection and the viewing of aired episodes—participants are able to offer an overall evaluation of themselves on the series.

The series constructs the specials like a "time-out," a moment when we get to hear participants comment directly on their experiences, reflect on their presentation of self, and answer questions from the studio audience, the host, and fellow participants. "The Women/Men Tell All" is the second-to-last episode aired in the season, before the finale. When this special airs, we do not know whom the star (the bachelor or bachelorette) has chosen. "After the Final Rose" airs once the series ends.

The specials are in "talk show" format, taped in front of a live studio audience. The host, Chris Harrison, interviews participants, and audience members ask them questions. In "The Women/Men Tell All," all rejected participants from that season are present except the final two participants selected by the star.[10] Participants who were most recently eliminated, and those who became central on a season are invited onstage.[11] Toward the end of the special, the star of the season is brought onstage to be interviewed by the host and answer questions from participants and from the audience. In the special "After the Final Rose," the host usually interviews the final runner-up alone and then the star for that season. The interviews are conducted onstage or in a room behind the stage. The series then reunites the happy couple for that season, and the host interviews them together onstage.

In the specials, immediately after the host invites a participant onstage, the series airs a montage of clips of the participant in selected moments from episodes aired. The host then asks the participant to reflect on his or her experiences on the series, explicitly suggesting that an edited montage of surveillance footage can capture a person's experiences in a given context. Although the series depicts participants as having complete autonomy in how they present themselves under surveillance (in the aired footage from the series), it elides the editing and production process and how these factor into the representation of participants. Thus, during the montage sequence, the series does not mention the process (involving many choices by workers on the show) of putting together the montage, let alone of assembling each episode in the series.[12]

THERAPEUTICS OF THE SELF IN THE BI

Now a look at how the "therapeutics of the self" work in the BI. In "The Women Tell All" special on the second season of *The Bachelor*, Gwen Gioia, third runner-up, eliminated the previous week, tells the host, in a some-times wavering voice, that as far as she and Aaron Buerge (the bachelor) are concerned, there are "so many unanswered issues, so many things I'd like to ask him that I don't have clarity on." When asked by the host if she feels her past divorce was a factor in her not receiving a rose, she answers, "Look, it's who I am, it's what made me who I am. I learned a lot from that and it made me look at who I am, and it made me look at relationships. So, either he [Aaron] likes me for who I am or he doesn't."

Gwen uses therapeutic language to maintain a sense of self, her pride in her self and her self-knowledge: I have confessed myself adequately, I have shown my emotions, I have revealed my inner feelings, and I have been (on the show) who I truly am in "real" life, consistently and unchanged. My reward, if nothing else, is that I am who I am. Gwen affirms that she is comfortable with who she is and that she ultimately loves herself (even if the bachelor does not). Although Gwen is eliminated before claiming the bachelor as her prize, she does not go home empty-handed: she knows who she is and is confident in who she has displayed under surveillance, and this knowledge, the series suggests, will accomplish a therapeutic good.

Bob Guiney, one of the bachelors on the first season of *The Bachelorette* and the starring bachelor on the fourth season of *The Bachelor*, provides another useful example of how a participant's experiences in the BI are claimed as therapeutic, especially in the book he wrote *What a Difference a Year Makes: How Life's Unexpected Setbacks Can Lead to Unexpected Joy* (2003). No other BI participant has published a book specifically about his or her experience on the series.[13] Throughout the book, Bob asserts the importance of the affirmation of a consistent self:

> I had been myself on the show, and that was the important thing. I've never tried to pretend I'm something I'm not. It isn't hard for me to act natural, because who I am at heart has been pretty much unchanged since I was a kid. I'm not a complicated person. I have never taken myself too seriously, and that's the way I was on the show. (P. 134)

Bob maintains that while on *The Bachelorette* he never pretended to be someone he was not, that he always acted naturally and that he remained consistent as a person—unchanged since he was a kid. Bob does not, in this quotation or in the book, explicitly frame his experience as therapeutic. But the book is presented as a therapeutic tool. It reveals how much Bob has learned and grown from the past year of his life (evidenced by the title of the book), a year marked by a divorce and his appearance in the BI shows. He finds great value in his experiences and hopes others will as well. In the introduction, Bob explains that the publisher of the book felt that sharing his experience "might inspire others who needed help recovering from a broken heart" (P. 3). He says, "if what I learned can help you lift yourself up at a time when you might be feeling a little down, nothing would make me happier" (Guiney 2003, 3). Bob learned something and changed as a result of the experience. This, of course, contradicts his statement that he has been the same person since childhood, but the contradiction is reconciled with the "therapeutics of the self." What Bob has learned is that he is the same man he has always been, and what he gains through this realization is contentment.

Part of what Bob learns is how to affirm a consistent self, which yields a therapeutic result—helps him live a better life, transforms him so he can move on from the sadness of his divorce, and this helps others do the same (or so he and his publisher anticipate). Of his impending appearance on the fourth season of *The Bachelor*, he says, "Who knows? I'm going into it with an honest and open heart, ready to see what happens. If nothing else, it's bound to be a valuable learning experience, just like every other thing that's happened to me over the past year or so" (Guiney 2003, 153). Toward the end of the book, Bob writes, "People often ask my friends how all this media attention has changed me, and I've heard them say it hasn't changed me at all—and that's a huge compliment" (Guiney 2003, 143). Paradoxically, Bob's book is both an expostulation on how much he has been transformed for the better by his experiences and an elaboration of how he has remained true to himself, been the same all his life: about how much he has *not* changed.

Both Gwen and Bob use the language of therapy. Gwen says she and Aaron have "unanswered issues," she feels she needs "clarity," and she talks about how her experiences in life have taught her much about herself and relationships. Bob claims his time on the show has been a valuable learning experience. Bob and Gwen strongly affirm who they are and claim that they will not change. Gwen says, "Either he likes me for who I am"; Bob says he remains "unchanged since I was a kid," "it [the BI] hasn't changed me at all." Both believe they have consistently displayed their "true" selves under surveillance (consistently been the same self while in the BI and in "real" life). Whether or not they are able to access the rewards of love through the BI, they have earned the reward of knowing who they are and they are proud of who they are.

SURVEILLANCE IN THE SERVICE OF THE THERAPEUTIC

Michel Foucault did not discuss the intersection of confession, the therapeutic, and surveillance of the self on camera, but his elaboration of the historical role of confession is useful for an analysis of how surveillance works in the service of the therapeutic in the BI. This is because one of the central activities surveilled[14] in the shows is a participant confessing, and the participant often uses therapeutic language to do so. However, this public confession is highly mediated. Although participants articulate the "therapeutics of the self" as an accomplishment carried out by revealing (confessing) their "true" and "real" self (as Gwen and Bob posit), as reality-based shows are the result of many hours of labor by television workers, the "therapeutics of the self" is realized through the technology of surveillance and through the editing and production process.

I begin by reframing Foucault's (1990) ideas about confession, to extend these to an understanding of surveillance as a technology of confession. Foucault writes that confession is required by an "other":

> for one does not confess without the presence (or virtual presence) of a partner who is not simply the interlocutor but the authority who requires the confession, prescribes and appreciates it, and intervenes in order to judge, punish, forgive, console, and reconcile; a ritual in which the truth is corroborated by the obstacles and resistances it has had to surmount in order to be formulated; and finally, a ritual in which the expression alone, independently of its external consequences, produces intrinsic modifications in the person who articulates it: it exonerates, redeems, and purifies him; it unburdens him of his wrongs, liberates him, and promises him salvation. (P. 62)

Confession, Foucault notes, is always part of a dynamic between two or more presences—one of which can be virtual. Surveillance fits the same mold—it is always required by an other (virtual or real), someone who will watch. In the BI, interestingly, a participant can also occupy the position of watcher by viewing footage of him- or herself on the series and doing this while on the specials (when viewing montages). All that is surveilled by the cameras can be used to confess the self, and all that is selected during the editing and production process can be used to represent a confessed self. How the self is ultimately confessed on reality-based shows is contingent on how the show constructs a participant under surveillance once the editing and production process is complete.

Foucault (1990) writes that the ritual of confession changes the person who is confessing: "it exonerates, redeems, and purifies him; it unburdens him of his wrongs, liberates him, and promises him salvation" (P. 62). In the BI, it is the representation of the confessed self under surveillance that does this work (aided by the production process). This is articulated most clearly by participants on the specials when they reflect on their tenure on the series. Indeed, the narrative in the series is built around how well or poorly participants confess themselves under surveillance: Have they done so "well enough" to gain access to the rewards of the series? Well enough to claim the "therapeutics of the self"?

The presence of the cameras, the constant knowledge of surveillance, also means that participants self-discipline. Briefly, I turn to Foucault's

(1995) notion of the panopticon to explain how this works. He argues that the panoptic structure's imperative is

> to permit an internal, articulated and detailed control—to render visible those who are inside it . . . an architecture that would operate to transform individuals: to act on those it shelters, to provide a hold on their conduct, to carry the effects of power right to them, to make it possible to know them, alter them. Stones can make people docile and knowable. (P. 172)

Although the environment in which the action of the reality-based show takes place is not panoptic in its architecture, strategically placed cameras and participants' knowledge that what they say and do will be on camera perform work similar to that of the panopticon.[15] In this sense, participants self-monitor, police themselves, like the inhabitants of the panopticon. In the BI shows (and in many reality-based shows), those inside the surveilled environment are completely visible first to the crew of the show and then, in an edited version, to the television public and to themselves. The fact that their every move can be recorded by a camera works to control the activities of participants, to transform them in some sense: they know they are being watched and that they are there to be watched, which serves to regulate their behavior.

Most important for my argument is how participants' behavior is quite literally disciplined through the production and editing process, which makes "it possible to know them, alter them" (Foucault 1995, 172). Although Foucault suggests that "stones can make people docile and knowable" (Foucault 1995, 172), cameras, and the editing of surveilled images that is part of producing reality-based television, can also "make people docile and knowable" (Foucault 1995, 172). In this instance, people become knowable to others and to themselves through the use of the technology of surveillance to confess the self, which performs a therapeutic good.

But what is the therapeutic good realized through this process? Mimi White (1992) outlines the main imperative of therapeutic discourse in U.S. culture as a "process of therapeutic engagement" (P. 12), where the therapeutic cure itself has become less important. What is most important are the therapeutic strategies to help people negotiate the problems in their lives, not finding a final cure (White 1992, 12). White maintains the importance, in the therapeutic process, of confession and social subjectivity: "recognition, acknowledgement, and confession of these problems—even to oneself—play a crucial role in the process. In other words, therapy has come to refer to the processes of negotiating and working through one's social subjectivity" (White 1992, 12). She suggests that on television, the therapeutic dynamic, which was traditionally a "private exchange between two individuals—in a church or a doctor's office, for example"

(White 1992, 9), has become "a public event, staged by the technological and signifying conventions of the television apparatus" (White 1992, 9). In reality-based television, this dynamic happens through the use of the technology of surveillance, allowing participants to have a therapeutic interaction with a virtual other in public.[16] This virtual other can take several forms: the camera, the audience, and, most important for this article, participants watching clips of themselves on the specials.

In the BI, an important part of the "television apparatus" (to use White's words) is surveillance. Andrejevic (2004) writes that in reality-based television, there is a "euphoric rhetoric of experience" (P. 145) that equates "surveillance with self-fulfillment: that being watched all the time serves to intensify one's experiences, and thereby to facilitate self-growth and self-knowledge" (P. 145). Hence, participants on reality-based shows articulate their experiences under surveillance as good because being on the series has been a learning experience with some kind of therapeutic end. Andrejevic (2004) suggests that revealing the self under surveillance is a means of proving—verifying—one's self-knowledge and self-awareness and that this works in a therapeutic capacity (P. 143). However, he does not note the importance of affirming self-sameness across disparate spaces—key in the BI (and in other media as well, as we see with the Jennicam example above), where participants affirm that who they are in the clips, on the aired episodes, onstage now (in the specials), and in their real lives is who they "really" are. This affirmation of consistency across disparate social spaces, verified by surveillance, is what allows participants to claim the "therapeutics of the self" and enables the therapeutic process White describes: participants view footage of themselves and recognize, acknowledge, and confess in public and to themselves who they are (White 1992, 11). Surveillance becomes a strategy that, to use White's words about the therapeutic, helps "people negotiate the problems in their lives" (White 1992, 12). The problem that is solved or rather, the need met by surveillance and confession is to publicly affirm self-consistency: to prove to oneself and to others that one is consistent.

Here is an example to illustrate how surveillance, confession, and the production and editing process come together to perform a therapeutic good. In the "After the Final Rose" special for the fifth season of *The Bachelor*, the host speaks with Tara Huckeby, the runner-up for the affections of the bachelor, Jesse Palmer. After bringing her onstage, he introduces a montage of clips with the words, "let's take a look at your journey on the bachelor,"[17] suggesting that this edited montage represents the entirety of her time on the series and, concomitantly, herself (her "real" self). This montage serves as the opening point to a conversation about how Tara feels about her presentation of self on the series.

After the montage is screened, the host says to Tara, "We saw you and Jesse slowly falling in love. And it took you a while to open up, but finally you did. Did you love Jesse?" Tara responds, "Um, I think I did fall in love with him. Um, I definitely, I was very happy at the time and I would have said yes to him." The host then comments, "One of the things that, ah, everyone has talked to me about is how well you spoke your mind to Jesse. Do you feel proud of the way you handled it?" to which Tara responds, "It's not necessarily that I'm proud of it. I just think that's who I am. If I have something to say to somebody, I'm gonna say it. I just, you know, I hope somebody else would do the same." The host interrupts her to comment, "You did say something that stuck with me, that I thought was really sad, because you said 'this always seems to happen to me.'" Tara says, "Ah, yeah, I always seem to be, um, in that relationship that just never works for the very worst reasons." The host then says, "The impression I got the final night, you did all the talking. He got away with a lot of listening and head shaking," and Tara responds, "I think I pretty much put everything out there that night. I don't think I left anything unsaid (laughing)."

By having Tara comment on her experiences immediately after showing a montage, the show situates her not only as commenting on the representation of herself but also as asserting that this representation is of her "real" self. In so doing, Tara affirms the consistency between how she is represented on the series and who she is in real life—"I just think that's who I am. If I have something to say to somebody, I'm gonna say it"—and that the events on the show were consistent with events in her life ("I always seem to be . . . in that relationship that just never works")—but also that the entire process of the BI (surveillance, editing, production) can do the work of representing a "real" consistent self.

Tara is enacting the "therapeutics of the self," but the series shows her demonstrating very little self-consciousness about the constructed nature of the moments that figure in the final televisual product.[18] Tara reveals herself in many different ways on the series. It is not simply that she revealed her feelings through confession, by speaking (not leaving "anything unsaid"), but that she confessed herself through her surveilled behavior: by taking her time to open up to the process, by falling in love with the bachelor, by speaking her mind.

As Tara comments on her presentation of self, she reflects on the process of surveillance—how well she appeared under surveillance, how well she confessed through the technology of surveillance, and how well she was represented through the editing and production process. And ultimately, she comments that this process was therapeutic because it affirmed self-sameness.

Here, we see television verifying a self as "authentic" and the production, editing, and all the work that goes into creating a show becoming a "natural" way of doing this under surveillance. Concomitantly, television works as a therapeutic tool: the verification of authenticity under surveillance instills confidence that one is always consistent, and knowledge (and proof) of this results in a therapeutic good.

CONSISTENCY IN REPRESENTING THE SELF

Trish Schneider's behavior on the fifth season of *The Bachelor* is one of the most striking examples of how asserting a consistent self under surveillance is represented as a good in and of itself. She is self-reflective about her presentation of self, and though the series constructs her as a dislikeable woman, it also shows her being unabashedly her "real" self at all times; and so she emerges as admirable for her ability to enact the "therapeutics of the self." The creators paint Trish as the villainess of the season: on the first episode of the season, before we meet Trish, the host warns that she will be the most hated bachelorette ever. In the "Women Tell All" special, the host describes her as the "most despised woman in *Bachelor* history."

The series puts Trish center stage. She is embroiled in most of the narrative action. In an unprecedented move, producers bring Trish back to the show, after being eliminated the previous week, to try to win back the bachelor (he turns her down). In the "Women Tell All" special, the host interviews Trish first, and her interview lasts as long as that of the most recently eliminated woman (Trish was eliminated two episodes earlier) and as long as the interview with the bachelor. Trish figures prominently in most of the discussions, even when she is no longer onstage. Many of the questions posed to participants are about their feelings about Trish. In the special "After the Final Rose," in another unprecedented move, the series brings Trish onstage. Generally, the only participants who appear on this special are the second runner-up, the final woman or man chosen by the star of the season, and the star. Indeed, the special opens with a "candid" behind-the-scenes discussion between Trish and the host about her plans to confront a fellow participant, the second runner-up, Tara—the same Tara as in the earlier example.

Once Tara and Trish are brought together onstage, we are shown a montage of clips of each woman talking about the other woman. In sum, Tara calls Trish a "slut," "pond scum," "unattractive," and "disgusting" and says that Trish has "no morals or values." Trish calls Tara a "spoilt and sheltered brat" and "a bitch" and says that Tara "spits venom," is "too young," is "insecure," is "ugly on the inside," has a lot of "issues," and puts on a "good front" but is "not nice" behind the scenes. The discussion onstage centers not on the specific comments made by each of the women but rather on whether they have presented consistent selves on the series, hence giving Trish the advantage. Trish accuses Tara of saying things behind Trish's back and of being "two-faced," of acting nice, prim, and proper in one setting but being completely different in another. Trish claims she is a better person than Tara because she can stand by what she has said on camera. In Trish's words, "I've been the same person the entire time on this show and in my life. I am the same person." Tara responds by claiming that she also stands by who she was on camera: "I speak my mind. I don't think there's anything wrong with speaking your mind," to which Trish responds, "But you wait until I leave the room to speak your mind. That's the difference." Trish adds, "You actually went so far out of your way to say these things. I didn't say anything like that about you . . . I'm sorry . . . you radiate unhappiness. I know who I am and I like who I am."

Trish's last statement ("I'm sorry . . . I like who I am") illustrates the ways that knowledge of the self and the ability to assert a consistent self under surveillance translates into performing a therapeutic good. Trish equates what she perceives to be Tara's unhappiness with Tara's inability to be consistently herself under surveillance and equates her own satisfaction with and her knowledge of herself with being consistent under surveillance. The display of a consistent self is articulated by Trish as a healthy self and, indeed, a therapeutic self, allowing her to know and like who she is.[19] Although Trish clearly failed to access the explicit rewards of the series (finding love) and although she is represented as disliked by virtually everyone on the show, the focus is not on the kind of self that has been represented but on whether this self is consistent and "real" under surveillance—that is, consistent on the series and consistent with who Trish is in "real" life.

The series gives Trish substantial airtime to assert the "therapeutics of the self" and to receive kudos from fellow participants for her ability to display a consistent and "real" self under surveillance. Jean-Marie, another participant, says during "The Women Tell All" special:

> I commend Trish. [And says to Trish] this is the only thing I commend you for, is being who you are . . . be who you are, and this is what I commend you for the whole time. You said I want this, this is what I want, don't fold in now honey, if that's who you are, stick with it.

Another bachelorette on this same special, DeShawn, says of Trish, "She's completely held her ground, stood by who she is. You may not agree with it, but we all have our skeletons." Furthermore, Jenny, the bachelor's spy in the house (a first on the series: Jenny lives with the women and pretends she is vying for the bachelor's affections when really she is a friend of the bachelor's), when asked by the host about her thoughts on Trish, says Trish is the wrong person for the bachelor because Trish does not have the right values to make a good wife for the bachelor. In other words, Trish is unsuitable for the bachelor because she is "truly" a bad match for him: she revealed herself to be the wrong kind of person for the bachelor.

Because Trish has been able to affirm a consistent self—she affirms it in how she assesses her representation on the series, and this is confirmed by fellow participants—she can ultimately feel good about the self confessed under surveillance, even if it is one the series shows nobody liking and that is not a suitable match for the bachelor. Conversely, Tara, whom the series represents as liked by fellow participants, does not fare well on this special because she is unable to defend a consistent self. Indeed, viewers actually see her leaving the stage shortly after the above exchange with Trish, refusing to defend her presentation of self, refusing to claim the "therapeutics of the self". Tara agrees to return to the stage only to complete the final segment of the show, not to continue her exchange with Trish.

EXPANDING THE DEFINITION OF THERAPEUTIC DISCOURCE

What do we make of participants professing that they have been therapeutically transformed by not changing? Bob's, Gwen's, Tara's, and Trish's articulation of their experiences in the BI run counter to the logic of the therapeutic, which demands that the self be transformed as a means of gaining happiness. I am not suggesting that traditional notions of the therapeutic do not occur in the BI. Participants on the series certainly do at times maintain a focus on changing the self. The "therapeutics of the self" and more conventional notions of the therapeutic can occur at the same time: they are not mutually exclusive. I am arguing that we need to expand notions of the therapeutic to include the idea of affirming self-sameness across disparate social spaces and the use of surveillance to verify sameness. This is becoming a part of contemporary therapeutic discourse in the United States, a trend we can see clearly in many reality-based shows. This trend may be a symptom of a shift on TV from a valorization of a therapeutic self to a valorization of a consistent self or to the valorization of a consistent self as therapeutic. Thus, in the BI, the representation of the self unchanged comes to embody idealized therapeutic change. Janice Peck (1995) outlines that "therapeutic discourse proposes that we change ourselves without conceding that our identities and actions are determined by social conditions that will not change just because we interpreted and handled them differently on an individual basis" (P. 75). However, in the "therapeutics of the self," the suggestion is not only that we not focus on the social conditions of our existence but that we not change ourselves, as a verified and affirmed consistent and unchanged self brings about a therapeutic transformation.

The "therapeutics of the self" works to keep people content exactly as they are—to stop any impetus for change,[20] to equate not changing with an important experience that can transform the self for the better. Contentment with social, political, and economic structures is the consequence of traditional notions of therapeutic discourse and of the "therapeutics of the self," but the "therapeutics of the self" adds a new layer by advocating solely for self-knowledge and acceptance. The therapeutic impetus in the "therapeutics of the self" is the process of affirming the self, but the end result is less important. If we learn to be happy with the self as it is and to love this self, then it does not matter what that self is actually like. This is a step beyond what Peck (1995), Cloud (1998), White (1992, 2002), and Jane Shattuc (1997) note and moves us further into stasis, but this time on both the political and the personal front.

NOTES

1. This chapter was reproduced from *Televisions & New Media*, vol. 8, no. 4 (2007).

2. The term *reality-based* designates programming that films "real" people over time with the aim of developing a narrative about their activities segmented into serial episodes. The history of reality-based television and its roots are complicated, as scholars include different types of shows in this category—in addition to the contemporary form of reality-based television (shows such as *Survivor, Big Brother,* and *American Idol*), talk shows and game shows are sometimes included in the genre. My use of the term does not include the latter two types of shows.

3. A season of a reality-based show generally lasts two to three months, with six to twelve episodes. Often in a single year, a reality-based show will air two to three seasons. *The Bachelor* has been on the air for six years, with twelve seasons (and a thirteenth in the works)—a long run compared to most reality-based shows.

4. Please see Bellah et al. (1996), Ben-Yehuda (1990), Cancian (1987), Cushman (1995), DeFranciso and O'Connor (1995), Ehrenreich and English (1978), Gergen (1991), Grodin (1991), Kaminer (1992), Katz (1993), Lasch (1979, 1984), Payne (1989), Rapping (1996), Riessman and Carroll (1995), Schilling and Fuehrer (1993), Simonds (1992, 1996), and Starker (1989).

5. In Alcoholics Anonymous, the twelve steps to recovery emphasize the need to admit there is a problem (drinking), one that causes other problems, and to commit to fixing this problem. Details about the twelve steps can be found online at http://www.alcoholics-anonymous.org/default/en_about_aa_sub.cfm?subpageid=17&pageid=24.

6. Scholars have noted the connection between the self-help movement and neoliberal politics (Cruikshank 1996; Ouellette 2004; Rimke 2000), suggesting that the self-help movement encourages people to learn to take care of themselves and behave as responsible citizens, to self-discipline. Elayne Rapping's (1996) work makes important links between the self-help movement and the women's consciousness-raising movement in the United States, suggesting that the self-help movement borrowed from the women's movement, especially notions of

empowerment. Rapping writes that although the women's movement is about identifying a personal malaise and finding the social cause of the malaise, the self-help movement is about identifying a personal malaise and finding a personal solution (curing the self through work on the self). Steinem inverts this set-up by pointing to the self-help movement to resolve problems traditionally addressed by the women's movement through social and political activism.

7. The private, how one behaves when one is alone, becomes interchangeable with the "real," "true," and "authentic."

8. The term *reality-based romance show* designates reality-based shows that follow the development of a romantic relationship (including dating, engagement, marriage, or other romantic liaisons) over an extended period of time.

9. The tenth season did not include "The Women Tell All" special, and seasons one, seven, eight, and nine did not include the "After the Final Rose" special.

10. On the first season of *The Bachelorette*, a participant was absent (no reason given), and in the fifth season of *The Bachelor*, the special was aired when there were still three women remaining.

11. Presumably, participants invited onstage are those most likely to generate high ratings.

12. The scenes immediately after participants are eliminated (often in the limousine ride as they leave the show) afford insight into how participants feel about their time on the series. However, these reflections are immediate. I am interested in participants' assessments of themselves after a period of reflection and once they have seen aired episodes.

13. Two bachelorettes from the second season of *The Bachelor*, Helene Eksterowicz, the final woman the bachelor selects (they break up shortly after the finale), and Gwen Gioia, the third runner-up, wrote an advice book titled *Nobody's Perfect: What to Do when You've Fallen for a Jerk but You Want to Make it Work* (Eksterowicz and Gioia 2004).

14. Although "surveilled" does not exist as a verb, I use it as such because in reality-based shows, the work done by surveillance is central, productive, and active.

15. On *The Bachelor* web site (http://thebachelor.warnerbros.com/bachelor/eligibility.html), items 9 and 10 of the eligibility requirements stipulate that participants must subject themselves to twenty-four hour surveillance and allow the series to use, as it sees fit, any information it gathers (from footage for the series or from other sources).

16. For instance, the clinical psychoanalytic dynamic is predicated on the construction of a narrative between analyst and analysand, it is "the codification of what takes place in the analytic situation and, more precisely, in the analytic relationship" (Ricoeur 1978, 185). Describing the therapeutic model as it develops in the West after World War II, John Durham Peters (1999) writes that it involves a process between a therapist and a patient to improve communication between the patient and his- or herself. The therapeutic process for participants on the specials mimics the psychoanalytic dynamic and maintains the second part of Peters's therapeutic model: communication with the self.

17. These words are used to introduce most of the montages.

18. Participants in "The Women/Men Tell All" and "After the Final Rose" do at times explicitly reference the difficulties of being under surveillance and of being

in constructed situations (i.e., having to compete with so many other participants for the affections of the star, not having time alone with the star, or having events edited out), but the series does not show this having any impact on participants' assessments of how they were represented on the series.

19. In his discussion of *Big Brother*, Andrejevic (2004) notes that online posters judge participants based on whether they perceive them to be "authentic" in their presentation of self and that the worst way to be "inauthentic" is to be inconsistent (two-faced). He also comments that participants are concerned with presenting a "real" self not tainted by an attempt to "play the game" or strategize (Pp. 117–41).

20. If we view the television text, as Laurie Ouellette and James Hay (Hay 2003; Ouellette 2004; Ouellette and Hay forthcoming) suggest, as a tool for neoliberal lessons about how to live our lives, how to be responsible citizens, then the BI texts tell us we are fine exactly as we are—that is, as long as we can proudly assert who we are and make a claim to consistency across disparate social spaces.

REFERENCES

Andrejevic, Mark. 2002. The Kinder, Gentler Gaze of Big Brother. *New Media & Society* 4: 251–70.

———. 2004. *Reality TV: The Work of Being Watched*. New York: Rowman and Littlefield.

Azote, Abigail. 2006. Heart, Be Still: ABC's "Bachelor" Revives. *Media Life*. <http://www.medialifemagazine.com/cgi-bin/artman/exec/view.cgi?archive=170&num=3309> (accessed March 8, 2006).

Bellah, Robert N., Richard Madsen, William M. Sullivan, Ann Swindler, and Ateven M. Tipton. 1996. *Habits of the Heart: Individualism and Commitment in American Life*. Los Angeles: University of California Press.

Ben-Yehuda, Nachman. 1990. *The Politics and Morality of Deviance: Moral Panics, Drug Abuse, Deviant Science and Reversed Stigmatization*. Albany: State University of New York Press.

Brenton, Sam, and Reuben Cohen. 2003. *Shooting People: Adventures in Reality TV*. New York: Verso.

Cancian, Francesca M. 1987. *Love in America: Gender and Self-Development*. Cambridge, UK: Cambridge University Press.

Cloud, Dana L. 1998. *Control and Consolation in American Culture and Politics: Rhetoric of Therapy*. London: Sage.

Corner, John. 2002. Performing the Real: Documentary Diversions. *Television & New Media* 3 (August): 255–70.

Couldry, Nick. 2002. Playing for Celebrity: *Big Brother* as Ritual Event. *Television & New Media* 3 (August): 284–91.

Cruikshank, Barbara. 1996. Revolutions Within: Self-Government and Self-Esteem. In *Foucault and Political Reason: Liberalism, Neoliberalism, and Rationalities of Government*, ed. Andrew Barry, Thomas Osborne, and Nikolas Rose, 231–51. Chicago: Chicago University Press.

Cushman, Phillip. 1995. *Constructing the Self, Constructing America: A Cultural History of Psychotherapy*. Boston: Addison-Wesley.

DeFranciso, Victoria Leto, and Penny O'Connor. 1995. A Feminist Critique of Self-Help Books on Heterosexual Romance: Read'em and Weep. *Women's Studies in Communication* 18: 217–27.

Dovey, Jon. 2000. *Freakshow: First Person Media and Factual Television*. London: Pluto.

Dubrofsky, Rachel E. 2006. The Bachelor: Whiteness in the harem. *Critical Studies in Media Communication* 23: 39-56.

Ehrenreich, Barbara, and Deirdre English. 1978. *For Her Own Good: 150 years of Expert's Advice to Women*. New York: Anchor Press.

Eksterowicz, Helene, and Gwen Gioia. 2004. *Nobody's Perfect: What to Do When You've Fallen for a Jerk but You Want to Make it Work*. New York: CDS Books.

Foucault, Michel. 1990. *The History of Sexuality: An Introduction, Volume 1*. New York: Vintage Books.

———. 1995. *Discipline and Punish: The Birth of the Prison*. New York: Vintage Books.

Gergen, Kenneth J. 1991. *The Saturated Self: Dilemmas of Identity in Contemporary Life*. New York: Basic Books.

Glynn, Kevin. 2000. *Tabloid Culture*. London: Duke University Press.

Grodin, Debra. 1991. The Interpreting Audience: The Therapeutics of Self-Help Book Reading. *Critical Studies in Mass Communication* 8: 404–20.

Guiney, Bob. 2003. *What a Difference a Year Makes: How Life's Unexpected Setbacks Can Lead to Unexpected Joy*. Los Angeles: Tarcher.

Hay, James. 2003. Unaided Virtues: The (Neo)Liberalization of the Domestic Sphere and the New Architecture of Community. In *Foucault, Cultural Studies and Governmentality*, ed. Jack Z. Bratich, Jeremy Packer, and Cameron McCarthy, 165–206. New York: State University Press of New York.

Hill, Annette. 2002. *Big Brother*: The Real Audience. *Television & New Media* 3 (August): 323–40.

Kaminer, Wendy. 1992. *I'm Dysfunctional, You're Dysfunctional: The Recovery Movement and Other Self-Help Fashions*. New York: Addison-Wesley.

Katz, Alfred H. 1993. *Self-Help in America : A Social Movement Perspective*. New York: Twayne.

Kilborn, Richard. 2003. *Staging the Real: Factual TV Programming in the Age of "Big Brother."* New York: Manchester University Press.

Lasch, Christopher. 1979. *The Culture of Narcissism*. New York: W.W. Norton and Company.

———. 1984. *The Minimal Self: Psychic Survival in Troubled Times*. New York: W.W. Norton.

Lisotta, Christopher. 2005. Is Honeymoon Over for ABC's "Bachelor"? *Broadcasting & Cable*, April 18: 10–11, 16, 24.

McGrath, John E. 2004. *Loving* Big Brother*: Performance, Privacy and Surveillance Space*. New York: Routledge.

Murray, Susan, and Laurie Ouellette. 2004. Introduction. In *Reality TV: Remaking Television Culture*, ed. Susan Murray and Laurie Ouellette, 1–18. New York: New York University Press.

Oldenburg, Ann. 2004 "The Bachelor" Tries New Twists. *USA Today*. <http://www.usatoday.com/life/television/ reviews/ 2004–09–21-bachelor_x.htm> (accessed September 21, 2004).

Ouellette, Laurie. 2004. "Take Responsibility for Yourself": *Judge Judy* and the Neoliberal Citizen. In *Reality TV: Remaking Television Culture*, ed. Susan Murray and Laurie Ouellette, 231–50. New York: New York University Press.

Ouellette, Laurie, and James Hay. 2008. *Television for Living*. Malden, MA: Blackwell.

Palmer, Gareth. 2002. *Big Brother*: An Experiment in Governance. *Television & New Media* 3 (August): 295–310.

Patsuris, Penelope. 2004. The Most Profitable Reality TV Shows. *Forbes*. <http://www.forbes.com/home/business/2004/ 09/07/cx_pp_0907realitytv.html> (accessed September 7, 2004).

Payne, David. 1989. *Coping with Failure: The Therapeutic Uses of Rhetoric*. Columbia: University of South Carolina Press.

Peck, Janice. 1995. TV Talk Shows as Therapeutic Discourse: The Ideological Labor of the Televised Talking Cure. *Communication Theory* 5 (February): 1, 58–81.

Pecora, Vincent P. 2002. The Culture of Surveillance. *Qualitative Sociology* 25: 345–58.

Peters, John D. 1999. *Speaking into the Air: A History of the Idea of Communication*. Chicago: University of Chicago Press.

Rapping, Elayne. 1996. *The Culture of Recovery: Making Sense of the Recovery Movement in Women's Lives*. Boston: Beacon.

Ricoeur, Paul. 1978. *The Philosophy of Paul Ricoeur*. Boston: Beacon.

Riessman, Frank, and David Carroll. 1995. *Redefining Self-Help: Policy and Practice*. San Francisco: Jossey-Bass.

Rimke, Heidi Marie. 2000. Governing Citizens through Self-Help Literature. *Cultural Studies* 14: 1, 61–78.

Rocchio, Christopher, and Steve Rogers. 2007. The Bachelor: Officer and a Gentleman *Ends with a Ratings Bang*. <http://www.realitytvworld.com/news/the-bachelor-officer-and-gentleman-ends-with-ratings-bang-5263.php> (accessed May 31, 2007).

Rogers, Steve. 2003. *"Star Search," "Bachelorette," & "Celebrity Mole"* Continue Week Of Strong Reality TV Show Ratings Premieres. <http://www.realitytvworld .com/index/articles/story.php?s=859> (accessed April 28, 2004).

———. 2004. ABC Orders Two More *The Bachelor* Installments for 2004–05 Schedule. Accessed April 28, 2004, from <http://www.realitytvworld.com/index/articles/story.php?s=2525>

———. 2006. *Report: ABC Greenlights Production of a Tenth 'The Bachelor' Edition*. <http://www.realitytvworld.com/news/ report-abc-greenlights-production-of-tenth-the-bachelor-edition-4423.php> (accessed November 17, 2006).

Ross, K., and S. Moorti, eds. 2004a. Commentary and Criticism: Introduction. *Feminist Media Studies* 4 (2): 203–31.

Ross, K., and S. Moorti, eds. 2004b. Commentary and Criticism: Introduction. *Feminist Media Studies* 4 (3): 333–64.

Scannell, Paddy. 2002. *Big Brother* as a Television Event. *Television & New Media* 3 (August): 272–80.

Schilling, Karen Maitland, and Ann Fuehrer. 1993. The Politics of Women's Self-Help Books. *Feminism and Psychology* 3: 418–22.

Shattuc, Jane M. 1997. *The Talking Cure: TV Talk Shows and Women*. New York: Routledge.

Simonds, Wendy. 1992. *Women and Self-Help Culture: Reading between the Lines*. New Brunswick, NJ: Rutgers University Press.

——. 1996. All Consuming Selves: Self-Help Literature and Women's Identities. In *Constructing the Self in a Mediated World*, ed. Debra Grodin and Thomas R. Lindlof, 15–29. Thousand Oaks, CA: Sage.

Starker, Stephen. 1989. *Oracle at the Supermarket: The American Preoccupation with Self-Help Books*. New Brunswick, NJ: Transaction.

White, Mimi. 1992. *Tele-Advising: Therapeutic Discourse in American Television*. Chapel Hill: University of North Carolina Press.

——. 2002. Television, Therapy, and the Social Subject: Or, the TV Therapy Machine. In *Reality Squared: Televisual Discourse on the Real*, ed. James Friedman, 313–22. New Brunswick, NJ: Rutgers University Press.

The Socioalgorithmics of Race: Sorting it Out in Jihad Worlds

LISA NAKAMURA

"Interest in profiling is at an all-time high in the United States—in films, in books, and on television news programs, but the practice remains surprisingly abstract." (Elmer, 2004, p. 75)

"Reynard is a seedling effort to study the emerging phenomenon of social (particularly terrorist) dynamics in virtual worlds and large-scale online games and their implications for the Intelligence Community. The cultural and behavioral norms of virtual worlds and gaming are generally unstudied. Therefore, Reynard will seek to identify the emerging social, behavioral, and cultural norms in virtual worlds and gaming environments. The project would then apply the lessons learned to determine the feasibility of automatically detecting suspicious behavior and actions in the virtual world" (*Data Mining Report (unclassified)*, 2008).

As Greg Elmer wrote in 2004, the topic of profiling is both irresistibly compelling yet usually understood in only the most broad and vague terms; it is indeed "surprisingly abstract." There is no shortage of media representations of profiling, and these are often extremely gendered ones. On the one hand, profiling implies feminine intuition; the tradition of female profilers in media texts starts with Clarice Starling of the film *The Silence of the Lambs* and continues today in television programs like *The Profiler*, *Bones*, and *Medium*. On the other, the spectacular appearance of sophisticated information processing machines associated with such narratives signals a move towards a different register of emotion, one displaced onto artifacts of and for identification. Emotions are pressed into service as tools for profiling (i.e. "I had a funny feeling about that man"); people who are profiled feel strong emotions about being watched and classified, populations endorse yet fear profiling as a means of protecting their precarious sense of security and safety, and digital technologies are pressed into service to bear the weight of this psychic burden. Profiling also carries the emotional charge of social inequality—to be "profiled" is to be identified as a criminal in advance of having committed a crime. Computers "simulate surveillance in the sense that they precede and redouble the means of observation. Computer profiling…is understood well not just as a technology of surveillance, but as a kind of surveillance in advance of surveillance, a technology of 'observation before the fact'" (Bogard, 1996, p. 27). When the job of profiling is given to a digital machine, no human is needed to do the watching, or even to do the feeling. Instead, surveillance has become a digital, algorithmic process.

The topic of surveillance has been amply addressed as a thematic focus and a set of stylistic concerns within filmic media texts, as summarized in Gates and Magnet's excellent introduction to this book. In contrast, surveillance practices such as fingerprinting, facial recognition systems, Closed Circuit Television (CCTV), reality television, cloud computing, and border patrolling have not been viewed as media practices *per se*. For to view them this way would mean acknowledging their status as media production practices and texts rather than as more or less accurate tools for getting at the truth about bodies, identity and deviance. The chapters in the book that you hold in your hands (or perhaps read on a screen) make a compelling case for viewing surveillance as a medium, like television, film, or the Internet, with its own particular distinctive history, politics, and visual culture. As the chapters in this book demonstrate through multiple examples and methods, surveillance is a signifying system that *produces* a social body, rather than straightforwardly reflects it. Fingerprint scans, retinal scans, facial recognition software images, and CCTV images are digitally produced visualizations, virtual spectacles or surfaces that represent a compellingly limited, easily manipulated identity or profile. Until now, new surveillance technologies have predominantly been described in the language of scientific discourse rather than in the language of media studies. However, even this scientific discourse is shot through with mediatic discourse referring to image quality and the acceptability of the body as a digital artifact. Heather Murray's excellent chapter makes this link explicit in her account of contemporary biometric science's handling of "abused" and illegible hands, biometrically "problematic" dark eyes, and Asian, female, and elderly bodies that are too "soft and fragile…lacking definition" to scan properly (Murray, 2008). Understanding surveillance as a visual digital media practice, industry, and technology that creates socially unequal bodies means having to understand it like other digital media representations, as "depthless images." As Andrew Darley writes, "the spectator of visual digital culture is positioned first and foremost as a seeker after unbridled visual delight and corporeal excitation"(Darley, 2000, p. 169). Digital images do not necessarily "lie" more than analog ones (see Mitchell, 1994). However, they create an articulated version of the world that lacks "symbolic depth," and as Darley notes, they operate on the viewer in a primal fashion that belies their supposedly neutral scientific status.

Digital media technologies have had a profound effect on the ways that race is performed, experienced, and defined. Early journalistic and academic accounts of the Internet stressed its utopian, democratic potential for erasing (or at least hiding) race and creating a "level playing field," celebrating its abilities as an anonymizing and thus egalitarian technology. Commercial and industrial narratives about the Internet created during the 1990s portrayed it in the most utopian terms, exemplified by MCI's Anthem and Microsoft's "where do you want to go today" campaign. These advertisements posited a radically democratic world where physical differences would be erased, leaving "only minds." Radical anonymity was the selling point of the Internet in those early adoption years (See Nakamura, 2002).

Internet users were prone to view their experiences online as post-racial, finding that they could "pass" by creating avatars that either were or weren't taken for normative white/male, or could simply omit any mention of race and accomplish the same thing. There was much at stake in avoiding appearances of profiling, particularly racial profiling, in the US at this time, and the Internet was identified as a technological solution to this key problem. The notion of "profiling" in the US acquired an especially nasty taint as several incidents of racial violence overlapped with the rise of the Internet as a popular technology, this all concurrent with the rise of neoliberal policies regarding media regulation and an officially "colorblind" Clinton presidency (Nakamura, 2007). The visual culture of surveillance in regards to race skewed towards the digital as a means of evening out social relations. The Internet's ability to conceal the user's body as the origin of communication was viewed as a curative to the problem of racial inequality—by rendering race invisible, it was thought, the "profile" or identity of the Internet users could omit race as a factor. Users could engage in social life without needing to bring race into the discourse, allowing us finally to all just get along. Of course, the varied and often conflictual nature of online interaction quickly demonstrated that racial passing and identity tourism were no solutions to the problem of racism.

It took another highly racialized act of violence—the events of 9/11—to transform the visual culture of digital identity in the US and elsewhere yet again, creating a craze for biometrics similar to the craze for photography that gripped the nineteenth century. While early proponents of the Internet as a racially equalizing technology had stressed its ability to hide bodies or create new "virtual" ones, after 9/11 political, technological, and cultural discourses emphasized the necessity of their radical revelation. The convention of the "reveal" taken from make-over reality television programmes showcased the new and improved version of the self, achieved as the result of intense self-cultivation and improvement; so too did our identities require to be stripped bare through digital, mediated means in order to be whole, to prove authenticity and loyalty, and to repair the damage to the national psyche. Biometrics creates spectacular images of an idealized self-sameness verified by science; just as reality television's therapeutics celebrate the "consistent self" (Dubrofsky, 2008).

Dubrofsky's striking insight that only "self-sameness across disparate social spaces (such as the show and 'real life')" can read as legitimate self-transformation in the logic of reality television points out how this therapeutic ethos requires us to stand completely still in order to be read as moving forward. Self-sameness has replaced identity play as a therapeutic value in digital culture, buoyed by an increasingly biometric cultural turn. As the British slogan regarding CCTV goes, "if you have nothing to hide, you have nothing to fear." The transformation of the Internet from an identity-constructing technology to an identity-confirming one has been remarked upon by *New York Times* journalist Clive Thompson, who writes "when cyberspace came along in the early 90s it was celebrated as a place where you could reinvent your identity—become someone new. 'If anything, it's constraining now,' a teacher told me, 'You can't play with your identity if your audience is always checking up on you. I had a student who posted that she was downloading some Pearl Jam, and someone wrote on her wall, 'oh, right, ha-ha—I know you, and you're not into that.' On the Internet today, everybody knows you're a dog!'"(Thompson, 2008).

The "therapeutics of the self" affirmed by social networking sites such as Facebook and MySpace require the constant tending and cultivating of the user profile, immaterial labor that must be performed under highly constricted, menu-driven conditions in front of an audience of witnesses. The myth of the "virtual world" as a space of identity re-invention was put to rest approximately ten years after its improbably utopian beginnings, just as the digitization of identity in real world, increasingly networked spaces such as airports, highways, malls and border stations continued apace to meet it. Populations learned to tolerate and accept previously unimaginable amounts and types of monitoring and searches—new conditions for new times—just as they had the "ambient intimacy" engendered by social networking sites and the Internet. The "work of being watched," as elaborated in Mark Andrejevic's groundbreaking work in the area of surveillance and media studies, has circulated freely between reality television and all forms of participatory digital media (Andrejevic, 2004). And as Lisa Parks and Simone Browne write, the act of airline travel has become inseparable from acts of monitoring (Parks, 2007; Browne, 2005).

The power of race as a social identifier is both amplified and reduced when it is turned into a data point in a digital profile. It becomes both more and less visible. This striving towards transparency that Rachel Hall identifies in her excellent chapter on the visual cultures of surveillance is accomplished by transforming the human body into both data and spectacle. Likewise, race becomes both visual phenomenon and invisible data, something to be both seen and processed. Race is a social algorithm in addition to and sometimes instead of a physiognomic or phenotypic feature, a form of genotypic media as well as phenotypic appearance. Race has been a spectacle from the beginning, constructed through technologically mediatized means such as photography as well as through older forms such as minstrels and museum sideshows (Fusco & Wallis, 2003; Gilman, 1985). Race as a socioalgorithmic process produces spectacular effects—depthless images—in and through digital data as well as within spatial locations such as grocery stores, city streets, and airports. As a foundational piece of the story and origins of the digital profile, race functions as a field of information, or as Matthew Fuller describes it, an identity "fleck" of data within a database.

Fuller describes the role of race within automated profiling systems as follows: "An element, cluster, or concatenation of data, flecks of identity—a number, a sample, a document, racial categorization—are features that identify the bearer as belonging to particular scalar positions and relations"(Fuller & Malina, 2005, p. 148). These "flecks of identity" are the indispensible building blocks of computer assisted profiling, "standard objects…within databases [that serve] as a primary compositional element within surveillance systems"(Fuller & Malina, 2005, p. 148). Fuller and other scholars in the emerging discipline of software studies identify the database as the key cultural form of the computer age, one that replaces hierarchical narrative forms such as the novel and cinema with "collections of individual items, where every item has the same significance as any other"(Manovich, 2001, p. 194). Manovich writes that a database is "anything but a simple collection of items," but is instead a "cultural form of its own" that presents a distinctive "model of what the world is like." He thus calls for the creation of a "poetics, aesthetics, and ethics of this database"(Manovich, 2001, p. 195). The chapters in this book extend this project by developing a *politics* of the database.

Biometrics, the measurement of the human body and coding of the result as data, transforms the body into a digital media object. The construction and deployment of databases are part of a political project of identity formation and regulation—they augment without replacing the visual image as the medium of identification. Being "in the database," be it in a no-fly list, a preferred shoppers club, or a "friends" list on a social networking service, results in differential social treatment that is nothing if not deeply politicitized, in ways that are less visible than they have ever been in their actual workings, yet more intensely visible in their effects (whose heart has not broken to see a toddler sobbing as her stroller is broken down and run through a scanner and her teddy bear confiscated and examined during a routine airport screening procedure?). The disavowal of agency rightly claimed by airport official parallels the "racism without racists" phenomenon noted by Bonilla-Silva and David Theo Goldberg (Goldberg, 2008; Bonilla-Silva, 2006). The decision as to which bodies must undergo which screening process is informed by both acts of seeing and acts of database usage and machinic data processing; it is both visible and invisible, with the latter tending towards the former in informationalized societies. As Fuller writes, "surveillance in the present context applies very little to acts of seeing. Surveillance is a *socioalgorithmic* process" (Fuller & Malina, 2005, p. 149).

As described by many of the authors in this book, the mediatization of the body characterizes life in informationalized societies, and it continues apace. Up until now, the bodies that users create to use in virtual worlds such as Linden Labs' *Second Life* and Blizzard's *World of Warcraft* have been more or less free of systematic forms of governmental surveillance or dataveillance. In her excellent chapter on border control and the economies of bodies, Simone Browne writes that "bordering is one of the key disciplinary practices of the nation-state, with classificatory identity/mobility documents playing an important role" (Browne, 2005). Until now, virtual worlds have been relatively free of these types of borders and documents permitting travel between virtual spaces within their worlds. While it is certainly not the case that entirely free movement is possible in either of these virtual worlds— *Second Life* allows space to be coded as private and *World of Warcraft* effectively locks content until users have acquired the requisite skills, abilities, and number of co-players to access them—these are algorithmic functions that do not involve knowledge of the user's "true" identity, but rather of an avatar's identity or player account characteristics. If airports and border checkpoints are spaces where users are sorted out based on their ability to provide the proper documents, until now virtual worlds have sorted users through other means, such as membership in social groups or "guilds," choice of player class or race, payment type, or choice of computer server. The attraction of travel through beautifully detailed and richly ornamented virtual worlds are appealing enough to compel almost 11 million users to pay significant monthly or hourly fees to Blizzard, the owner of *World of Warcraft*. Linden Labs' *Second Life* has produced a burgeoning economy that supports a whole new class of entrepreneurs who build virtual objects to sell or give to other players. *Second Life* also attracts users by letting them construct new content, encouraging them to create appealing navigatable spaces and virtual objects. These virtual worlds are thriving, partly because of the freedom of movement and pleasure in role-playing that they offer within rule-bounded environments.

While all kinds of data about players and player behavior are collected by Linden Labs and Blizzard, up until now they have not been systematically monitored by governmental agencies. Virtual worlds have been treated as spaces at least nominally exempt from surveillance, though as digitally mediated worlds, dataveillance is built into the structure of the world. Yet, if Linden and Blizzard's claims are to be given any credence at all, users live "second lives" online. Thus, the line between dataveillance and surveillance is an exceedingly tenuous one in the case of virtual worlds. As the unclassified February 15 Office of the Department of National Intelligence Report notes, "many enterprises collect information that can used to identify their individuals...the customer must be willing to share some information (Personally Identifiable Information (PII) in particular) in order to obtain desired services." Linden and Blizzard collect significant amounts of PII from their users.[1] This dataveillance has differed from surveillance in that it refrains from watching actual users, only their avatars. But since a human being in real time controls each avatar, this amounts to a form of surveillance. As Clarke writes "dataveillance is automated monitoring through computer readable data rather than physical observation...Dataveillance is the systematic use of personal data systems in the investigating and monitoring of the actions or communications of one or more persons" (Elmer, 2004). The line between "physical observation" and "automated monitoring through...data" may become radically blurred when a pilot project codenamed Reynard is implemented in virtual worlds.

Reynard, a fledgling initiative announced by ODNI in February of 2008 is charged with uncovering terrorists in virtual worlds, including—but not restricted to—*WoW* and *Second Life*. As a *Wired Blog Network* article puts it rather sensationally "US Spies Want To Find Terrorists in *World of Warcraft*." Other news outlets such as the BBC, Thirteen/WNET, and fan blogs such as *WoW Insider* have covered this story as well, attracted no doubt by the weirdness of the project (Vallance, 2008; Carr, 2008; Schramm, 2008). A *BBC World News* feature by Chris Vallant entitled "US Seeks Terrorists in Web Worlds" includes interviews with several experts from the "intelligence community," among them Andrew Cochran, founder and co-chairman of the Counterterrorism Foundation, and Roderick Jones, a "vice president of Concentric Solutions and a former special branch officer." According to Mr. Cochran: "'All of the major terrorist treatises have been distributed through the internet so taking it to a virtual world with multi-player role games is really an easy step.' 'It was inevitable that terror groups would make greater use of the internet and the possibilities that virtual spaces offered them,' said

Mr. Jones. 'There's more a chance of things like Jihad worlds coming online in the next five years I think,' he said" (Vallance, 2008).

By this logic, all virtual worlds are potentially "jihad worlds" and must be monitored as such. The notion of the "jihad world" has particular resonance given the thousands of Arabs and Muslims in the US who have been "preventively detained," compelled to give "voluntary interviews," and made to enroll in "Special Registration," a biometric procedure that "required the interviewing, fingerprinting, and photograph in of more than 170,000 men from twenty-four Muslim-majority countries (and North Korea). Special Registration initiated deportation proceedings for almost 14,000 people...none of the policies produced a single terrorism conviction" (Bayoumi, 2008a, p. 267). These individuals, many of whom are not virtual world users, are nonetheless already living in a "jihad world."

Virtual worlds have been both touted as democratic social spaces that provide innovative tools for learning and critiqued as time-wasters, family-destroyers, and killers of sleep-deprived young Asian men in PC gaming parlors. They have not, however, been identified as havens for terrorists until recently. The ethos of transparency that underpins the visual culture of surveillance is stretched to its limit in the Reynard project—and indeed, the project of "spying on" virtual worlds is itself a limit case for surveillance studies. On the one hand, the project acknowledges the sweep and importance of virtual worlds as populous spaces where strategizing, socializing, and meaningful social activity occur. On the other hand, it signals the ongoing elimination of spaces of ludic possibility through digital play and interaction that make these worlds so appealing to so many. The most common critique of Reynard among *World of Warcraft* players who posted to the *Wired News Blog* article is a pragmatic one—many are unopposed to the notion of surveillance as a general principle, but almost all are quite skeptical that it will work. As "Rumrunner" posted on February 22, "Good luck getting a baseline of 'cultural norms' from fifteen year olds hopped up on bong hits. Maybe they can start by data-mining Barrens chat. lmao" (Singel, 2008).[2] Many fear being incorrectly identified as terrorists because of decisions they made long ago in constructing their avatars or social groupings. As "Duncan" remarked wryly in a comment to the *Wired News Blog* on February 23, 2008, "I knew that I shouldn't have named my (*sic*) guild al Qaeda!" The freedom to parody, satire, or in any way reference politics, nation, race, and the "war on terror" is not guaranteed by Blizzard's End User License Agreement (EULA), but nor is it entirely restricted. However, in the future the possibility of surveillance by government agencies may make this a dangerous activity. Reynard is an experimental, still unimplemented "seedling" project as of February 2008 that carefully restricts its aims to conducting "unclassified research in a public virtual world environment" rather than surveilling individual users (*Data Mining Report (unclassified)*, 2008). However, its mission to "study the emerging phenomenon of social (particularly terrorist) dynamics in virtual worlds and large-scale online games and their implications for the Intelligence Community" implies that terrorists are to be found in virtual worlds *without a doubt*, and that social dynamics *per se* are inseparable from terrorist ones. This would fail to exempt any type of "social interaction" from scrutiny. The step from this type of pattern matching dataveillance to more intrusive types of surveillance is a short one, as game avatars are examined and profiled just as their users have long been in public spaces. As "Bob" posted ironically "The Next Step will be a required retina scan to login to WoW, with presentation of identity papers before you are allowed to create a character. There is nothing more important than the pursuit of terrorism" (Singel, 2008).

The absurdity of implementing this data-mining project in a virtual world based on bloody battles, duels, the accumulation of vast arsenals of weapons, armor, and explosives and a system that rewards users for killing as many other avatars and mobs or "mobile monsters" as possible in the name of "warcraft" has not been lost on the *WoW* playing community. The idea that a fantasy simulation game based on *war between two racially and culturally opposed factions* could be an appropriate site to record patterns of "suspicious behavior" is so patently absurd that it has been gently mocked by a video segment of the *Bill Moyers Journal* entitled "Government Spying...on World of Warcraft?"[3] In it, Rick Carr reports "Now a federal intelligence agency wants to spy on people in [virtual worlds] in the name of the global war on terror." As he delivers this line, the visual imagery cuts from his face to a clip of *World of Warcraft* game play featuring massive armor-wearing jackal-headed monsters marching en masse across a desert, then dissolves to an image of the Office of the Director of National Intelligence seal. Carr goes on to say, "The announcement came from the Office of the Director of National Intelligence in February, in a draft proposal for a new project that would monitor these online worlds. The project would study their social, behavioral, and cultural norms then try to build a system to try to detect suspicious behavior. It was not clear what qualified as suspicious in *World of Warcraft*." The visual commentary that accompanies this statement again cuts to a clip of *WoW* game play, showing an avatar lopping off another avatar's head with a massive sword. As the victim falls to the ground in a bloody heap, Carr asks, "In *Second Life*, would attending a peace studies seminar count?" (Carr, 2008) The idea that virtual worlds might function as spaces of exception to surveillance and social sorting was never based in reality, and with the development of programs such as Reynard, clearly well past us. As T. L. Taylor demonstrates in her work on surveillance in *World of Warcraft*, both Blizzard and other players have long had the ability to gather information about each other in ways that influence styles of game play and sociality (Taylor, 2008). Virtual worlds were always spaces of surveillance. Reynard departs from this, however, in that it posits a "jihad world" that must be uncovered through data mining. The automated mapping of "suspicious behavior and actions in the virtual world" may claim to be free of racial or cultural bias. However, as "Rick O'Connor" posted to the Wired blog on February 22, "This is bullshit. It's spreading racism and exploitative."

The desire to declare race irrelevant is both perennially strong and far from new. As David Eng writes, "At a time when race appears in official political discourse in the United States only as ever 'disappearing,' it becomes increasingly urgent to contest such sanguine pronouncements with, among other things, this simple fact: ever since the Enlightenment, race has always appeared as disappearing" (Eng, 2008, p. 1479). This turn towards the post-racial in public discourse has been much in evidence during this year's US Presidential race. Pundits, academics, and journalists all addressed the question anew in 2008 (Williams, 2008; Steele, 2008). In 2008 the term "postracial" has circulated widely to describe the effects of Barack Obama's run for the US presidency. In "Race Will Survive the Obama Phenomenon," American historian David Roediger writes that "race is a far more fluid category, both popularly and at law" partly because a huge share of the 'white' population now regards itself as identifying with 'nonwhite' peoples or culture in some way that respondents regard as central to their lives" (Roediger, 2008). It makes less sense to attribute the surge in popularity of biometrics technologies to their increasing accuracy—indeed, as Shoshana Magnet has compellingly argued, they are much less accurate than had been thought—and more sense to link it to the "fluidity" of racial categories (Magnet, forthcoming 2009). The immense funding and investment in biometrics technologies signals both a socio-political crisis and a crisis in racial categorizations.

Computers have long shaped and been shaped by racial policy, law, and categorization. Some of the first computing machines were born in the U.S. Census Office, which in 1890 "hired Herman Hollerith to design a machine capable of collating demographic information about millions of people" (Friedman, 2005, p. 35). The result was a calculating device that used holes in paper punch cards to collate demographic information—the earliest flecks of identity—and the company would later change its name to IBM. Thus, computing culture's history is intimately connected to the history of racial classification and sorting. The need to sort populations was engendered by mass immigration of peoples whose racial status needed to be classified precisely because it challenged existing ideas of racial classification. Slavs, Italians, Greeks, and other "approximate whites" stretched the definition of whiteness, as Arabs, Japanese, and Filipinos challenged the definition of citizenship in the post-war period. The struggle for whiteness and the claim to citizenship have always been intimately linked in the US context, for it was on the basis of purported racial whiteness that the latter group claimed citizenship. As Moustafa Bayoumi writes, the struggles of Arab-Americans to become naturalized citizens of the US proceeded through a series of stops and starts, punctuated by changes in racial classification. "When an immigration judge ruled in 1942 that the Yemeni Ahmed Hassan—perhaps the first Arab Muslim to face the court (the others had been Arab Christians)— could not petition for citizenship, the community faced a setback" (Bayoumi, 2008b, p. 263). He quotes Judge Arthur Tuttle, who wrote, "Arabs are not white persons within the meaning of the Immigration Act." A reversal was soon to come, however—in 1944, Mohamed Mohriez succeeded in naturalizing as a citizen, with the justification being "to promote friendlier relations between the United States and other nations." As Bayoumi explains, the US's need for oil "changed the supposedly immutable facts of the Arab 'race'" (Bayoumi, 2008b, p. 264). Thus, racial classification has always been subject to both political exigency and the related activity of automated sorting, with the needs of one motivating the development and application of the latter.

The chapters in this book demonstrate that surveillance is itself a new medium that needs to be studied as such in order to understand the shifting terrain of identity. The socioalgorithmics of gender, race, nation, class, and belief operate within digital spaces such as virtual worlds and Google Gmail as well as at border checkpoints and transportation control centers. In a slight modification of the claims of the software studies movement, the databases that underpin and underwrite socioalgorithmic surveillance practices have *politics* as well as poetics, aesthetics, and ethics. Massive databases such as Blizzard's and Linden Labs' contain intimate details of users' computer usage time, forms of social interaction, sexual preferences and practices, economic status and habits, and "known acquaintances"—flecks of identity that may have once been viewed as merely virtual, but are now suspect as all too real. Bogard defines "hypersurveillant control" as both the intensification of surveillance and the "effort to push surveillance technologies to their absolute limit" (Bogard, 1996, p. 4). As new methods of surveillance and new ways of sorting us out come into being in a variety of worlds, such research is of the greatest importance.

NOTES

1   Scholarly projects have engaged in automated data collection in virtual worlds for several years now. As Taylor writes, "the PlayOn project at XeroxPARC deploys extensive data-

mining techniques for their social science research on player communities within the game (http://blogs.parc.com/playon/.)" (Page 199) In addition, players use software programs or "mods" to "constantly monitor, surveil, and report at a micro level a variety of aspects of player behavior." (Page 191)

2 Conversations that occur in public or trade channels in *World of Warcraft* are called "chat." The Barrens is one of the starting areas for new players in *World of Warcraft*, and is well known for a particularly juvenile and tedious style of humor based on Chuck Norris jokes. "Lmao" is a common abbreviation for "laughing my ass off."

3 *World of Warcraft* is full of racialized and racist depictions of avatars, environments, and other cultural artifacts that map onto U.S. depictions of Afro-Caribbean, Native American, and Asian cultures and people. The distinction between the Euro-American identified races in the "good" Alliance faction and the "bad" or non-white Horde is described in detail by Jessica Langer in her essay in the World of Warcraft Reader. Langer, J. (2008). The Familiar and the Foreign: Playing (Post) Colonialism in World of Warcraft. In H. A. J. W. R. Corneliussen (Ed.), *Digital Culture, Play, and Identity: A World of Warcraft Reader* (pp. 87-108). New York: Routledge.

REFERENCES

Andrejevic, M. (2004). *Reality TV: the work of being watched*. Lanham, Md.: Rowman & Littlefield Publishers.

Bayoumi, M. (2008b). *How Does It Feel to be a Problem? Being Young and Arab in America*. New York: The Penguin Press.

Bogard, W. (1996). *The simulation of surveillance: hyper control in telematic societies*. Cambridge ; New York: Cambridge University Press.

Bonilla-Silva, E. (2006). *Racism without racists: color-blind racism and the persistence of racial inequality in the United States* (2nd ed.). Lanham: Rowman & LittlefieldPublishers.

Browne, S. (2005). Getting Carded: Border Control and the Politics of Canada's Permanent Resident Card. *Citizenship Studies, 9*(4), 423-438.

Carr, R. (2008). Government Spying on...World of Warcraft? *Bill Moyers Journal*. Retrieved from http://www.thirteen.org/newsandpublicaffairs/government-spyingonworld-of-warcraft

Darley, A. (2000). *Visual digital culture: surface play and spectacle in new media genres*. London and New York: Routledge.

Data Mining Report (unclassified) (2008). Office of the Director of National Intelligence.

Dubrofsky, R. (2009). Therapeutics of the Self: Surveillance in the Service of the Therapeutic. In S. Magnet and K. Gates (Eds.), *The new media of surveillance*. New York: Routledge.

Elmer, G. (2004). *Profiling machines: mapping the personal information economy*. Cambridge, Mass.: MIT Press.

Eng, D. L. (2008). The End(s) of Race. *PMLA, 123*(5).

Friedman, T. (2005). *Electric dreams: computers in American culture*. New York: NewYork University Press.

Fuller, M., & Malina, R. F. (2005). *Media ecologies: materialist energies in art and technoculture*. Cambridge, Mass.: MIT Press.

Fusco, C., & Wallis, B. (2003). *Only skin deep: changing visions of the American self*. New York: International Center of Photography/Harry N. Abrams.

Gilman, S. (1985). Black Bodies, White Bodies: Toward an Iconography of Female Sexuality in Late Nineteenth-Century Art, Medicine, and Literature. In H. L. Gates (Ed.), *"Race", writing, and difference* (pp. 223-261). Chicago: University of Chicago Press.

Goldberg, D. T. (2008). Racisms Without Racism. *PMLA, 123*(5), 1712-1722.

Magnet, S. (forthcoming 2009). Using Biometrics to Re-Visualize the Canada-US Border. In I. Kerr (Ed.), *Lessons from the identity trail: anonymity, privacy and identity in a networked society*. Oxford: Oxford University Press.

Manovich, L. (2001). *The language of new media*. Cambridge, Mass.: MIT Press.

Mitchell, W. J. (1994). *The reconfigured eye: visual truth in the post-photographic era* (1st MIT Press paperback ed.). Cambridge, Mass.: MIT Press.

Murray, H. (2009). Monstrous Play in Negative Spaces: Illegible Bodies and the Cultural Construction of Biometric Technology. In S. Magnet and K. Gates (Eds.), *The new media of surveillance*. New York: Routledge.

Nakamura, L. (2002). *Cybertypes: race, identity, and ethnicity on the Internet*. New York: Routledge.

Nakamura, L. (2007). *Digitizing race: visual cultures of the Internet*. Minneapolis: Minnesota University Press.

Parks, L. (2007). Points of departure: the culture of US airport screening. *Journal of Visual Culture, 6*, 183-200.

Roediger, D. R. (2008). Race will survive the Obama phenomenon. *The Chronicle of Higher Education*. Retrieved October 14 2008, from http://chronicle.com/free/v55/i07/07b00601.htm

Schramm, M. (2008). PBS covers the government's intrusion into online worlds. *WoW Insider,* (June 11, 2008). Retrieved from http://www.wowinsider.com/2008/06/11/pbs-covers-the-governments-intrusioninto- online-worlds/#comments

Singel, R. (2008). US Spies Want to Find Terrorists in World of Warcraft. Retrieved from http://blog.wired.com/27bstroke6/2008/02/nations-spies-w.html

Steele, S. (November 5, 2008). Obama's post-racial promise. *Los Angeles Times*. Retrieved from http://www.latimes.com/news/opinion/commentary/la-oe-steele5-2008nov05,0,6553798.story

Taylor, T. L. (2008). Does World of Warcraft Change Everything? How a PvP Server, Multinational Player base, and Surveillance Mod Scene Caused Me Pause. In H. Corneliussen and J. Rettberg (Eds.), *Digital culture, play, and identity* (pp. 187-201). Cambridge: MIT Press.

Thompson, C. (2008, September 7, 2008). Brave New World of Digital Intimacy. *The New York Times*.

Vallance, C. (2008). U.S. Seeks Terrorists in Web Worlds Retrieved October 7, 2008 from http://news.bbc.co.uk/2/hi/technology/7274377.stm

Williams, P. (2008, August 10). Talking About Not Talking About Race. *New York Magazine*.

Index

American Civil Liberties Union
   (ACLU)
   and US-VISIT program, 52
Agamben, Giorgi
   bio-political relationship
      between citizen and state, new,
      42, 45
   "body without words", 42, 61, 63
   and social control, 41
   and US-VISIT program, 41-2
   "words without a body", 42, 63
airport security, new, 44-5
   bio-political relationship
      between citizen and state, new,
      42,45
   compensatory heterotopias, 44,
      65n.4, 66n.13
   and fear, 44
   and foreign visitors, 45-52, 154
   and hygiene, 44, 65n.5
   and US-VISIT program, 45-52
Amazon.com
   and target marketing, 23, 34

biometrics
   *Biometrics: Implications and
      Applications for Citizenship
      and Immigration* forum, 119
   and biases 74-8
   bodies, 12, 69-85
   and borders, national, 70
   and class, gender, age and race
      implications, 73
   and criminology and

   monstrosity, 75-8
   cultural construction of, 69-85
   and the digital enclosure, 37
   and evidentiary role, 75, 84n.15
   face recognition technology,
      69-70
   fingerprint scanning, 69-70, 72
   genealogy, 74-8
   and illegal bodies, 69-85, 150
   iris scanning, 69-70, 73
   and mobility, prevention of, 70
   as non-innocent actor, 70
   and normative notion of body,
      13, 73-4, 80, 113, 151
   and Permanent Resident Card
      (PRC), 112-113, 115, 123
   and police use of, 5
   and racial profiles, 73
   and reduction of deployability,
      72-3,78, 150
   retinal scanning, 69-70, 150
   and social sorting, 78-83
   and Special Registration, 156
   and transnational flow of bodies,
      70
   using social norms as control
      mechanisms, 70
   US-VISIT program video, 42,
      46-52,54
   and virtual border, 45
   and wanted posters, 74
bio-political relationship between
   citizen and state, 42, 45
border control, 159

LaVergne, TN USA
11 November 2009
163832LV00002B/3/P